FIGHTING IN THE
JIM CROW ARMY

FIGHTING IN THE

JIM CROW ARMY

Black Men and Women
Remember World War II

Maggi M. Morehouse

ROWMAN & LITTLEFIELD PUBLISHERS, INC.
Lanham • Boulder • New York • Oxford

ROWMAN & LITTLEFIELD PUBLISHERS, INC.

Published in the United States of America
by Rowman & Littlefield Publishers, Inc.
4720 Boston Way, Lanham, Maryland 20706
http://www.rowmanlittlefield.com

12 Hid's Copse Road
Cumnor Hill, Oxford OX2 9JJ, England

British Library Cataloguing in Publication Information Available

Library of Congress Cataloging-in-Publication Data

Morehouse, Maggi M., 1953-
  Fighting in the Jim Crow Army : black men and women remember World War II /
Maggi M. Morehouse.
    p. cm. — (Voices and visions)
  Includes bibliographical references and index.
  ISBN 0-8476-9193-4 (alk. paper)
    1. World War, 1939-1945—Afro-Americans. I. Title. II. Voices and visions (Lanham,
  Md.)

D810.N4 M67 2000
940.54'03—dc21   00-055257

Printed in the United States of America

♾™ The paper used in this publication meets the minimum requirements of
American National Standard for Information Sciences—Permanence of Paper for
Printed Library Materials, ANSI/NISO Z39.48-1992.

To the special memory of my father,
Lee Sinclair Quarterman.
Thanks, Dad.

Enjoying the western terrain. Lee and Liz Quarterman
in Fort Huachuca, Arizona, in 1942.

CONTENTS

FOREWORD

"Postwar America" was not simply a historical abstraction when I was growing up in the 1950s and 1960s. Everyone, kids and adults, knew which war we were "post"—it was the Big One, World War II (Korea, somehow, didn't seem to count). Everybody's fathers, it seemed, my own included, had found themselves in uniform at least for some of the years between 1941 and 1945. In fact, all the significant males in our lives—our teachers, coaches, Boy Scout leaders, ministers, and the like—were veterans of World War II, as were the presidents we saw nightly on television. Digging out old military gear and apparel from their mothballed existence in the attic and then dressing up in the old man's reflected glory (even if he had never left a training post in the States) was a favorite way to pass a rainy weekend afternoon.

Indeed, the whole culture of the era was saturated with imagery from the war, ranging from the realistic to the fanciful. On our bookshelves at home we had a big red-covered, folio-sized edition of Life's *Picture History of World War II*, which I pored over endlessly, stirred by the pictures of heavily burdened paratroopers preparing to be dropped over Normandy and grimly fascinated by the pictures of emaciated survivors liberated by American forces from concentration camps in Germany. I also read comic books like *Sergeant Rock*, where the information conveyed was not always as reliable (a regular reader of the genre would come away with the impression that a well-aimed shot from Sergeant Rock's .45 automatic could easily knock an attacking Messerschmidt fighter plane out of commission). My favorite movies were all about the war—*The Longest Day*, *The Guns of Navarone*, and *The Great Escape*, among many others. And I regularly watched two weekly half-hour television action shows, *Combat* and *The Gallant Men*, the one devoted to the experiences of an American army platoon fighting in the hedgerow country of France in 1944, the other to a similar platoon slogging its way up the rocky Italian boot. With such resources at my command, like many other boys, by the age of twelve I considered myself quite the expert on the war.

And by that same age, in my case around 1963, I was absorbing another set of images of a dramatic conflict being waged in freedom's cause: long-suffering black sharecroppers and idealistic black southern college students, standing up at that very moment to bullying white sheriffs and hooded Ku Klux Klansmen in not-so-faraway places such as Birmingham, Alabama, and Greenwood, Mississippi. And although I was from a white family, and lived in a nearly all-white community in rural Connecticut, those nonviolent freedom fighters also became my heroes, just like the veterans of my father's generation.

It would be many years before I made any connections between the two sets of images and two sets of heroes. It simply did not occur to me that black American men had also fought in Europe and the Pacific in the 1940s and that their experiences in the war years had anything to do with the struggles being played out in the churches, courthouses, and streets of the South twenty years later. In retrospect, that is not surprising. There were no blacks in *Combat* or *The Gallant Men*. There were no blacks in *The Longest Day*, *The Guns of Navarone*, or *The Great Escape*. There were no blacks in *Sergeant Rock*. There was one black serviceman represented amid the hundreds of photos reprinted in Life's *Picture History of World War II*; he was a U.S. Navy musician in Washington, D.C., in April 1945, weeping as he played "Nearer My God to Thee" on an accordion in honor of the just-deceased President Franklin D. Roosevelt. It was a powerful image, to be sure, and one that I appreciated much more as the years passed, but not one destined to figure largely in a twelve-year-old's imagination.

If future generations of twelve-year-old American boys—and their sisters, and their parents, and their teachers—are spared my ignorance, Maggi Morehouse will surely deserve a significant share of the credit. For in *Fighting in the Jim Crow Army* she illustrates the crucial link between World War II and what has sometimes been referred to as the Second Civil War, the black freedom struggle of the 1960s. For what we learn in these pages is that a generation of black men, hundreds of thousands of them, began the most important struggle of our time for equal protection before the laws and for simple human dignity when they donned their army khakis or navy blues between 1941 and 1945. That didn't mean that they were consciously battling for civil rights (though some were). But they began to think of themselves in new ways. As one veteran of the army's black 93rd Division recalled, after a year of rigorous training at Fort Huachuca, "[We were] no longer a conglomeration of men, we were soldiers in a military organization. We sensed the growth of our consciousness, unity, and strength, a unified consciousness."

Mustering out in 1945 did not destroy that sense of unified consciousness, nor did the indignities heaped upon returning veterans, especially those returning to the Jim Crow South (where it was not uncommon, in those first postwar years, for uniformed black veterans to be lynched for their refusal to resume the humble demeanor demanded by Jim Crow's laws and customs). And if children growing up in white families in the years that followed did not learn from their school books or popular entertainment that blacks as well as whites had risked their lives in freedom's cause in World War II, their counterparts in black families certainly learned of it from the most authoritative possible source—their own fathers and mothers. As Maggi Morehouse argues in the concluding pages of this book, it was an alliance of those fathers, their wives, and their children that spearheaded the civil rights revolution of the 1960s, and in doing so made "postwar America" a more decent place for all of us to live in.

Maurice Isserman

PREFACE

The black "Citizen Soldiers" who participated in the "Good War" also form part of the "Greatest Generation," yet they continue to be invisible in the general histories of World War II. Why have recent popular representations of World War II—books and films—overlooked the multitude of black experiences and voices? I suspect it is because this history is a complicated story, one filled with moments of glory as well as moments of shame. Black combat soldiers in World War II fought in a segregated army to "keep the world safe for democracy." In the historiography of World War II we have traveled from self-congratulatory analyses of the war, to examinations of individual battles and leaders, and now to a virtual cottage industry of first-hand remembrances from the perspective of the foot soldier. But in all of these phases of remembrance, scant attention has been paid to the contributions of the individual black soldiers of World War II.

One of America's first war heroes, Dorie Miller, a black navy man, was in the bombing of Pearl Harbor. Black soldiers came ashore at Omaha Beach for D-Day, and two whole divisions of black soldiers slogged through the jungles of the Pacific and fought through the bitter battles of the Italian campaign. Black Americans participated in most of the same battles as white Americans, yet we continue to gloss over or ignore their participation. This book highlights the experiences of black combat soldiers through the words and experiences of these men, intermingled with official government documents. The personal narratives demonstrate the irony and ambiguities of fighting a war for democracy within a segregated army. To understand World

War II, that watershed event that affected all Americans, we must add in the voices of the black men and women who also served in the armed forces.

This book is based on several years of research started primarily as a project for a graduate history seminar. The assignment called on each student to use primary sources and relate something "new" about politics and society in twentieth-century America. Like everyone else in the seminar, I was bereft of ideas. I struggled just to identify a topic I was interested in researching. Only when I started digging through some of my father's papers did I find a link between the personal and the political, between "book" history and personal history. My recently deceased father had served as one of 275 white officers in the mostly all-black 93rd Infantry Division. I mentioned this in passing to my history professor, and he suggested that the history of black soldiers in World War II would be a good topic for a research paper. He could recommend only one book on the topic, but it gave me a starting point. Thus I embarked on a research project that I have always viewed as family history.

My father was a career army officer, a lifer. My position growing up in a military family was always partially determined by the privileges that go along with being an officer's daughter. To those privileges I would add all the constraints and expectations placed upon a young girl in the male-dominated military world of the 1950s and 1960s. I ran from the army life as soon as I had the opportunity. I viewed the stories of my father's military life as something not worth investigating. Although I had always known that my father served with black soldiers, I never sat down and talked with him about that time. I never saw the significance or benefit. When my father's health failed to the point that he required assisted living, my mother told my younger brother to find a residence for him, and then she instructed me to clean out my father's things from his room. While completing this task, I discovered all of the World War II mementos that he had kept through the years. During all of the twenty or more moves our family made across the United States and abroad, and despite all of my mother's reorganizations and spring cleanings, my father had managed to keep a box of mementos, mostly World War II memorabilia. He could have kept Korean War memorabilia, or reminders of his days of serving with the occupation forces in Germany or Japan, but he did not. The evidence suggested to me that World War II was the most defining period in his life. Not his thirty-five years with me, nor his fifty-two years with my mother, nor his twenty-five years in the Civil Service, or any other time in his twenty-year military career meant as much to him. Just that time period in World War II when he was with the 93rd Infantry Division. He had newspaper clippings, personal photographs, and dog-eared articles about the "Tan Yankees" and the "All Negro Division" from *Time* and *Life* magazines.

I slept on the floor of the assisted living residence for several nights while my father settled in. He never got used to the place; he was totally disoriented, and near the end of his life he had vivid recollections of World War II, including nightmares from which he woke up screaming that he had lost his battalion. I know a nursing home is not the place to do historical research, especially when the interviewee is the researcher's father, but during his calmer moments we talked about history and his activities in the war. Overall, it was too emotional for me—I was not ready to hear about the events of that time period or to think of my father telling me his story for the last time. Still, I did ask him about the papers and pictures I found, mentioning them in order to elicit a response. I told him I was studying foreign policy and history at the university I was attending. Many of the things he had lived through were topics of research papers for me. I tried to engage him, but his thinking was not all that clear, and, as I said, I was not ready to hear it all anyway.

I did not look at the mementos and clippings again until I was in graduate school a few years later. Only then did I discover the dearth of information on the topic of black soldiers in World War II, most especially from a participant's point of view. My father was always a background character, standing in support of others or organizing systems of management. He would not have wanted me to write a history of him or of the few other white officers who served with black troops. He would have considered his participation insignificant. He would have wanted the black men he served with to get top billing, and it is to this end that I have endeavored to write the story.

For me this has always been a family history, and I approached the story in that manner. I was always looking for the soldier who could tell me about my own father. I was aching to hear a story about how dad was one of the "good ones." Everybody was remembering World War II, and I was looking for a way to bring my father back to life and insert him into history. On the way to finding my father, I discovered the story of the men who served alongside him. All of these men fought the "good fight" for their country and for their families. The men gave me their stories, a gift I lovingly pass on.

ACKNOWLEDGMENTS

I have been able to work on this exciting project because of the love and support of many people. The most important person in my life and in this project has been my dear husband, David Weintraub. He did yeoman service on this project during all of its numerous phases. He listened to me, met and photographed some of the men, edited multiple versions of this work, and supported me through my extended stay in graduate school. He gave me the love and confidence to pursue this project, and my thanks are inadequate to express my gratitude.

I became interested in this topic while taking a graduate history seminar at San Francisco State University. The paper I researched and presented to the class provided the spark for this work and introduced me to a topic that has become a vibrant part of my life. I would like to thank Professors William Issel and Robert Cherny for their patience, interest, and advice as I developed that seminar paper into a master's thesis. Other people have read and reread sections of this work, and I would like to thank them for their many cogent comments. I thank them in the order of their assistance: my graduate buddy, Bob Bionaz; my fieldwork "assistant," Jim Finley at the Fort Huachuca Museum; my inspirational mentors at San Francisco State University (who did not have to read my papers), Professors Dwight Simpson and Robert C. Smith; my research "subjects" turned editors-friends, Felix Goodwin, Spencer Moore, Bill Payne, Nelson Peery, Bill Perry, and Hank Williams. Three professors at the University of California–Berkeley have commented on this work in its various forms: Professors Bil Banks, Charles

Henry, and Stephen Small. Thanks also to my Cape Cod readers Vincent Kenny and Paul Fox.

The most brilliant scholar I have met to date, and the person to whom I owe the most thanks, is Dr. Robert L. Allen, visiting professor at University of California–Berkeley. He needs to be thanked separately and given the full acknowledgment that his treatment of my work deserves. He carefully guided this project by listening to ideas, talking through problems, and recommending my proposal to the publisher. He recognized the weaknesses in my work but accentuated the positive. He believed in my abilities as a writer and researcher, and he encouraged me to continue developing the soldiers' stories. His fine caretaking undergirds this final version of the work. While none of the errors are his responsibility, much of the book's sensibilities are due to his support and thoughtfulness.

In January 1998 Rowman & Littlefield expressed interest in a finished manuscript of *Fighting in the Jim Crow Army* based upon my proposal. In the two years that I have been collecting data and writing the manuscript, they have maintained a keen interest in the topic. Also during the two years of work on this project, many people supported me. Several people gave me writing space: in Cleveland, Kamla Lewis and Ian Heron lent me a cozy room to sit back and think; in Tucson, Felix and Barbara Goodwin provided a real home-style writing retreat; in Santa Fe, my good friends Carl and Charlotte Berney let me hole up in the back room and empty my mind; and in Palm Springs, my friend Joanne Lilley provided a writing retreat complete with cocktails at five. I want to thank my friends and colleagues who actively listened to my "reports from the road" and sent me clippings and citations from all over the world: Page Evans, Amalia Gonzales, Maurice Isserman, Halle Lewis, Carla Palmer, Posy Quarterman, Susan Rouder, and Elisa Joy White—my special love and thanks to you all. To the Roe-Quarterman family I extend my appreciation for all the love and cheering over the years. This project is an oral history, and I owe a debt of gratitude to my two transcribers, Denise Rehse and Deborah Devitt. For the beautiful handcrafted maps, I send my thanks to Jackie Aher.

My life was enriched because of my interaction with the "old soldiers" of World War II. Many of the men and women whose stories are contained within the book, in effect, have adopted me as their daughter. I cherish the love and friendship of my new family. I realize that I have been entrusted with their stories. I hope they will recognize my labor of love in crafting and combining their histories. This book stands as a legacy to their contributions during one of the most formative times of American history.

I dedicate these pages to their honor.

WE'RE IN THE ARMY NOW

THE "NEGRO PROBLEM"

When the white paratroopers dropped out of the sky and into the military maneuver area around the Pee Dee River in South Carolina, they had no idea that some of the troops waiting for them on that summer day in 1941 were black combat soldiers. The paratroopers were prepared to out-maneuver their opponents in war-preparation training, but when they discovered that one of the opposing teams was black, many of the white paratroopers became enraged.

Felix Goodwin, one of the black combat soldiers, described the encounter:

> Some of those white boys were not really accustomed to the idea of black combat soldiers like us. . . . They were jumping out there without realizing that a black unit was down in those woods. We had little bags of flour to throw on the opponent, and when they got hit, they were supposed to be "dead." When those white boys jumped into that field, we were all over them. It was their worst nightmare. They didn't like the idea of black guys throwing flour on them. So we had a big fight.

In that fight, as in many other altercations between white and black soldiers during the war years, according to Goodwin, "somebody had some live ammunition and some shots were fired." Even though no one was injured in the fracas during the Carolina maneuvers, military officials quickly assigned the black troops to another area.

The army moved the black troops deeper into the South—from South Carolina to an area around Augusta, Georgia. This change of venue was supposed to diffuse the hostile situation the black troops faced. In fact, the move exacerbated tensions, because the local Georgia farmers did not want armed black men in their fields. Goodwin said:

> Those old farmers were raising hell about what they were gonna do with us and all that kind of nonsense. They came down to talk to our [white] commander about getting us out of there. And they brought their hunting dogs with them, too. When the captain went out there to talk to them, well, one of our guys started firing a machine gun into the area. I don't know where the ammunition came from, but I saw one of our guys mounted on top of a truck just firing away. You have never seen dogs and men run so fast in your life. Everybody was hitting the dirt, getting into the ditches, or running like hell. Those farmers were running back toward Augusta as fast as they could. Three of those hunting dogs didn't make it, and of course, our guy got sent to jail. Now this was all before the war even broke out!

Goodwin was a private serving in the 25th Infantry Regiment of the U.S. Army. All service personnel in World War II served in a newly constituted national army—one that was organized differently from those in earlier eras because of the National Defense Act of 1920. The first peacetime draft was implemented in 1940, and National Guard units were federalized, making the World War II army not only a completely national army, but one that was constitutively different from those of other war times. The black soldier served under a new and experimental set of racial policies crafted and re-crafted during the war years. Yet he served much like every other soldier in World War II, without thinking too much about the War Department's policies. At the beginning of World War II, black infantry soldiers were limited to service in only a few units of the Regular Army. All of the units were segregated, and most of them were filled to the maximum allotment for black soldiers. Four all-black units had been in existence since the Civil War: the 9th and 10th Cavalry and the 24th and 25th Infantry. In the period between World War I and World War II, total army personnel stood at 188,000 men, with about 3,700 black soldiers serving in segregated units. The army at that time was maintained strictly by volunteer enlistment handled though recruitment offices around the nation. In 1939, two more all-black units were added, designated as quartermaster or service units. In 1940, more all-black units were added, including more quartermaster units and units in field artillery, antiaircraft, engineer, and chemical warfare.

SEGREGATION WITHOUT DISCRIMINATION

Before World War II, many government agencies studied possible options for racial policies within the armed forces. By the outbreak of the war, no agency or military office had resolved "the Negro problem," as the black soldier population was referred to at the time. After much research, numerous acrimonious debates, more research, presidential edicts, committee reports, and more committee reports, the War Department constructed a segregated policy for the enlistment and usage of black Americans within the armed forces. The department called its approach "segregation without discrimination." True to the time period, military planners did not consider segregation to be inherently unequal. The army of the 1940s was a microcosm of American society—it was segregated and thoroughly racist.

The military segregated its troops, creating separate and usually unequal conditions. Military planners and government officials agreed that segregation was the most efficient manner of dealing with perceived racial differences. Many official documents of the War Department confirm the military's belief that segregation did not constitute discrimination. This is not surprising, considering that *Plessy v. Ferguson*, the 1896 Supreme Court ruling that affirmed "separate-but-equal" as a legal precedent, was still in effect. Many white Americans, in social settings and in government institutions, believed that black people were inferior in intelligence, character, and ability. Racist attitudes prevailed in all strata of American society and also throughout the military. War Department officials constantly stated they were not going to solve the racial problem—a social problem—within the military. *Army Service Forces Manual M5* clarified the official position:

> War Department concern with the Negro is focused directly and solely on the problem of the most effective military use of colored troops. It is essential that there be a clear understanding that the Army has no authority or intention to participate in social reform as such, but does view the problem as a matter of efficient troop utilization.

Efficient troop utilization meant keeping the black soldiers in segregated units, while also attempting to restrict them to service jobs rather than give them combat assignments.

All across America, black infantry soldiers were separated from white soldiers as a result of the army's policy of segregation without discrimination.
Black soldiers were separated from white troops in troop training, work situations, and social settings. Bill Perry even experienced the policy while a
patient at a U.S. Army hospital. He recalled, "I caught pneumonia and got
hospitalized in Alabama. For the first week that I was bedridden they
brought my food to me." Then the next week the white nurses told Perry to
go down to the mess hall and get his own food. When he got to the door he
saw six black soldiers standing outside the door. As he entered the room one
of the black men tapped him on the shoulder and asked where he was going.
Perry replied that he was going in to "fetch" his meal. The soldier shook his
head and told Perry, "You gotta wait until the white guys finish." Perry was
offended. He said, "I had never experienced anything like that, and it was as
if a veil had been lifted, and I began to see things more clearly."

Ultimately, the military's policy of segregation without discrimination
failed in World War II, as it had in every other military engagement since
colonial times. The policy failed to produce military efficiency. Work stoppages on military bases, labor problems with war industry workers, and racial
friction within army units dragged down the efficiency of the war machine.
The policy resulted in both the misuse and the underuse of the black Americans who served in the military during World War II. Rigid segregation dis-
advantaged the black soldier in all social and military settings. Added to the
emotional cost of segregating soldiers was the economic cost of building separate facilities and structures. The multiplicity of government agencies
charged with addressing "the Negro problem" failed to construct a universal
policy approach that did anything more than reflect the general prejudice
rampant in the American ethos.

The Selective Service Act of 1940 was introduced in the House of Representatives by Republican Representative Hamilton Fish, a commander in
World War I of the "Harlem Hellfighters," an all-black infantry regiment.
The debates within Congress and the War Department make it clear that the
final Selective Service bill, Public Law 783, was a compromise reflecting the
prevalent racial attitudes of the day. The original wording of the bill allowed
the president to assign men—white or black—to various units within the
army as situations arose and also to induct any number of men. Secretary of
War Harry H. Woodring responded to the proposed bill by asking Congress
to strike the presidential authority provision from the legislation.

> Its retention . . . might result in the enlistment of Negroes in numbers out
> of all proportion to the colored population of the country. Such a result
> would demoralize and weaken the effect of military units by mixing

colored and white soldiers in closely related units, or even in the same units. It might also have a dangerously adverse effect upon discipline. . . .

The bill, if passed as written, would have given the president the authority to bring black men into every branch of the army, rather than simply the all-black Regular Army units. Additionally, it would have allowed black men to serve in the military in numbers disproportionate to their percentage of the American population. The final compromise bill contained specific instructions to recruit black Americans commensurate with their percentage of the overall population. In the 1940s, thirteen million black Americans made up approximately 10 percent of the country's population. The final bill included provisions that banned discrimination in the recruitment of black men. Sections 3a and 4a of the Selective Service Act specified that, regardless of race, all persons were to be afforded the opportunity to volunteer for induction and that no discrimination in the training or selection of men was to be practiced. However, this policy left intact the racial restrictions whereby black men could only be assigned to one of the all-black Regular Army units. Because very little turnover occurred within those units, new army hopefuls, if they were black, had to wait for someone to retire or for the armed forces to expand before they were inducted into the service.

This technicality kept many black men out of the army. Although the armed forces were expanding, black men were relegated to segregated units, and their processing to active duty was delayed. Between 1940 and 1942, despite the nondiscrimination clause of the Selective Service Act, less than 2 percent of volunteer enlistments came from the black population. Recruitment offices deterred black enlistment by rejecting applicants due to lack of space in the six black-only regiments. Applicants were also rejected due to housing concerns. Because black soldiers had to be segregated, and most bases did not have sufficient space to provide segregated housing, the army was unable to accommodate the number of black men attempting to enlist for service. By the end of World War II, more than two and a half million African Americans had registered to serve in the military, but only about one million were accepted. By 1945, 650,000 black soldiers were serving in the army, with approximately 50,000 in some type of combat capacity. A black soldier in the army could expect routinely to encounter white officers and enlisted men who felt that he was not fit to be in the armed forces except in a service and support capacity. He could also expect to be constrained by the military's racist policies, which limited his opportunities for advancement.

As Congress was passing the Selective Service Act, the army released a new plan for the utilization of black troops, the 1940 Army Plan for Mobilization. The plan contemplated the mobilization of black soldiers equal to their proportion of the total population. Furthermore, the plan called for assignment of black soldiers to all types of units for which the men were qualified. Both combat and service assignments were to be open to black recruits. The army ordered its men into separate and supposedly equal facilities. This experimental plan had little practical consequence: by the end of 1941, only 5 percent of the army's infantry personnel were black. For most of World War II, the army struggled to meet the goals of its 1940 plan and the Selective Service Act. Only in 1944 did the percentage of black army men get close to the stated goal of 10 percent enlistment.

FIGHT AGAINST THE "WORST FORM OF SLAVERY"

Whatever the push or pull factors bringing the men into the armed forces, and despite the restrictions of segregated service, many black men wanted to help protect their nation through military service. The 1940 Army Plan for Mobilization, along with the first peacetime Selective Service Act, ostensibly made volunteering for induction more democratic, because it allowed all groups to participate equally in the armed forces. These new policies and new conditions of service did not create equality between white and black servicemen, but black men still continued to volunteer for or were inducted into the service. Despite the racial restrictions, military constraints, social mores, and inherent distrust that surrounded enlistment in the armed forces, many black men sought to wear the uniform of the United States during the war years. Most Americans, white and black, were swept up in the patriotism of the day that called on men to protect the nation. Many black Americans were thoroughly committed to the fight against fascism, although it is not clear how many believed that it was "the worst form of slavery ever imposed upon the world," as the War Department propaganda charged. In general, black men enlisted in the army for the same reasons as white men did: first, to serve their country; second, for steady employment and better job opportunities; and third, because they felt conditions would be better for them after military service. Of course, the sense of adventure and the inevitability of wartime service were also major reasons for participating. Several black World War II veterans commented on their reasons for serving.

Nelson Peery said he felt that soldiering was a respected profession with secure employment. He noted the prevalence of segregation and discrimination within the army, but he thought conditions were even worse outside of the armed forces. A. William "Bill" Perry, explained how "some things you accepted, you would say 'this is a fact.' When they began to

A. William "Bill" Perry, 1945: "To Mother and Dad"

build up for World War II by adding white units and Negro units, we always figured we'd get the short end of the stick because that's the way life was. We expected, like after every other war, things would improve a little. And I did think that the army would try to live up to a separate-but-equal thing."

Woodrow Walton said he too felt blacks would come up short in the seg-regated army, but he was advised by his friends to just "keep going, and keep cool." Jim Williams said:

> I just thought up until that time the whole world was prejudiced. I thought that even though the army was segregated, if we went in and proved ourselves, in some small way, when we got back home they would have to recognize us. And I thought that in a sense they would have to recognize our deportment in the army and say, "Well, hey, look. These people are A-number-1, so we'll have to treat them as citizens."

Black Americans faced obstacles on their way to becoming soldiers that most whites never encountered. Despite the obstacles, most remained loyal to their country. Perhaps the sentiments of famed boxer Joe Louis best ex-pressed the reasons black men volunteered in the fight against fascism: "There may be a whole lot wrong with America, but there's nothing that Hitler can fix." In 1941 the War Department declared:

> Negroes have been notably a loyal and patriotic group. One of their outstanding characteristics is the single-mindedness of their patriot-ism. They have no other country to which they owe or feel any degree of allegiance. Therefore, they have built in America a fine record of loyalty and willingness to support and defend their native land.

In the press, particularly in the seventy or more newspapers that catered to a black audience, journalists debated the merits of black men fighting for the nation. In a syndicated article titled "A Negro Looks at the War," jour-nalist J. Saunders Redding spelled out the reasons black men should engage in the fight against fascism.

> The issue is plain. The issue, simply, is freedom. Freedom is a precious thing. It used to seem shamefully silly to me to hear Negroes talk about freedom. But now I know that we Negroes here in America know a lot about freedom and love it more than a great many people who have long had it. We see that in the logic of a system based on freedom and the dignity of man we have a chance. This is a war to keep me free. The very fact that I, a Negro in America, can fight against the evils in America is worth fighting for.

While articles in the black press were reporting debates on the merits of service in a segregated army, groups such as the National Association for the

Advancement of Colored People (NAACP), the Congress on Racial Equality (CORE), and the Urban League pressured the War Department to create a racial policy that would address the issues of black service to the nation. The NAACP used its paper, *Crisis*, to induce black Americans to serve in the war effort by equating defense of the country with full citizenship rights. But other papers and individuals questioned why black Americans should serve in a segregated army to protect a racist government.

THE "DOUBLE V" CAMPAIGN

White and black leaders exhorted the black population to participate in the war effort to fight fascism. Black soldiers were asked by some black spokesmen to participate in the war for "Democracy at Home and Democracy Abroad," the so-called "Double V" campaign. Black leaders such as Walter White and A. Philip Randolph used the pages of the Pittsburgh *Courier* to argue the merits of victory against the fascists abroad, as well as victory against racism at home. Many black leaders, government officials, and average citizens believed full participation in the war would bring enhanced rights to America's black citizens after the enemy was defeated. Government officials spoke at public gatherings and worked with the media to garner black support for the war effort. Journalists directed the following message to their black readership: "Today we are engaged in a war in which the freedom of all men is at stake—men of all races and nations. Negroes have a natural and legitimate interest in the fate of oppressed peoples everywhere."

Several issues confronted the average black man with regard to military service in World War II. Besides the ambiguous Double V campaign, black men were confronted with service in a segregated army and the prospect of combat assignments. In black newspapers, and among the men themselves, a plethora of opinions existed. Clyde Whitted said he knew a few men who did not want to serve in the armed forces, but most of his friends and acquaintances "ended up just doing what they were told." Perhaps Spencer Moore's words best reflect the prevailing mood:

I was a kid. I was into having a good time; I wasn't trying to be a hero. I was just following orders. They'd say, "Go here," and I went there. If they said, "Come back," then I would come back. I mean, I didn't know anybody inside the army who was an activist against the Jim Crow situation. We just felt that was the American way. My leaders were my commanding officers, not the race leaders at the time. And personally, my wife and I were our own leaders; we didn't follow the advice of those spokesmen. We would all say "V for Victory," but I wasn't thinking about my civil rights at home. I was thinking about keeping from getting killed, and from my men getting killed. I was thinking about victory abroad for me.

As surveys revealed, black soldiers were not unified in agreement about integration in the military. Because of an individual soldier's background—including his degree of politicization before entering the army, his religious values, and most importantly, his social position and experience—a diversity of opinions prevailed among black Americans. A rift developed among various spokesmen. Some leaders promoted accommodation—acceptance of segregation for now—whereas others agitated for full and immediate integration of America's armed forces. This rift was primarily among elite spokesmen rather than among rank-and-file members of the black community. When the army asked thirteen thousand soldiers whether "white and Negro soldiers should be in separate outfits," only 36 percent of black respondents, and 12 percent of white respondents, answered that blacks and whites should be in the same units. Thirty-eight percent of blacks said they wanted to be in separate units, and 26 percent registered indifference. Government officials were not in agreement over which black leader's views should be given priority. Within the Office of War Information members commented to each other: "As anyone in this field soon discovers, there is no little political pulling and hauling between the various factions of Negro leadership in the government. The current fight for power . . . is indicative. It would be a mistake [for the War Department] to align itself even implicitly with any one group."

Bill Payne said he did not care whether he served in a segregated army. In fact, he never gave much thought to the dispute over integration versus segregation in the military. Payne's goal in life was to be a soldier. He went into the service with the idea of getting a job, learning as much as he could, and advancing up the ladder. He had some quasi-military experience in the Civilian Conservation Corps (CCC), the New Deal make-work program instituted during the Depression. He devoured war stories in pulp-fiction magazines and followed daily radio and newspaper accounts of international affairs. When he learned that black men were being drafted, he and a group of friends went to the local recruiting office and signed up. After the physical and mental exams, two of his friends were rejected, but Payne was accepted into the U.S. Army. He was on his way to fulfilling a boyhood dream, and the army's policy of segregated service was far from his mind.

With American entry into World War II in late 1941, civilian and military planners became concerned about creating a universal, servicewide policy to counteract rising discontent among black soldiers. Given the state of the international emergency, military planners were especially concerned about designing an effective policy to utilize black troops. The War Department was pressured from all sides to do something proactive to increase enlistment of black soldiers. However, there was not a general consensus among the public voices, nor a united push from within the War Department, to change the segregationist policies in effect at the time. Military planners were confused with the multitude of opinions and voices, so they did very little to change existing policies. Still, many black Americans wanted to serve in the armed forces, segregated or not. A majority of eligible black males attempted to enlist in the military. The reasons they gave were patriotism, a spirit of adventure, and a hope for improved employment and educational opportunities. In 1942, the War Department finally activated two full divisions of black soldiers, with about eighteen thousand men to each division, and the nature of race relations in America changed forever.

MY COUNTRY 'TIS OF THEE

Black men came into the army from all regions of the United States. Some "got the greetings from Uncle Sam," and others volunteered for service. One army newspaper, reporting on the black soldiers who were convening at a new training camp, printed the following: "The Negro soldiers here come from all walks of life. Some of them are college graduates and some have only gone as far as the third grade. Here, there are former porters, waiters, teachers, newspaper reporters, entertainers, lawyers, doctors, boot blacks, etc." Many of the men were raised in the same town where they were born, then made their first trip through America on an army troop train. Some men came from industrial cities in the Northeast; some came from farms and fields in the South. Before World War II, many black families had migrated out of the South looking for better job opportunities; yet, at the start of World War II, more than 75 percent of black Americans still lived in the South, and about half of those lived in rural areas. When black recruits were inducted into the service and brought together into segregated units, they had to overcome their regional differences in order to form fighting units. They had varied educational backgrounds, ranged in age from eighteen to thirty-six, and differed culturally because of their regional distinctions. In short, the men had nothing in common except the color of their skin.

Some of the black soldiers were young, or not yet born, when their families chose to migrate out of the South. The pre–World War I depression in the South and a string of natural disasters such as floods and infestations of boll weevils forced many families to leave the only homeland they had ever known. Not all of the migrating black families moved to the industrial regions of the North, but most moved into areas more urban than the ones they had left. Woodrow Walton's family members were "sharecroppers run out of Georgia by the boll weevil." They migrated to the western part of North Carolina and took up farming cotton, corn, and wheat. Walton went to school in split terms—one term for school, one term for farming. He was working on the family farm and also in a sawmill when the army sent him his draft notice.

Many black families were forced to leave the South. Allen Thompson described one such forced move that is indicative of the situations faced by other black families. Thompson said his family came from Mississippi to Ohio via Kentucky. Getting out of Mississippi was an ordeal:

> Oh, I know why my grandparents left the South, if that's permissible for me to say now. Well, it had to do with race and prejudice. My grandfather was an excellent farmer. And my grandmother, who was half Irish, kept the books for his farming. He dealt with a commissary in town for things he could not grow. At the end of the year when he'd go to the commissary to check out the balances for the year, he found he was always behind. My grandmother told him: "Jim, you do not owe that man anything." She said, "Your balance is good. You don't owe him any money."
>
> So Grandpa took his books down to the commissary to show the man. The man got upset, abusive, and violent. He got a poker from an old pot-belly stove and went after my grandfather. My grandfather took it away from him and beat the man. That's why my grandfather had to leave Mississippi. And the townspeople knew my grandfather and liked my grandfather and knew what the conditions were and what they had to do. So they put Grandpa in a pickle barrel and shipped him to Kentucky and then he made his way to Ohio. He went to Kentucky to get out of Mississippi to avoid getting minced. That's the way he got out; he left with assistance, you could say.

More than one million black southerners migrated to the North at the beginning of the previous century in what would later be labeled the "Great Migration." Black families migrated from predominantly rural communities to urban areas. Here, the breadwinners developed new work skills to fit the growing demands of a modernizing America. Others already had the new skills but could not find work in their new hometowns. William "Ted" McCullough described how his father came North looking for work.

I was born in Birmingham, Alabama, but I was raised in Gary, Indiana.
My dad came looking for work in the steel industry. He was an un-
skilled laborer. When the mills starting closing down in Birmingham,
my father hopped a freight train and came all the way to Indiana looking for work. He was a Mason and some of the watchmen on the trains
were Masons. When he got ready to hop the freight, he threw the
Mason's distress signal, and the watchmen just acted like they didn't
see him when he got on the train.

Dennett Harrod's father and grandfather also worked in steel mills, although his family had been in the North for some time. Harrod described the
changing conditions in the post–World War I Pennsylvania steel mills. "Things
changed dramatically for blacks because of a large influx of southern Euro-
peans into the job market. The unions locked in jobs for union members, and
blacks were not allowed to join the unions." When the Depression of the
1930s hit the steel towns, Harrod's father was laid off. The stress of unem-
ployment on the Harrod family "broke them up," so young Harrod and his
mother went to live with his grandparents in Washington, D.C. Harrod
worked after school as a delivery boy for a drugstore, making a dollar a day,
relatively good money at that time. His mother had a part-time job cooking for
women who worked in the government, and she also worked at a local hotel.

When McCullough and Harrod joined the army, they felt that the difficult conditions of life in the military would certainly be better than the economic deprivation that had been the hallmark of their lives during the Depression. Although both had attended college before they were drafted,
neither McCullough nor Harrod had met so many people with diverse backgrounds until they went into the service. The same was true for Bill Perry
when he first joined the service.

A bunch of guys from Cleveland were on the train with me going down
to Fort McClellan, Alabama. When we got settled into the fort, then I
met men from all over the country. I met some guys from South Carolina, one kid from Birmingham—we were about the same age so we
made friends pretty fast.

The common bonding experience of military service helped all of the men
form long-lasting relationships with recruits and draftees from other regions
of the country.

Many families and individuals were assisted by the make-work programs instituted during the Depression by the Roosevelt administration. Some of these
jobs pulled black families to new locations, while others assisted families in

their own hometowns. The separate but similar experiences of Fred Watt and Felix Goodwin illustrate the ways in which the federal government assisted families in distress. After his father died when Watt was only five years old, he and his mother went to Tennessee to live with an aunt. Watt went to a segregated school—combined grammar and high school—with about three thousand other students.

> The Negro schools down there did not have people to clean up or do the engineering tasks like fire up the boiler. The principal knew about my mechanical skills and abilities, so while I was going to high school they got me this National Youth Authority job taking care of the stoker for the boiler at my school building. So in my high school training I had what we would call manual training. That included electricity, building homes, plumbing, and also two years of chemistry.

After high school, Watt worked at a munitions plant loading TNT into shells. Drafted when he was nineteen years old, he had not previously thought of military service in terms of a career, even though his grandfather had served in the Civil War and his uncle had been in World War I. He indicated to the officer at the induction center that he wanted to obtain medical training, or perhaps even learn dentistry, during his military stint. He wanted to expand his opportunities. The officer asked Watt if he wanted to be a paratrooper, and he said no—that was more than he had bargained for. So he was assigned to the 364th Engineering outfit in the army, where his mechanical and engineering skills could best be utilized.

Felix Goodwin, like Fred Watt, advanced his knowledge and opportunities through a Roosevelt Depression program. Facing a lack of job opportunities, Goodwin joined the CCC in 1937 after high school. The CCC, a military-style training program in which army officers commanded units of civilian men, performed public service tasks, such as getting alligators out of the swamps of South Carolina, building hiking trails in the San Francisco Bay Area, and supporting black cavalry troops in Kansas. Goodwin's father, a Baptist minister, died when Goodwin was a young boy, and his mother was working at a small school district in Kansas, running the cafeteria and teaching in the home economics department. After his two-year stint in the CCC, Goodwin came back to his hometown of Kansas City and tried to get a job, but there were few opportunities. With his CCC experience, he thought himself "better than any of those low-paying jobs"—the only ones available for a young black man. So he took a job working in a restaurant as a busboy just to survive. His experience was not uncommon for a young black man, yet it was formative. One day, three white men who had been drinking entered the restaurant and told Goodwin to dance:

"Come here, boy. Do the 'buck-and-wing' for us."
"Sir, I am sorry, but I do not know how to dance," Goodwin replied.
"Oh, come on, now. All niggers know how to dance."

When Goodwin turned his back to walk away, the man started cussing and "a little altercation took place." Goodwin lost his restaurant job but soon found another doing yard work for a doctor's wife. Goodwin noticed that she entertained gentlemen visitors during the day, while her husband was at work. "She decided I was available, and I can tell you I was scared. This was back in the days of the Scottsboro Boys [the 1930s case of nine black youths convicted of raping two white women], so naturally I was nervous. My mother told me to get myself out of there and I did." With fifty-one cents in his pocket, Goodwin hopped a freight train going to Arizona to try his luck with the army. Like many other black men of that era, Goodwin viewed service in the armed forces as a means to learn new skills and maintain steady employment.

When Goodwin decided to enter the service, he knew he did not want to join one of the two black cavalry units. He had spent two years of military-style life in the CCC around the 10th Cavalry at Fort Leavenworth and the 9th Cavalry at Fort Riley, Kansas. His jobs in the CCC kept him busy trimming trees, crushing rocks, cutting officers' lawns, and doing other yard work. He also learned clerical skills while working as an assistant to the educational adviser of the camp. Goodwin noticed that in addition to yard work, the cavalry soldiers were taking care of the horses belonging to the officers and their wives. "I had never seen so much horse manure in my whole life. And I had never seen such big shovels. So right then I decided I wanted to be in the infantry, not the cavalry." The cavalry was located in Kansas, and the infantry was in Arizona. This meant Goodwin had to go to the area where the infantry was located and hope for an opening in one of the units stationed there.

Goodwin got lucky and was inducted into the infantry, but his first assignment was as unglamorous as the manure-shoveling cavalry he cast aside. He was assigned to be a "striker" in the officers' quarters. A striker is just a "houseboy," Goodwin explained, and his tasks included waxing all the oak wood in the officers' quarters as well as serving drinks at cocktail parties. Goodwin was chosen for the job when his commanding officer assembled all the light-skinned soldiers in the all-black company, including Goodwin, and inspected their fingernails for signs of manual labor. After passing that examination, Goodwin lasted only a weekend on the job. Then, in what could

have been a career-limiting move, he told the captain's wife that he did not
want to be a houseboy. He told her he was in the army to be a soldier. "She
was a typical, old-Army-type wife," Goodwin recalled.

> She started drinking in the morning, and she drank until evening, all
> the while ordering you around like she was the captain. When I quit,
> she got mad as a hornet and called the captain on the phone telling
> him about me. He called me in and said, "If you think you are too good
> to do this kind of work, then just what do you think you can do in this
> army?" And I told him about the things I did in the Three Cs, includ-
> ing typing and taking shorthand. The next thing you know he's dictat-
> ing, and I'm taking a test.

Goodwin did so well on the test that instead of being punished for quitting
his job as a striker, he was assigned as a clerk in the judge advocate's office
on the post.

Spencer Moore came into the army after the 1940 mobilization plans
opened up more opportunities for black men to serve, and his army experience altered his life in a positive way. Moore had not been out of his hometown until he was in the service. In fact, Moore's family had been in the
Cherry Hill, New Jersey, area for more than two hundred years, and they
were deeply entrenched in both the white and black neighborhoods of the
town. Moore describes the black–white marriages in his family as "God's
will, because if He didn't want intermarriage, He would have made it so the
parts don't fit." Moore's father was a country doctor, and his mother was a
nurse—they both provided health care to the local community. Moore graduated from high school in 1940 and then enlisted in the New Jersey State
Militia. That September, the militia changed into a National Guard unit, the
first black guard unit in the state of New Jersey. The unit even had black
commanders, including a full colonel.

In February 1941, they were called up to serve their year. "You know,
good-bye dear, be back in a year," Moore said. His unit formed the 372nd
Infantry Regiment, one of the six all-black regiments in the Regular Army.
Moore was still in the service and still stateside in 1943 when he married his
fiancée, Susie, on a weekend leave. Susie was just a senior in high school,
and her family was upset with her marrying a "fly-by-night soldier boy."
Moore had seen Susie's picture and arranged to meet her where she attended church. He put pressure on Susie to marry him before he was sent
overseas to war. Susie was swept away and succumbed to Moore's proposal,
marrying him one week afterward. Susie finished her senior year in high
school and then joined Moore at his training base in Arizona.

"I DIDN'T EXPECT TO BE ANY HERO"

Although many blacks were eager to serve in the military, some were not. Lawrence Johnson said he "did not want to go into the military, period." In Johnson's Chicago neighborhood there were several World War I veterans who told him war stories and instilled fear in him. "It wasn't my choice to go in, and when they called me, I didn't expect to be any hero." He was tested and told he had mechanical aptitude. The army sent him to a base in Maryland and put him to work on jeeps, light tanks, armored cars, half-tracks, and tank destroyers. Nominated for Officer Candidate School (OCS), Johnson refused to go because he "wasn't making a career out of the army." He was one of many not-so-eager men who served in World War II. Even men raised on military bases or in military families did not automatically choose the military as a career.

Reuben Horner was born at Fort Ethan Allen, where his father served with the 10th Cavalry, more commonly known as the Buffalo Soldiers. Horner's father was intrigued with the military life because his father had fought in the Civil War, and he had grown up hearing stories of a soldier's life. Rather than go to college as his parents wanted him to do, Horner's father went to Norfolk, Virginia, to enlist in the navy.

> When he got there two things decided him against the navy. One, was the day he arrived they were doing personal laundry and washing. He didn't want to do that. Then, most of the sailors he talked to were stewards. He decided that was not for him, so he enlisted in the army.

Horner's father married while stationed in the Philippines and brought his wife back to live in the United States. The family lived in Fort Huachuca (pronounced Wa-chu-ka), Arizona, where young Reuben went to the black school on the post. As an officer's son, he could go to the stables, saddle up his father's horse, and ride all through the countryside. The Buffalo Soldiers watched out for the officers' kids and even allowed some of them onto the firing range after the soldiers had fired. There, Horner says, he learned to shoot while "playing army." Yet, when it came to choosing a career for Horner, his father wanted him to prepare for something better than a $21-per-month soldiering job. So Horner went to college, graduated from the University of Arizona, married, and got a job working for the U.S. Postal Service. When the army established a volunteer officer candidate program prior to World War II, Horner's father encouraged him to sign up because he could expect to be paid $50 a month when he finished the course. Only then did Horner begin to think of the military as a career choice.

There were various ways that men attempted to get out of military service, from marriage and job deferments, to educational rejections, to outright refusal to register. Conrad Lynn of New York reported for duty but sued the military because he felt its segregation policies were unconstitutional and in violation of the antidiscrimination clause of the 1940 Selective Service Act. Lynn told the draft board: "I am ready to serve in any unit of the armed forces of my country which is not segregated by race. Unless I am assured that I can serve in a mixed regiment and that I will not be compelled to serve in a unit undemocratically selected as a Negro group, I will refuse to report for induction." Although his case was taken up by the NAACP and supported by A. Philip Randolph's March on Washington Movement and the Workers' Defense League, Lynn lost the case when the court upheld the army's quota and segregation system.

Although antiwar or antiarmy sentiment was not that widespread, it was still a point of discussion among many men, both civilian and military. No matter how few black men read C. L. R. James's writing in the 1940s, his sentiments capture the attitude of many less-than-enthusiastic soldiers.

> Why should I shed my blood for Roosevelt's America, for Cotton Ed Smith and Senator Bilbo, for the whole Jim Crow, Negro-hating South, for the low-paid, dirty jobs for which Negroes have to fight, for the few dollars of relief and the insults, discrimination, police brutality, and perpetual poverty to which Negroes are condemned even in the more liberal North? When the working Negro asks this question, what can the warmongers say to him? Nothing. Nothing but lies and empty promises of better treatment in the future. Why must I die for them? I am not afraid to fight. Negroes have been some of the greatest fighters in history. But the democracy that I want to fight for, Hitler is not depriving me of.

Reuben Horner said some men talked about resisting the draft because they knew about the rough conditions black men faced in the army. "In our local barbershop the Pittsburgh *Courier* was distributed, and that led to some real heated arguments about whether we should volunteer to fight or not." Nelson Peery echoed that sentiment with his description of men in his unit. He wrote, "Drafted, they came grumbling and cursing." All grumbling aside, most black men who were drafted subsequently reported for duty. Military authorities noted that very few men failed to report for induction, citing only a "few hundred individuals among three million Negro registrants" indicted for evasion of the draft. Men who intentionally failed the test, whom the army termed "malingerers," were few, yet army officials still worried they would affect the morale of the other men. Hank Williams noted mixed feelings among his friends regarding military service. He said:

> Maybe once in a while when we would get together we would talk about what was going on in Europe, and what was going on at home. But mostly I had to concentrate on my job and getting there and getting back home. I wasn't particularly fearful. We didn't have people that I ran across who said "I don't want to go." There may have been some, but I didn't know them, and nobody talked like that around me.

Most men simply accepted the wartime inevitability of military service.

Still, the quota system that limited the men to slots in black-only units hindered their enlistment overall. Twice the number of men were on the available registry than were accepted into the armed forces. The "Order to Report for Induction" began with "Greetings;" and continued with "you are hereby notified that you have been selected for training and service in the _____." Most black men who were drafted found "Army" filled into that blank. Many who were inducted—whether through the draft or by volunteering—thought they were going to be given a choice of service. "I enlisted in the service when I was promised that my choice of service would be honored," said Donald McNeil. "That promise was not kept." Bill Perry volunteered for the draft at eighteen. He explained his "choice" of the army in this manner:

> In the navy you could only be a mess man, and I didn't want that. There were very limited opportunities in the air corps. You didn't really have a choice—you thought you did, but you really didn't. They assigned you where they wanted you to go. It wasn't like now, where you go in and pick a branch of the service that you want to enter. Then, they mostly assigned blacks to the army, so that's where you went.

At one point, the Perry family had three sons in the army—they displayed three blue stars in the living room window for all the neighbors to see.

Clyde Whitted was drafted into the army. He did not have the least desire to go into the service—he had four children with another on the way and was suffering from asthma. Whitted said he figured the army would not want a thirty-four-year-old man with asthma and all of the complications of family life, but they sent him the "Greetings" during Christmas. Whitted hoped to be assigned to one of the two black cavalry units so that he could utilize his blacksmith skills. However, neither the 9th nor the 10th Cavalry was operational by the time Whitted was drafted. He was first assigned to be a slinger, "where you sling cargo off the freight trains onto the ships." After a short while, he was assigned as a chauffeur, driving personnel and, at times, heavy weapons. "I was in the army," he recalled. "Whatever I was asked to do, that's what I did."

Edgar Whitley was eighteen years old and just getting ready to graduate from high school when the army tapped him for service. True, it was wartime, but Whitley believed he was safe from the draft while in high school. Not true, he learned. One day after he had come home from school his mother said, "Son, you got a letter." "Who'd be writing me?" he asked. His mother broke down crying and sobbed, "It's from Uncle Sam; he's sent you the Greetings." After Whitley recovered from the shock, he went down to the induction office to take a battery of tests. Like other inductees, Whitley answered questions about his preference for the navy or the army, believing all the while that he had a choice in the matter. "I heard that the army was very tough, so I told the man that I wanted to be in the navy. Then the guy stamped 'army' on my papers, and Ha! That was it. I was in the army!"

Cleother Hathcock was also a young man with aspirations to go to college and learn a trade when he was drafted out of high school. Hathcock had been brought up in a hardworking household, yet he knew he could not do the same type of hard, physical labor as his father for a career. Hathcock's father worked on the railroad in Florida, and after a full day of backbreaking work he would "throw a cross-tie on each shoulder and bring them home. He didn't have any other way to haul them—no truck or anything." Hathcock said his father could haul twenty railroad cross-ties a quarter of a mile in a half hour. "It was nothing for him to pick up one of those cross-ties on one shoulder and one on the other and bring them home. Nothing." Hathcock's mother had also done exhausting physical work, having grown up in a sharecropper's family. Hathcock heard stories about his mother plowing in the fields just like the men. He was in awe of both his parents, realizing all the time that he could never do the type of work his father and mother had done. Hathcock said he could barely pick up one cross-tie— certainly not two—and he was not interested in farming as a career. His plans for advancement through college were disrupted when he got drafted as an eighteen-year-old high school junior. He quickly modified his plans for the future.

At that time, I guess being young I wanted to see the world and everything. And I thought I could do that in the navy. Once I was called, they gave me a card that said "army or navy." I asked for the navy, but the navy had taken up more than their quota the day before. They didn't tell me that they were not putting me in the navy. They just said,

"Stand over here." There were about ten of us, and they told all of us the same thing. Then when we looked, we had cards saying "army." We thought we had made a request, but all of us went into the army.

Before the outbreak of World War II, William Banks was involved in a teacher education program at Fort Valley State College in Georgia. As the supervisor of the project, Banks crafted the curriculum that taught educators in the predominantly rural and agricultural state of Georgia how to implement improved farming techniques in their communities. Aware of the growing world unrest, Banks was not about to run down to his local recruiting office to volunteer for service. His two brothers had already been called up, which left Banks shouldering the responsibility of caring for his parents. He felt that he was already contributing to the war effort by training and teaching young students how to improve themselves. He had high hopes for the new agricultural program at the college. Banks was not gung ho about the military; he had a good job, and he was already burdened with extra responsibility. But like many Americans at that time, when Banks received his notice to report to the local recruitment office, he settled his affairs at the college, said good-bye to family and friends, and headed off to "make the world safe for democracy."

ONE WAY OUT

Joe Stephenson had dreams of coaching football and teaching science in his hometown of Greensboro, North Carolina. "The only jobs I could get after graduating from North Carolina A&T were in the lumber mills or the tobacco farms. The opportunities were just not there. So I went down to the draft board and got on the list, but they were slow in drafting me. And nobody wanted to hire me because I was classified 1-A, ready to go. So I just went in and volunteered. I enlisted and they inducted me into the army in Fort Bragg, North Carolina."

Another young inductee, Levi Hill, called himself a "baby-in-arms." He enlisted in the army at a young age in order to escape the ghettos of Philadelphia. Gang wars and rough crowds were pulling him in, so he secured his family's permission to enlist. Hill saw the army as an opportunity—an avenue to success. The only black workers he saw in his neighborhood were bus drivers and laborers. He decided his chances for better employment lay in military service. Before Levi Hill and Joe Stephenson entered the service, both remembered their impressions of meeting World War I veterans. Stephenson said, "I was just a young kid, and I was impressed when these two heroes came to our school. They had really done something during the war, and they were in the history books!" Both Stephenson and Hill said that the military offered them opportunities they could not find in their own hometowns.

Like Stephenson, Edward Price tried to get in the army, but the recruiters said they had met the quota and would not accept his application. Price was on track to be a barber, like his father and grandfather. He shined shoes at his father's barbershop until he was eleven, when his father unexpectedly died. Price then worked odd jobs until he was sixteen, when he forged his mother's name on a CCC application and was assigned to duty at a camp at Mammoth Cave, Kentucky. The CCC team was building up the cave, constructing right-of-ways and large living quarters, for possible human habitation. The CCC also worked fighting forest fires in the area. Price commented on the work:

> You met all types of people at the camp, a lot of types I was never exposed to, a lot of boys from the city. I was a country boy, and I wasn't used to all the fighting that those guys did. They all knew I was too young to be there, but they would protect me and tell the others, "Oh, yeah, he's eighteen you know." I tried to volunteer for the service when I got out of the camp, but they said, "We have our quota," so I had to wait until they drafted me, which they did.

Allen Thompson said military service did not enter his mind as a career choice. No one in his family had ever served in the armed forces or considered a military career. His father worked in the Cleveland area at a foundry, and after school Thompson did odd jobs like shining shoes and sewer work. His mother was "the best seamstress in town." He wanted to go to college because she had instilled that aspiration in him at an early age. She arranged a job for her son at Wilberforce University as a driver so he could attend that college. Thompson drove for a short time and then got a job taking care of the administration building. That job paid his room and board, and his parents paid the tuition. He studied history and political science, hoping to become a teacher.

He was drafted in October 1941 before he could finish college. His mother, Thompson recalled, had been orderly and precise, and that training assisted him in adapting to military life, although he still encountered situations for which he was unprepared. "Roosevelt brought me into the service, and that's where I got the shock of my life. I had white friends at home and at our high school. Plus my family is all mixed up with white and black. My uncles married Irish women. I wasn't brought up to be prejudiced about race. But when I got to the military camp around Columbus, Ohio, they said,

'You colored soldiers over there, and you white soldiers over here.' It was a shock. I did not expect that type of thing. Right there the army started separating men."

When the War Department reviewed its experimental policy of segregation without discrimination, they concluded that black soldiers were "happy and content under the existing policy" because they had continued to reenlist in high numbers. Despite the discussions of draft resistance and other modes of discontent, most black men entered the service and fulfilled their duty to the nation. The soldiers were admonished to "close ranks" in order to fight the real war. Major General Charles Hall, commander of one group of black soldiers, counseled the men: "We, the living, are engaged in the greatest war in history. This is no time for petty dislikes or internal bickering. We are fighting for the existence of our national family—and a family divided will surely fall." In case the average black soldier missed the general's message, the following plea, written by Frank E. Bolden, Pittsburgh *Courier* war correspondent, was widely circulated in the post newspaper.

I sometimes wonder if the men serving in this combat unit are aware of the great responsibility that rests upon their shoulders. In making my trips around the camp during the Division's activation, I have been impressed by those who are aware of the magnitude of responsibility and the opportunities that this Colored army unit affords. THEY ARE SOLDIERING FOR AMERICA AND THEIR RACE. As far as Colored citizens are concerned, they are duty bound to do their bit AS THEY ALWAYS HAVE WHEN THIS COUNTRY'S LIBERTIES WERE IMPERILED. This is YOUR COUNTRY AND IT IS WORTH FIGHTING FOR BECAUSE YOU WOULDN'T TRADE IT FOR ANY OTHER WHEN THE CHIPS ARE DOWN. You have never had another military opportunity in race history as you have now. Get in on the gravy train with biscuit wheels! BE A SOLDIER.

THE POLITICS OF RACE

Employment discrimination and underutilization of black troops were two major issues in the 1940 presidential election. During the campaign, Republicans included an equal-rights plank in their party platform. Wendell Willkie, the Republican candidate, directly addressed race relations in one campaign speech: "Our very proclamations of what we are fighting for have rendered our own inequities self-evident. When we talk of freedom and opportunity for all nations, the mocking paradoxes in our own society become so clear they can no longer be ignored." Black Americans had defected from the Republican Party in the 1936 national elections and were being lured back when Democrats co-opted the Republicans' traditional issues. While the concept of black Republicans might seem an anomaly today, Felix Goodwin described how they were viewed at the time.

> Beginning in the 1920s in Kansas, many black Republicans belonged to a group called the Sunflower Club. My dad belonged and many of his friends. They were Republicans, the party of Lincoln. When the Republican Alf Landon ran against Franklin Roosevelt, my whole family was out campaigning for Al. We would have been in Washington if he had made president. It was only when Roosevelt started using the government to help the black folk that we started voting Democrat.

During the 1940 election, garnering the black vote became crucial to Roosevelt's election success. A. Philip Randolph, leader of the Brotherhood of Sleeping Car Porters, threatened to lead a march on Washington to pressure the White House to end racial discrimination and increase public awareness about racial issues. Many spokesmen, including Randolph and W. E. B. Du Bois, wanted Roosevelt to appoint a black member to his cabinet of advisers. Many believed that a black cabinet member could deal with issues of concern to the black population. There was no discussion of appointing a black American to the cabinet simply because he or she could do a job, or any job not related to minority issues. Rienzi Lemus, a black combat veteran from the Philippine insurrection of the early 1900s, wondered why "colored persons could not be appointed to the President's cabinet as a person" rather than by race. Although President Roosevelt was pressured by many factions, he did not appoint a black person to a traditional cabinet post. From Roosevelt's executive office George Barnes commented to Ulric Bell at the Office of Facts and Figures that the president had not "succumbed to the perennial proposals to include a Negro in the White House secretariat," although he did appoint "special civilian advisors for Negro affairs."

In the 1940 election campaign, Roosevelt took advantage of his incumbency by expanding existing assistance programs to appease the black vote. Goodwin commented:

> The CCC, NRA, WPA—all those kinds of organizations helped black people who did not have jobs. Like in 1936 or so, when Kansas stopped paying its teachers. We got some sort of food coupons from the government, like food stamps today. My mother was too proud to

use them, so she just stored them in her bedroom. But one day when she was at school teaching, and my brother and I were at home for some reason, we decided to go into her room and get those coupons. We were hungry, and there was no real food in the house. We weren't supposed to go into Momma's room, but we did it. We got this old yellow flour container and a wagon and went down to the food center.

We couldn't come back through the white neighborhood or we would have been arrested. And we were afraid to go through the black neighborhood because bigger kids would beat us up to get the food. So we came back with our wagon through the alleys that divided the white and black neighborhoods. I'd go out front and check to see if there were any colored kids, then I'd check to see if any white kids were coming. We came all the way back to our street with our wagon loaded up with butter, flour, sugar, potatoes, all kinds of stuff including those red cans of stringy beef. We mixed some water in with the cornmeal, and cooked that on the griddle on top of the stove. We got out pots and pans, then boiled the onions and the potatoes. I made a pie crust and baked the whole thing together.

When Momma came in the door and smelled all that food cooking, she screamed out: "I knew you were going to get mixed up with those robbers! Where did you get that food?" I told her we had got those coupons from her room and gone down to get the food. She started crying and saying that I had disgraced this family and all that. I told her I had seen Mr. Brown there and Mr. Boardman, from the church, and so on. She started crying harder.

When we went to church the next time, one of the men told her, "Lucille, your boys are real nice. They were very well behaved when they came down to get their food." And then he told her the best time for us to come down there, when it wouldn't be so busy and when they would be expecting us. The next time I went down there I carried a hatchet tied to my waist with a little piece of leather. Like an old Indian hatchet. One time a kid came up like he was going to get the wagon, and I drew that old hatchet back over my head, and he went tearing off. We still had to defend ourselves because not everybody had even what we had.

On the eve of the election, in a 1940s-style "election surprise," President Roosevelt announced several concessions meant to build support among the black electorate. He ordered the immediate formation of black aviation and Regular Army combat units. He signed into law the antidiscrimination clause of the 1940 Selective Service Act, which was meant to provide equality in enlistment. He promoted Colonel Benjamin O. Davis Sr. to brigadier general—the highest position attained by a black man in the military. Roosevelt could have issued an executive order banning segregation in the military, which might have led the nation into a new era of race relations, but instead he chose to downplay the segregation issue, never acting to overcome the inherent discrimination involved in the separate-but-equal practice. When asked in a letter from the Reverend Dr. W. H. Jernagin, director of the Fraternal Council of Negro Churches, to explain the policy of segregation in the military, Roosevelt responded through his administrative assistant, Jonathan Daniels: "The policy of establishing separate units is based upon long experience and statutes of the Congress which authorize the formation of such units in our regular establishment." But, as a final vote-getting appeasement, Roosevelt appointed William Hastie, federal judge and dean of the traditionally black Howard University Law School, as "Advisor for Negro Affairs," an assistant to the secretary of war. Overall, the president's well-timed gestures rallied most black Americans to vote Democratic in the 1940 election.

Judge Hastie suspected that the motives behind his appointment were merely political machinations, and he accepted the position with some reluctance. He was convinced that any new military policies he recommended would be delayed or not implemented at all. One of his first assignments was to study the conditions of black Americans within the armed forces. Distrustful of the glut of studies previously commissioned by the military, Hastie gathered a team to redo the work. In the end he recommended the military integrate its troops for reasons of efficiency. About segregation he wrote: "This approach is not working. In the army the Negro is taught to be a man, a fighting man; in brief, a soldier. It is impossible to create a dual personality which will be on the one hand a fighting man toward the foreign enemy, and on the other, a craven who will accept treatment as less than a man at home." As Hastie predicted, the military hierarchy in the War Department rejected his recommendations. They restated the extant policy, which placed the issue of integration within the social, not the military, sphere. Army Chief of Staff General George C. Marshall wrote to Hastie: "Your solution . . . would be tantamount to solving a social problem which has perplexed the American people throughout the history of this nation. The army cannot accomplish such a solution, and should not be charged with the undertaking." Marshall said he wanted the War Department to focus on the larger issue of the war and drop discussion of the "vexing problem." Marshall also asked for recognition of what he termed the basic facts: The American people had established the relationship between the races through both custom and habit; rather than interfere, the War Department should honor that relationship.

In the 1940s, black Americans constituted approximately 10 percent of the overall population—13 million people out of 130 million total. In the military—predominantly the army—blacks represented only 5.8 percent of the total number of servicemen, even after the nondiscriminatory selective service standards were instituted. Many civil rights groups, as well as numerous individuals, pressured the White House to review the racial policies of the military. Secretary of War Henry L. Stimson wrote in his diary: "There is a tremendous drive going on by the Negroes, taking advantage of the last weeks of the campaign in order to force the army and navy into doing things for their race which would not otherwise be done and which are certainly not in the interest of sound national defense." Many black Americans also pressured Eleanor Roosevelt, the president's wife, to take up their cause with her husband. She had been sympathetic in the past; thus, many civilians as well as soldiers made a special appeal to her. Private Jubie Bragg, who had recently been passed over for promotion, wrote to Mrs. Roosevelt, asking her to look into his situation. He wrote: "I feel that I can be of invaluable service in some capacity. . . . I feel that you are the one person that can help me to realize that goal. I feel that your keen understanding of the sacredness of human personality will help me."

Another black soldier, Private Charles F. Wilson, wrote to President Roosevelt to protest the "undemocratic Jim Crow segregation" practiced in the army. He implored Roosevelt to recognize the contributions of black soldiers and develop a national policy to deal with discrimination. Wilson wrote: "In the interest of victory another Executive Order is now needed which will lay the base for fighting for democracy in the Armed Forces of our country." But Roosevelt, always the consummate politician, did not want to anger either southern voters or the military hierarchy, both of whom called for the maintenance of segregation, so he did nothing to change the status quo. While none of the pressure from individuals and groups changed the policy of segregation, the sustained pressure—and more importantly the need for manpower—pushed the military into activating two all-black infantry divisions.

OUTRANKED

Despite the restrictive racial policies within the military, there were more opportunities in World War II for black men to be commissioned as officers than there were in World War I. In June 1942 the Pittsburgh *Courier* printed an article about the new policies within the 93rd Infantry Division. "When the 93rd goes into action it will carry a living symbol of American democracy in action . . . this combat unit will be led by both colored and white officers—a distinct departure from the military policy of World War I. Colored officers, fresh from training, are arriving daily . . . and are ready to help the Tan Yanks keep their rendezvous with history." But even after the Reserve Officer Training Corps (ROTC, a college military-prep program), the newly instituted volunteer officer candidate program, or Officer Candidate School (OCS), black officers were not easily given commissions or allowed to utilize their leadership skills. Military planners usually placed white Southern officers in command of black troops. These officers were presumed to have an understanding of blacks because they had lived and worked with them in the past. One black officer in the 93rd commented that the "so-called southern aristocracy ran the army. The white upper echelon in the military would sit up nights trying to think of ways to keep the Negro soldier, particularly the officers, in 'their place.'"

Many black soldiers became aware that the army had a policy of placing white officers in command of black troops. Bill Perry encountered a few black officers, but he noted how little authority they were given. He was certain that some sort of policy to prevent black soldiers from advancement was in place. Most high-ranking black officers he encountered were either chaplains or doctors, who had no authority over white soldiers. "It appeared as if the army never let a black man outrank a white man in any kind of working relationship," he said. In fact, it was official policy. The army's 1940 Plan for Mobilization specified that black officers were to command only black troops. No black officer could command a white enlisted man, and no black officer could hold a position higher than any of the white officers in the unit. Major General Virgil L. Peterson, Inspector General of the Army, clarified the policy in a memorandum to the War Department. "Except for medical officers and chaplains," he wrote, "senior Negro officers will not be assigned to a unit having white officers of other arms and services in junior grades."

Military planners discussed the black officer policy in numerous top-level meetings. Field commanders complained that the policy was ambiguous: Could a black officer be in a higher grade than a white officer on the same base, or did the limitation apply only within the same unit? The War Department received so many letters and requests from white commanding officers asking for clarification of the existing black officer policy that the Inspector General finally redrafted it. In March 1943 the policy was amended to be more specific. An internal recommendation, written by the Inspector General and stamped "Approved" by the secretary of war, altered the policy to read: "Except for medical officers and chaplains, senior Negro officers will not be assigned to a unit having white officers, nor in any case will white officers be commanded by Negro officers."

This thinking, from top brass all the way down to white commissioned officers, limited opportunities for black leadership in the army. It restricted the advancement of black soldiers by limiting their commissions as officers. But in 1942 Roosevelt intervened, ordering an increase in the recruitment of black officers. However, he did nothing to change the existing policy, which limited black officers to commanding only black troops. Roosevelt still approved of segregated officer camps, segregated living quarters, and separate all-black units. He hoped that the army, by promoting white officers to more senior ranks, would open up slots for black officer candidates to fill.

All the rules, regulations, and restrictions did not keep Felix Goodwin from advancing. His story provides another, more human, dimension to the memorandums and statistics that remain in the official military record. He recalled:

> In June of 1940, we got word that the army had begun to expand and that we should prepare to send some of our men out on cadres. At that time, I was a clerk to the first sergeant in Company G of the 25th Infantry Regiment at Fort Huachuca, Arizona. On payday in June of 1940, the company clerk lost his money in a gambling game and lost the company's money after he pilfered that from the safe. The next morning he had gone to Mexico. He had a girlfriend there, and they both escaped to the interior of Mexico.

After the company clerk had been gone for two days, Goodwin went to see the sergeant major about replacing the clerk on the cadre going out to form the newly expanded units in Fort Bragg, North Carolina.

> I approached the sergeant major and said, "Sir, you know the company clerk was on the cadre to go to Fort Bragg, and he has been AWOL for two days. I wonder if I could get on the cadre." The sergeant major said, "Well, whatcha got?" You know, back in those days you bought everything. I said, "Sir, I have about five dollars." And he said, "Put it in my in-box then."
>
> Well, I did that, but then after I got outside I realized he hadn't promised me a thing. I was afraid to go back in there, and I don't think I slept but two hours that night thinking about my little money. The next morning I was trying to decide what to do when my orders came through, and I was on the cadre and on my way to Fort Bragg. After we were there for a few days I moved up from private to buck sergeant. All for only five dollars!

Like Goodwin, Arnett Hartsfield had prepared for military service before he entered the army in 1940. He joined junior ROTC in high school. At UCLA he continued with another four years of ROTC, a requirement for all male students at the state land grant college. Hartsfield had ambitions of attending the advanced ROTC program so he could be considered for an officer's commission. Yet even with all his previous experience, excellent grades, and proven leadership skills, Hartsfield was rejected four times for the advanced course. Speaking without resentment, he said that two Japanese students attending UCLA were told to take out citizenship papers and they would be advanced. The last time he was rejected for the program, Hartsfield recalled, he complained to his college friend Tom Bradley (later the mayor of Los Angeles), and the two of them appealed to the public on a local left-wing radio show. During the show they "lambasted the university for its bias and prejudice." Finally, the university succumbed to the pressure, and Hartsfield became the first black man to get advanced at UCLA.

The training course was held in the Monterey, California, area at what was then Camp Ord. Military bases on the West Coast, unlike those in the East, did not have separate facilities for black candidates. Howard, Wilberforce, Tuskegee, and many other black colleges in the East had ROTC programs that regularly fed black men into advanced officer courses. There were fewer black men in ROTC programs in the West, and military bases in that region were unprepared to provide separate facilities for black servicemen. When Hartsfield finally gained acceptance into the advanced course and headed off for training, he still encountered trouble.

> When they sent me to the camp, they immediately set me over to the supply tent with my duffel bag. I was furious. Like a slave auction, everybody there looking at me! I was separated from the rest of the men. I wanted to be assigned to a tent alphabetically like everyone else, but I was the only black that had ever shown up, and they did not know what to do with me.

Normally each tent contained four candidates, but the instructors did not want to assign white students to live in Hartsfield's tent. Finally, two white candidates accepted Hartsfield into their tent. Although a fourth student never joined the tent, that actually worked to the group's advantage. They won "best tent" and "best bunk" more than any other group in the camp. Generally, the three men got along, even though Hartsfield recalled feeling resentment that he had been "helped." Although he did not know it at the time, the father of one of Hartsfield's tent mates was a general, and he called the camp's commanding officer and requested that the candidates be treated fairly. "I thought for the longest time that I did it all on my own, but I learned about this kid's father, and now I realize I had a 'great white father' all along!"

WAR ON AMERICAN SHORES

For the men who were completing their year of military service, everything changed when the Japanese bombed Pearl Harbor. The army responded by assigning guards on both the East and West Coasts, as well at many other strategic locations within the interior of America. Fear of invasion, in retrospect far-fetched, was horrifyingly real to most American citizens. In New York, the army mobilized to guard the shores of Long Island and the tunnels and bridges that led to Manhattan. Spencer Moore's job as fingerprinter for the military police at Fort Dix, New Jersey, instantly changed when he was assigned to active guard duty in New York City. Moore speculated that the black troops were sent to guard the city because "they could tell we weren't spies"—other troops with German or Italian heritage might be suspected as sympathizers.

Felix Goodwin too served as military guard in New York City in the 372nd Infantry Unit. Both he and Moore were on the shores around New York City when the cruise ship *Normandy* was destroyed by fire. The official report claimed that the fire had started from a welding accident, but rumors circulated that spies were responsible for the damage. The army looked for submarines off the East Coast and checked beaches every morning for footprints coming out of the water. Most of the narratives of World War II describe warfare on foreign soil, but many Americans remember being fearful about the possibility of invasion at home.

Goodwin recounted his guard duty: "Our black unit caught some German spies off the coast of Long Island—you never heard about that." Moore guarded an airfield against intrusion—a tedious and boring job of walking the length of the field and looking for enemy spies. It was bitter, cold December weather in New York. His duty was lightened by the appreciation of the local women, who would bring the guards hot coffee and buns. Moore recalled: "The women out there, I'm talking about the young, white women, were crazy about us being out there because they said they felt so secure, that nobody was gonna come in off Long Island to hurt them." Then Moore's group was sent to guard Manhattan. He was in charge of a machine-gun section with a permanent emplacement sandbagged at the entrance to the Lincoln Tunnel. His troops were quartered in the heart of Harlem, at 124th Street and Seventh Avenue. In case of an alarm, they had fifteen minutes to get from Harlem to the tunnel and man the machine guns. In their rapid response, the troops displayed heavy military armaments so if the enemy was watching "they could see we were not playing around." The soldiers were always on the ready, poised to protect American soil. The fear that anyone could be an enemy of the nation was ever-present in the minds of the soldiers, and they took their job seriously. In fact, one of the black soldiers shot at a taxicab because the driver disobeyed military orders to clear the area.

Hank Williams was drafted in February 1941 and thought he was just going to serve his year and then go back home to Cleveland to work. His idea about service was the same as Moore's: "Good-bye dear, be back in a year." Williams "knew how to press clothes, hop bells, wait tables, chauffeur, and drive trucks and taxis." One of his summer jobs was as a water boy in a road construction crew. After several summers, he moved up to cement-bag loader and truck driver. He had been on his own for a while, completing college at Ohio State and working at odd jobs throughout the Depression years. Both parents were deceased, leaving Williams to fend for himself at an early age.

He was serving his year of duty at Fort Huachuca, Arizona, when he "got word that the United States was under attack by the Japanese somewhere in a place called Pearl Harbor." The men were immediately moved to Barstow, California, an area around Los Angeles, to guard nearby towns, reservoirs, and train stations. Williams received instruction from his commanding colonel to prepare for an attack. "You get out the machine guns and dig holes and mount them out there. Somebody will be around after awhile for instructions." Williams continued:

> We got out our manuals so that we could identify friendly planes and enemy planes. The hardest job I had until the commanders came down there was to keep my soldiers from shooting those guns off that they had been training on all this time. They wanted to shoot. One guy, a very good friend of mine, kept saying, "That's not a civilian plane, let me shoot it." That was my biggest headache, keeping everybody on alert but calm.

Fred Hurns was in Arizona at the same time as Williams, and he experienced a similar state of high alert just after the attack on Pearl Harbor.

> We stretched out along Route 66 with our headquarters in Kingman, Arizona. We did guard duty for three nights in a row, guarding tunnels and bridges. It was very cold in the open canyons there. It was below zero, and the water was freezing. We all slept in shifts in the canvas tent. We tried to get a little heat going by burning some wood, but

when we burned the railroad ties from the Santa Fe Railway, they sent
a letter to us about destroying their property. So they moved us back
to Fort Huachuca.

The American military was not ready to fend off a full-scale attack or defend its military bases and strategic civilian locations. Goodwin described his
immediate response after Pearl Harbor. The black infantry troops were just
returning from the Carolina maneuvers when war was declared. Goodwin's
outfit was ordered to move north into New Jersey and Pennsylvania to guard
the Delaware River from invasion. He said: "We weren't ready for war when
it started. We did not have adequate guns and ammunition to prevent an attack." Before Goodwin left the South, his unit cut down about a dozen pine
trees and covered them with creosote, then loaded the oiled-up, blackened
trees onto big military transport trucks. They got to the Pennsylvania National Guard station at night and immediately began unloading the logs and
moving them to the tops of nearby buildings so they were visible.

When everybody got up that morning they just assumed the logs on
the rooftops were guns. We thought Hitler was going to send some
planes over, so we set up all these defensive locations around the nation. We did have machine gun dugouts, but mostly we did not have
enough to stop anybody. But we looked like we did.

One woman commented that she thought her father was off on "Garden
Patrol" when he told her he was leaving for "Guard and Patrol." Americans
were simply unprepared and unable to comprehend the reality of being a
nation at war with the possibility of conflict on its own shores. In Florida, infantry units were deployed to defend power stations and bridges against possible enemy attack. Dennett Harrod, of the all-black 366th Infantry Unit,
was in uniform in Florida when a few white citizens rushed up to him in a
store and asked for any news. They wanted to know if he had seen the enemy
or if there had been battles. The fear of invasion was so pervasive that citizens would question any soldiers they met. Joe Stephenson also commented
on the change in the nation following the attack. "War had come, and the
whole nation seemed to have changed over night."

Charles Wesly was a reserve officer working full-time for the post office at
the time of Pearl Harbor.

I really wasn't drafted. I was called, you know, when you have a commission your stated preference is that in an emergency you will serve.
Really the war was kind of distant. It wasn't weighing heavily on too

many people's minds. As a matter of fact, I was at a football game, and the announcer came on and said something like, "Somebody just threw a pass only he dropped it. The Japanese just bombed Pearl Harbor. Now back to the game." And everybody wondered where was Pearl Harbor. A bunch of us with reserve commissions got together after the game, and then we realized that we were all going to get called up.

Since 1939 most Americans had been following the war in Europe in the news. Still, the bombing of Pearl Harbor and America's immediate declaration of war shocked many people—black and white, men and women. The distant European war and the Japanese aggression in Asia now involved Americans. Donald McNeil had not finished high school and was not thinking of military service, but Pearl Harbor shocked him into enlisting right away. He said he had a "great desire to be with the troops before the conflict was over," and his sentiments express the feelings of many young men of the time.

Women too felt the pull of military service after Pearl Harbor, and some tried to enter the service. Like their male counterparts, black women experienced acts of subterfuge meant to prevent them from entering the armed forces. Madine Davis Lane was a practicing nurse in Virginia when America declared war on the Axis powers. After watching so many young men going to war, Lane decided to enlist in the army's Nursing Corps. The Virginia State Nurses Association had a rule barring enlistment in the army unless a nurse belonged to the association, but Lane was barred entry to the association because she was black. It was the ultimate "Catch-22" situation. She was also barred from the Red Cross, another avenue of entry into the military. Several of her nursing friends advised her to go to New York, where the army was recruiting without the requirements of joining the state nurses association or the Red Cross. Lane was inducted within three months of relocating to New York and then was sent to a nurses training facility in Fort Huachuca, Arizona, where the all-black infantry divisions were training and preparing for war.

Ruth Jones Earl had graduated from the School of Nursing at Howard University at the time of the outbreak of war, and like Lane she was determined to get into the army. She felt her "family would love the idea of having somebody in the service," and her twin sister was not interested in serving. More importantly, Earl wanted to join the army because she had heard the army would not accept black women.

They did not have the right to say directly, "I'm not going to take you," but they would do things like flunk you on your physical or discourage you in other ways. I'd had a complete physical before I even went to see them, so I knew there was nothing wrong. But they kept calling me back for x-rays and all types of things. I went right up to headquarters and told them that I was not going to accept that type of treatment. Not because I was jumping up and down about going into the military but because they were denying me the right, and they were lying about it.

She told them "they were wasting valuable film that was needed by the soldiers across the pond," and they better put a stop to it. She was sworn in two days later and began training nurses for military service overseas.

BLUEPRINT FOR DESEGREGATION

No matter how many blacks signed up for military service, the army still perceived a morale problem among black Americans, considering them to be lackluster in supporting the war efforts. The Office of War Information (OWI) asked one of its high-ranking officials, Theodore Berry, to draft a report on the situation. His final report, titled "Blueprint for Strengthening Negro Morale in the War Effort," called on the military to desegregate its forces in order to boost black support for the war. Berry circulated the completed blueprint to numerous government agencies. It called on the president to declare that prejudice and discrimination were un-American. It also requested that all government agencies review the extra cost and waste of materials and manpower that resulted from segregation and other long-standing exclusionary practices.

Berry's recommendations were never fully instituted in the armed forces or in any government agencies. While "morale problems" among the black population were commonly investigated, no government agency was willing to undertake extensive reforms such as desegregating. OWI Director Elmer Davis made this comment about the blueprint: "Neither we nor anybody else can solve the Negro problem as an incident of the war effort." When Berry questioned segregation in the military, his opinions were dismissed. His ideas went against prevailing prejudices and included recommendations for the administration to "take the lead in eliminating . . . segregation in the armed forces, especially in the recreational and cultural facilities." His superior, Davis, added two question marks to Berry's report and asked "?? Why not segregate." Davis wrote that Berry had not provided any concrete evidence that segregation was discrimination. With this type of thinking in the senior command, it is not surprising that neither the White House nor the military hierarchy was anxious to reconsider their policy of segregation in the armed forces.

The OWI's mission was the control of information that affected the war effort. It was very much aware of the unrest in black communities across America and was reeling from the multitude of opinions on how to handle "the problem." Along with the War Department, it was struggling to enforce its own racial policies. In 1943, the OWI completed its report called "Government Policy on the Negro Problem." Instead of facing the issues of segregation and discrimination head-on, the report called on all agency personnel to deemphasize the "Negro problem." The OWI employed a soft-pedal approach by asking each branch of the military to deal independently with racial situations. The report's summary stressed that "the long-range problems of racial and minority–majority antagonisms cannot be settled during the war" and recommended that the "media should be fed all the material we can develop" to convince the black soldier he had a stake in the "institutions of liberty."

The War Department apparently believed that most people, both black and white, approved of their policies. When citizens complained about segregation in the military, the department branded them as extremists. When complaints of discrimination were raised, the department investigated and then issued proclamations and directives. The department stated over and over that segregation was not discrimination and usually answered complaints with a restatement of its overall policy objectives. For example, in 1944 when Governor Chauncey Sparks of Alabama complained to the War Department because he felt that the military bases in his state were allowing too much intermingling between white and black soldiers, he was sent a reassuring letter stating that the War Department would not interfere in local practices. Acting Secretary of War Robert P. Patterson responded, "The War Department has maintained throughout the emergency and present war that it is not an appropriate medium for effecting social readjustments. . . . [M]en who are fulfilling the same obligations, suffering the same dislocation of their lives, and wearing the identical uniform should, within the confines of the military establishment, have the same privileges." The intent of the policy was to provide equal treatment within separate facilities. No government agency, most especially the War Department, recognized the inherent inequality of segregating people by the color of their skin.

All of the studies and surveys that the army conducted validated its rationale for maintenance of the status quo. Segregation was a local practice that the army would respect, and it emphatically denied that the practice was an indicator of a belief in racial inferiority—a belief it abhorred. Army directives asked officers to have "frank and objective discussions of the subject of racial doctrines." It was felt that this openness would be particularly useful in countering enemy propaganda campaigns. The army called on white officers to discredit Hitler's Aryan race theory. Some were given special instructions in the course and manual entitled "Leadership and the Negro Soldier." The manual stated the army's policy on segregation:

> The army accepts no theories of racial inferiority or superiority for American troops but considers that its task is to utilize its men on their individual merits in the achievement of final victory. National doctrines of inborn race superiority are the product of a variety of specific situations. That they represent a prejudice, can be shown beyond any reasonable doubt. Scientific knowledge does not support the idea of the inherent superiority of any one race over another. The American Negro has lived for generations under the influence of such beliefs, and at the same time he has been taught, and has been benefited by American democratic ideals and practices.

This strong statement against discrimination and prejudice was never used against segregated service. And, regrettably, the ideology of racial inferiority was not erased from the minds of the white commanders simply because they attended sensitivity training. The views of Major General Edward M. Almond, a commanding general experienced with both black divisions in World War II, reveal the level of racism that existed in the minds of military planners of the era.

> I do not agree that integration improves military efficiency. I believe it weakens it. . . . The basic characteristics of Negroes and whites are fundamentally different. . . . There is no question in my mind of the inherent differences in races. This is not racism—it is common sense. Those who ignore these differences merely interfere with the combat effectiveness of battle units.

All through the war, military leaders struggled to maintain the segregation without discrimination policy. Surveys revealed public opinion was leaning toward integration, but there was still internal resistance to change in the War Department and within the military command. When battlefield generals asked for additional manpower—of any color—for what would be the final battles in Europe, a few black troops were voluntarily integrated into white combat units. This special exception situation did not reflect a change in policy as Assistant Chief of Staff Major General S. G. Henry warned in a memorandum. "The War Department policy," he reminded the troop commanders, "has been to assign colored personnel only to colored units. The reported action [of integration] if not checked will result in demands on the

War Department that such integration be established throughout the entire army." He was right, of course. The integrating of troops on the battlefields of World War II did provide the rationale for a policy change, although it would take another three years of intense debate and additional surveys to enact and many more years to implement.

Many black soldiers said they did not think too much about whether they objected to the military's practice of segregated service. Joe Stephenson commented: "I've often wondered what the heck we did think about in those days. Our prime objective was to make it into officer candidate school and not get busted out. So we didn't really have any serious conversations about the military policies at the time." During the war, black soldiers were more concerned about equality of assignments and fair enlistment and promotion policies. The subterfuge preventing the full enlistment of black men into the armed forces concerned many of the soldiers. Once they got into the service, they became concerned that their duties would be limited to service and support. Stephenson continued: "We were aware of the policy of not sending us into combat. We read in the black press about all the pressure put on President Roosevelt to get our boys into the fight. I remember some of our people who were wishing that they wouldn't push that too strong."

Dennett Harrod's memories differ from Stephenson's. Harrod also recalled the newspapers putting pressure on the War Department to get them into combat. "My unit, the 366th Infantry Regiment, was black from the colonel straight on down to the private. We had been trained, and we were ready to go. And we were sick and tired of playing games. We kept getting more badges and citations for good training, but they would just send us back to do some more training."

Robert Madison summarized the discussions of the day: "Let's put it this way. The debate was basically about whether black troops were going to be sent into combat. That was number one. Number two was whether or not we would get promoted in rank as others. Well, as far as the first debate, we weren't concerned about that at all because we thought we were *not* going to be sent into combat. Did we want to go into combat? I'm not sure we did, but that was the debate going on in the country." The concerns and debates of the black Americans who served in the segregated armed forces during World War II were multilayered and complex.

Despite segregation and restrictive enlistment policies, black Americans signed up in record numbers to serve their country. A 1944 public opinion poll conducted by the army revealed overwhelming support for the war. Of the thirteen thousand respondents, 66 percent of black soldiers and 89 percent of white soldiers responded "yes" when asked whether they thought the "war was as much [their] affair as anybody else's." Nelson Peery enlisted in the army after the Japanese attack on Pearl Harbor. He wanted his enlistment to be his own decision rather than a response to a selective service directive. "I deeply believed war would give us a chance to be free." His reasoning was based on the notion that the War Department would have to utilize black troops in an all-out war. Reflecting the attitude of some black newspapers of the day, Peery believed that black soldiers could then bargain with the government for more enhanced rights after they returned from war. With prescient wisdom he told his high school teacher, "I have to go, Miss O'Leary. Part of it is so I can say, this is my country. I fought for it and you can't deny me."

2

LIFE ON THE MILITARY RESERVATION

"SO THIS IS THE ARMY?"

In 1942, the army activated two all-black infantry divisions, the 93rd "Blue Helmets" and the 92nd "Buffalo Soldiers." The training base for the two divisions was located at Fort Huachuca, Arizona—a military reservation encompassing about 100 square miles of desert and mountain terrain. The fort was established in the late 1800s as a post in the Indian wars and originally only encompassed about 40 square miles. The harsh landscape, weather patterns, and general lifestyle proved difficult for many of the new residents of the Fort Huachuca area. Hank Williams remembers the day he arrived at the fort and the indignities he suffered in the following days.

> We stood in the worst sandstorm in twenty-four years. It was daylight when we arrived in our winter uniforms. And by evening, you couldn't tell who was who or what, because we were all whipped with that sand. One of the guys who cadred from the 25th Infantry showed us how to protect ourselves by putting our handkerchief around our face. And I thought, "Well, here I am. So this is the army?" I got my duffel bag of army issue stuff and struggled to carry it to the barracks. When they finally decided to feed us, we got boiled wieners and potatoes with a hunk of bread. The next day's fare was not much better, and we were all ready to shoot the cook, but we didn't have anything to shoot him with.

As the days went on, we became more and more oriented into what the military was all about. We read field manuals, and we had exercises that we had to go through on a daily basis. I had to pull KP [kitchen patrol] even as an acting corporal. One night they had me in the kitchen from 3:30 in the morning until after 10:00 that night. And I said, "To hell with this. I'm going home. No more of this for me!" And I took a shower and got dressed in my clothes and waited on my cot until I could sneak away. But I fell asleep, and when I woke up my platoon sergeant was shaking me saying, "How come you didn't make the formation this morning?" I had slept all the way through everything and never got to sneak away.

I told him, "Man, I've never worked so hard in my life, and I have worked highway construction and everything. I tell you, I'm not going to work like this anymore." Well, he told me to hang on, that he was sure they were going to make me corporal, a noncommissioned officer, and then I would not have to do dishes and KP. So from then on I started to turn into a soldier. I began to learn, and I just absorbed everything in the manuals, like the nomenclature and the types of weapons and even how to dress in the military fashion. Things changed for me. They knew I could read and write, and that tended to put me in a different category than some. I guess I was a corporal for about a month, and then I became a buck sergeant.

By the end of 1942, approximately eighteen thousand men of the 93rd Blue Helmet Division were on the post, or military reservation, at Fort Huachuca. The 92nd Division was training at four different locations around the United States. Supported by aircraft, ships, and armor, an infantry division provides the most fundamental task of any military: on-foot warfare. Ninety-two divisions served during World War II; all were constituted as triangular divisions, different from the square formation of World War I divisions. The new triangular formation divided each division into three regiments, and each regiment into three infantry battalions. Service and support units, including quartermaster battalions, signal companies, and medical units, constituted the full complement of personnel in a division. Selective Service recruits and volunteers filled the ranks of each division. The infantry regiments, and all of the attendant units, were called to the colors to begin basic training.

Although some elements of the 93rd had been on the reservation since 1941, most of the men in the division were recruits who arrived en masse by train. Fred Hurns described what it was like to be in one of the first large groups of soldiers assembled at the fort: "The train going from our collection point to the fort in Arizona was an eighteen-car troop train. All eighteen cars were black. We almost made up a whole regiment just on that train." Other soldiers arrived singly or in small groups, mixed in with civilians on regular passenger trains of the Southern Pacific Railroad. Nelson Peery had a first-class railway ticket, courtesy of Uncle Sam, when he left Fort Sill enroute to Fort Huachuca, but in Missouri he had his first taste of the army's "separate but equal" policy. The MPs came along to tell him to move to the segregated car. He refused, saying, "I'll go to the colored car if you tell me it's a first-class car like my ticket says." They sent over more authorities to try and convince him, but finally they put him in his own deluxe suite. He had a bathroom, bed, and small sitting area. The ultimate style of his transport and arrival at the military reservation is most unusual, however. He described the majority of the black men who arrived for service at Fort Huachuca:

> Some came with scars of shackles stamped into their eyes. They came with college degrees and parole papers. They came with pockets full of loaded dice. They came damning America, her Jim Crow, and her lynch law. They came cursing Hitler and the Fascists and eager to do battle for human rights.

Most of the black officers graduating from Officer Candidate School (OCS) arrived separately from the enlisted men. Lieutenant Arnett Hartsfield, a longtime Los Angeles native, arrived in Fort Huachuca and announced to the men who greeted him in the barracks: "Hey, so this is what the East looks like!" Although Hartsfield was joking, the officers in many ways were as naïve as their men in terms of what to expect at the desert fort. None of the men was prepared for life with scorpions, snakes, Gila monsters, mountain lions, skunks, ringtail cats, kiss bugs, or horned toads. No army training manual described what to do in case a soldier stumbled into a clump of cactus of the barrel, prickly pear, buckhorn, or organ-pipe variety. Charles Wesly gave this account of his first exposure to life in the desert Southwest.

> Four of us traveled together after our short leave in D.C. down to Fort Huachuca. I'll never forget that. I was totally ignorant of what to expect in the desert. My ideas of what it looked like were formed from movie images. I expected desert sand and that kind of blank terrain. I asked a lady who was a service attendant when we were going to get to the desert. She just rolled her eyes and said, "What the hell do you think this is?" All you could see was vegetation everywhere you looked. I didn't think there was supposed to be any vegetation in the desert.

Actually, the Arizona desert contains some very colorful vegetation when it is in bloom—the yellow blossoms on the massive paloverde trees, the fire-red flowers on the ocotillo, the little barrel-shaped rainbow cactus, and the green foliage on the towering ironwood trees are breathtaking. But when the desert is not in bloom, the traveler notices very little other than the preponderance of tumbleweeds.

Wesly was also surprised by the wildlife in the Arizona desert—nothing during ROTC training or at OCS had prepared him for the mammals and reptiles of the desert. "There were these things called coatimundis. I had never seen that, a catlike raccoon thing. And then there were these rats we called 'trader rats' because they would steal things in your packs, but they would leave something else in its place. I lost a cigarette lighter; they liked shiny things. If you took off your bars, your officer's insignia, they would steal that and maybe leave a stone in its place." Wesly had to learn how to cope with some of the dangerous wildlife, such as rattlesnakes.

> You didn't dare sit down under the shade of a tree. You would take your rifle butt and push the bushes around and look under the tree. Because sometimes the rattlesnakes would be in there like spaghetti. As you traveled along you could hear "ttss, ttsss," and you're walking and getting stuck by a cactus bush. You wouldn't know whether you were bitten by a snake or stuck by cactus. I will never forget the first time I went through that, I was so tense, when I got to the end of it, I just fell down on the ground and threw up all over everything. I mean, it was horrible. "Ttss, ttsss," and then something would stick you, and then "ttss, ttsss" again. It went on the whole way.

Many of the soldiers stationed at Fort Huachuca agreed that the landscape and the wildlife of the desert prepared them for the hard life of the army.

TURNING A JOHN DOE INTO A JOHNNIE DOUGHBOY

"Doughboy" was a common nickname among soldiers for a new recruit who completed infantry training. The yearlong training turned a "John Doe" into a "Johnnie Doughboy." Basic training lasted seventeen grueling weeks and was followed up with thirteen weeks of unit training. Then the doughboy could expect another fourteen weeks of specialized arms training and finally eight weeks of division rehearsal or review time. After these fifty-two weeks of training, an infantry division would then normally be sent on maneuvers against another division to test and refine its skills. The 93rd Division received the same type and approximately the same length of training as the other newly formed divisions. The 92nd received a little less training than the 93rd because the latter went through more rehearsal or maneuver training than most divisions. One soldier grumbled accusations that the 93rd was only a "maneuver division," rather than an infantry division. However, even accounting for the extended period of maneuvers, training time for the 93rd was roughly equal to the training time of the newly constituted white divisions. By the time the 92nd Division moved to Fort Huachuca for unit training, the army had reduced its training schedule for new divisions to a period of ten months including a shortened maneuvering period.

Known as the Buffalo Division, the 92nd Infantry was organized in October 1942, with the slogan "Deeds Not Words." The official shoulder patch was circular, with a black border and a black buffalo on an olive drab background. At first members of the 92nd were housed at four separate locations: Alabama, Arkansas, Indiana, and Kentucky. Usually infantry divisions train together in one location; however, only Fort Huachuca was designated for black troops, and thus the 92nd was parceled out among four separate locations. In 1943, after the 93rd Division had moved out of Fort Huachuca to go on maneuvers, the 92nd Division was finally assembled together and moved to Arizona. Joe Stephenson said:

> I think I was a little on the naïve side in regards to why the 92nd Division had to train at four separate places. I figured it was a matter of space. I didn't think about it in racial terms. I thought it was a matter of space, and eventually they would pull us all together. I knew the 93rd was in Fort Huachuca, and so I thought there was no place to put us. But, really, they did not want to put a black division so close to the white population, so they had to wait until Huachuca opened up.

It took readjustment, along with some hard lessons, for many of the men in the 92nd Division to learn to enjoy life at the Arizona reservation. Even getting to the fort presented a challenge. Troop trains could go right into Fort Huachuca, but passenger trains, used by men traveling alone or in small groups, stopped at the little town of Hereford, Arizona, 25 miles away from the fort. Jehu Hunter joined the division after his specialized training at OCS.

> When I was at the Hereford, Arizona, railroad junction I thought, "Man, this is one lonely place." I thought the train had stopped to let another train go by, because there was no reason to be stopping, there was nothing out there that I could see, other than some cactus and some open space. I had never even seen cactus before. The conductor came along and said, "Hey, you. It's time to go." And I said I didn't realize we were so close to the fort. And he said, "You're not." So I got out with my duffel bag, and I saw this old school bus there. I thought,

there must be a school close by. But, in fact, that was the bus waiting
to take me to the fort. It was a long and bumpy ride. Dirt roads like a
washboard, all rutted out.

Bill Perry described his experiences traveling to his first military base.
"We went to Fort McClellan, Alabama, by train. I remember when I woke
up that morning on the train. I saw a bus parked at this crossroads with a sign
that said 'Rome.' And I said, 'Hell, I'm in Italy!' But, of course, it was just
Rome, Georgia, a little southern town on the Alabama–Georgia border. That
was the first time I had been south of the Ohio River. It was a new experience. Then, after a while, we moved to Fort Huachuca." At first, Perry found
life on the Arizona reservation better than in Alabama.

> When we arrived in Huachuca, I thought it was beautiful. All the red-
> roofed buildings and big purple mountains behind them. But almost
> as soon as we got settled in, things began to unravel. There was dis-
> sension among the guys and problems with the officers. There was a
> policy that if you asked too many questions you would get busted and
> transferred. If there was some kind of friction, you'd get transferred
> rather than court-martialed.
> I learned that the hard way. I guess my attitude had deteriorated,
> and I started laughing at some of the things and the people. Not really
> defiant, but enough to get me transferred. I had to make the adjust-
> ment to calling people "sir." It upset me, but I found out it was strictly
> army procedure, army courtesy. So you get used to it. I started to say
> "Yes, sir" and "No, sir" after that.

This lesson was even more difficult to carry out when Perry was transferred
to Captain "Iron Jaw" Reedy's company to be his personal messenger. Reedy
swaggered when he walked and talked with a southern accent, but by then
Perry had learned to "clean up his act" so that he would not be transferred
again.

Allen Thompson said that as an American soldier he was trained to survive, and that involved a lot of technical training and hours of grueling rep-
etition. He was familiar with hard work and hard ways because his mother
had been an orderly and precise woman, running their house with military
precision. "There were certain things that just had to get done, and I had
certain responsibilities in the house. One time as I was getting ready to go
out on a date, my mother called me back home and said, 'You better get back
in here and clean up your room.' I was walking down the street to my date,
and she called me from a block away. That's the way I was raised." For

Thompson, as well as for many other soldiers, the army training was rough, but he was up to the challenge. Many black Americans had experienced tough conditions and strict discipline before entering the service.

Whether he was going through literacy instruction or learning to use unfamiliar equipment, much of the young soldier's day was spent in some sort of educational activity. In the modern World War II army there was so much technical knowledge to impart, so many strange terms, and so much unfamiliar equipment. Charles Wesly instructed new recruits.

> I remember the hardest part of it was there was no real classroom and no shade. You did your instruction out in the desert sun. There were guys just sitting on the ground out in the desert sun, and you're doing everything to keep them alert. The educational level was so low overall, and you're trying to teach technical stuff like map reading for instance. You're teaching fractions, and here's a guy sitting there who can't put two and two together, and he's out there boiling in the desert sun. It was a challenge to get any kind of instruction across.

SMACK DAB IN THE MIDDLE OF NOWHERE

At Fort Huachuca during the war years, all of the black soldiers of both the 93rd and 92nd Divisions were segregated from white troops—no white divisions or infantry units were stationed with them—and they were segregated from the local towns. Jim Finley described the situation: "The men were stationed at the far reaches of Arizona at the very edge of the map, segregated—their apartness was emphasized." The fort is located in Cochise County, about 70 miles southeast of Tucson and 20 miles north of the Mexican border town of Nogales. Many of the roads between the fort and the local towns were still unpaved in the forties. The post paper for the 93rd Division, *The Blue Helmet*, carried a story that described the terrain: "You ride along a gravel road and then finally a paved road for miles and all of a sudden you come up over a hill and before you lies Fort Huachuca. On all sides of this army post in the Arizona desert are high purple mountains."

The military reservation was about as far away from any American city as you could get and still be within the borders of the continental United States. It was "smack dab in the middle of nowhere," as many soldiers commented. Although most of the men were unimpressed with the landscape, Ernestine Hughes was more idyllic in her description of the area. "Encircled by stately mountains, with bright lights visible from miles afar, Fort Huachuca on a moonlit night is like a cluster of gems set in a diadem of

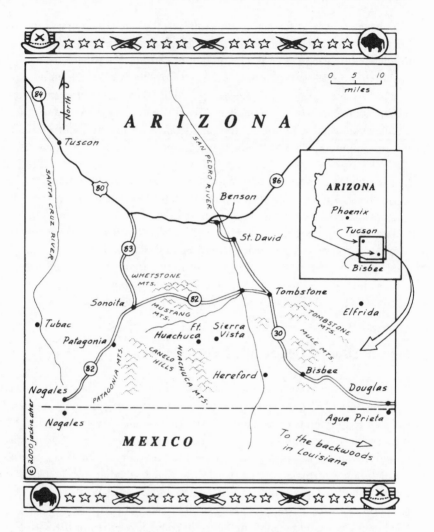

black velvet. You have never seen a more beautiful moon than the one that beams on Huachuca—so big, so starry, beyond the horizon where sweet memories lie."

No real post town existed anywhere close to the reservation. A car was an absolute necessity for visiting one of the local towns, but few enlisted men could afford a vehicle on pay of only $21 per month. But the ingenious GI could always find a way to get off the fort. Jim Williams used to trade his whiskey ration tickets with a lieutenant who had a convertible, "a real nice deal," he said. Fred Hurns knew a local woman with a car who used to transport a few soldiers for "a fee, like a bus fare." Eventually, the army provided truck transport if soldiers wanted to travel en masse to one of the surrounding towns. Tucson usually required a weekend pass. Bisbee, an old mining town, was 45 miles away and, at times, off limits to black soldiers from Fort Huachuca. And Tombstone, the Western town famous for the shootout at the OK Corral, was 25 miles away. Enterprising civilians in the area started up the Nogales–Bisbee Stage Coach, which was really a bus line, with three scheduled trips per day between the fort and the towns. For the most part, soldiers stayed on base and utilized the closer, though segregated, recreational facilities.

The name "Huachuca" refers to the nearby mountain range, known to the local Indians as the "place of thunder." The mountains, 7,600 feet high, provided fresh running water and strategic observation locations. Geronimo staged numerous raids from their security. Enterprising Indians and soldiers found plenty of game in the area. In fact, to supply the troops at the reservation—even up to World War II—resident soldiers were sometimes issued three-day hunting passes to provision the army with local fish, birds, deer, and javelina (a wild pig unique to the area). The fort was ill-equipped to handle the eighteen thousand troops and thousands of support personnel stationed there during World War II. There was plenty of space, but hardly any buildings to house the number of recruits being brought onto the reservation. The "Old Post," which had been in existence since the late 1800s, was generally occupied by white officers who were also being brought in for service. White soldiers had higher rank than the black soldiers, and housing was a benefit of rank. First Sergeant Andrew Jackson "Duke" Wells, a twenty-year veteran from the 25th Infantry, described the Old Post prior to World War II as an outpost with about a thousand men and a thousand mules.

The "New Post," or cantonment, was quickly conceived and constructed by a Phoenix firm before most of the recruits arrived. The firm received a contract in 1941 from the War Department to expand the post facilities by 1,200 new buildings. They left intact the Old Post "officers' row" and its supporting infrastructure but added an entirely new post on unused land of the reservation. New training facilities were constructed, including artificial lakes used for pontoon and bridge training as well as firing ranges, tank facilities, and classrooms. All the new facilities, including training centers, housing, hospitals, and entertainment areas, were equipped with modern power and sewage systems. Most of the living facilities on the New Post (barracks) were designated for bachelor soldiers, although a few quarters were designated for married officers. Most married couples—black and white—tried to find living quarters off base, although housing was scarce everywhere. There was a guesthouse that could temporarily house about twenty-eight visitors. Visitors could also stay at the Copper Queen Hotel in Bisbee (still a landmark today). When most new recruits entered Fort

Huachuca, they marched right into their new, never-been-occupied barracks and past a flurry of construction activity. Clarence Gaines described his arrival at the fort: "When we got off the train, the band from the 25th Infantry was playing 'South of the Border' for us. Our first duty was to take our mattresses to a place where we were instructed to stuff them with straw."

Although the construction continued for a while after the 93rd moved to the fort, the opening of the newly expanded post received substantial local press. Army journalist Private Chester A. Burrill reported on the new accommodations in the local paper, the *Apache Sentinel*. "Almost overnight the little village [of Fort Huachuca] blossomed forth a city, up from the desert . . . astonishing growth." Burrill also reported on the astonishing construction of numerous theaters, hospitals, bakeries, laundries, and storage buildings, all new necessities for the large incoming divisions of soldiers. More than eleven hundred civilians were employed to work at the fort. In total, approximately twenty-five thousand people were at Fort Huachuca, which made it the third largest city in Arizona at the time. The telephone switchboard operators handled more than twenty thousand calls in a routine day. The post laundry facilities handled the clothing of approximately thirty thousand "customers" each week.

Bernice Cosulich of the *Arizona Daily Star* reported on the inventory at the base, which included everything from "howitzers to toothpicks, bulldozers to aspirin, airplanes to floor polish, and mattresses to coat buttons." Daily food preparation was an enormous task as well: every day cooks baked thousands of pounds of bread and prepared six tons of fresh vegetables. At any one meal, the soldiers drank 1,500 gallons of milk. For the Thanksgiving holiday meal, the men at the fort consumed 20,000 pounds of turkey. Even with the massive, new, modernized facilities, the enterprising soldier could still make a few extra bucks augmenting the services of the army. Fred Hurns and a fellow enlisted man started a laundry business at the fort. "For thirty-five cents a fellow could get his shirt washed and ironed. Sometimes we would sew on buttons for a little bit more. And on payday, I used to set up right beside the pay officer and collect on my bills owed."

The post was so isolated that the army attempted to build a recreational infrastructure within the 100-plus square miles of the reservation. However, much of the new building was duplicated to maintain segregation. For instance, two officers clubs, two hospitals, separate recreational facilities, and dual living quarters for dependents were built during the new construction on the base. It was not necessary to build dual enlisted men's clubs, because the only white men on base were officers and thus would never use the facilities for lower-ranking soldiers. One aspect of the building boom at Fort Huachuca received considerable press, both locally and nationally. This was the construction of two officers clubs—Lakeside for white officers and Mountainview for black officers.

Black newspapers reported that Jim Crow segregation had flown across the desert and set up shop at Fort Huachuca. Actually, Lakeside had been in operation prior to the fort's expansion, but it was refurbished for the influx of white officers. What was newsworthy was the building of the black officers club, a new structure that would allow black officers to fraternize among themselves. Frank E. Bolden, correspondent for the Pittsburgh *Courier*, asked the post commander, Colonel Hardy, why there were two separate officers clubs. Hardy replied:

> The purpose of officers clubs are to provide places where officers can get away from the daily grind of their intensive training program, relax, freshen up, and be in a better state of mind and body to carry on the next day's work. Everybody recognizes that morale and relaxation of mind and body are necessary in building an efficient military organization. At Fort Huachuca we have to make our own fun. As to whether or not the War Department made a mistake in deciding that there would be two separate clubs for colored and white officers, presents a problem which is not up to the post commander, the division commander, or officers under them to decide. Having separate clubs follows a traditional pattern not only as pertains to the relationship between the white and colored races, but between all races. It has been the custom throughout the world for people to organize clubs according to their races. With the urgent and important problems which have to be solved in these critical times, the problem of separate officers clubs fades into comparative insignificance.

The Mountainview Club for black officers is no longer standing, but there are pictures of it at the Fort Huachuca museum, and many men remember going to it. The club was built on a hill overlooking a creek and, as the name implies, had a beautiful view of the surrounding mountains. Large windows capitalized on that asset. Rock walls bordered the club and enclosed a garden containing red-flowered oleanders and a green arbor vine. The club contained more than eighty paintings and other works of art by black artists from nine different states. The men also brought in their own paintings as well as posters from back home. But when one of the soldiers brought in some popular George Petty posters, which depicted voluptuous, buxom white women, several white officers objected, and the posters were removed. Evidently the top brass did not want black men looking at white women, even on posters.

At Lakeside, murals depicted the Indian warrior Geronimo in the local habitat. But these western-style murals were "whitewashed" to remove any indication that black soldiers were stationed at the fort when Geronimo and his men were active in the nearby mountains. When the murals were first unveiled, Gene Autry led a crowd of all-white officers in rounds of cowboy songs. The local Indian Scouts—all fully employed Regular Army soldiers—performed dances for the officers. This was the newly reconfigured "Wild West," all being overseen by the War Department.

The soldiers could expect a wide variety of weather—much of it bad—while stationed at Fort Huachuca. Extreme heat and freezing temperatures frequently occurred on the same day. The mountains made their own weather: fast-moving thunderstorms, snowstorms, and sandstorms frequently blasted the fort. One new recruit, Alfred Allanby, was killed instantly when lightning struck the tripod-mounted machine gun he was holding. The other soldiers on the training mission with Allanby were knocked unconscious by the strike, but they revived after the initial shock. Another soldier, Fred Brock, was killed by lightning while he was working in the rain to install signal equipment. Bill Payne also experienced extreme weather conditions at the fort.

> We arrived in Fort Huachuca on March 1, 1941, amid a giant sandstorm. I definitely remember that. We were wearing these old uniforms. I call them "Bully Woolies" because they were of such a heavy wool variety. We were standing in line amid this sandstorm, and the color of our uniforms changed entirely. When we got to the barracks we had to shake out our uniforms to get all the sand out.

DWELLING IN THE DESERT

All of the army wives daring enough to choose life at a military reservation were confronted with housing problems upon their arrival at Fort Huachuca. Established army bases around the country generally had housing facilities for officers and their wives and families. Naturally, with the build-up of manpower in World War II, all of the bases and housing accommodations around the country were strained beyond capacity. That was certainly the case at Fort Huachuca, where the small regimental outpost turned division cantonment barely provided sufficient housing for the new recruits. While some officers and their families were offered housing there, Fort Huachuca's dilemma was how to provide segregated housing for the white commanders. The men and their families were already segregated by rank, but the housing shortage did not allow for segregating by race. Thus, quarters for black officers' families were not available. The original, old fort and "officers' row," two-story single-family dwellings, were occupied by the white generals, colonels, and majors. Captains and lieutenants—a mix of white and black men—usually had to find accommodations for their families in the surrounding towns and neighborhoods.

The wives of the black officers generally traveled by passenger train to the Hereford station outside the fort. It was simply a depot and nothing else—a railroad station with a ramp and space to wait for the only activity in town, the arrival and departure of the train. Susie Moore was just nineteen years old when she went to Arizona to join her new husband, Spencer Moore of the 92nd Infantry Division. It was the first trip of such distance that she had ever made by herself. The train ride from Indiana through Missouri was exciting but uneventful, Susie recalled. However, in Texas, she was surprised to find that all of the black women were removed from the train in order to provide space for white soldiers. Even though Susie had arranged in advance to have a sleeper car all the way to Fort Huachuca, the porter reassigned her berth to a white major. Scared and unsure of herself, Susie was able to arrange passage on another train out of El Paso, which she rode all the way to Hereford, Arizona. She described that train stop as "pure wilderness" with "nothing but the stars shining." She met up with a few other military wives traveling to meet their husbands, and they all caught the school bus to the fort. Here they encountered the first of many shocks about life on the military reservation.

The women were driven to the gate of the fort, where the "red-light" district was located. Here they were let off the bus to fend for themselves among the prostitutes and their customers. Susie said the area at the gate, the "whorehouse," was filled with "criminal types and military police [MPs]"—two groups she had never before encountered in her young life. She had never seen "men so big" as the MPs. She was not mistaken; they were big men—the division recruited policemen over 6 feet tall and armed them with nightsticks. Susie's discomfort grew as she realized that Spencer was not there to meet her and take her to safety. (Spencer was not able to meet Susie at the train stop or at the gate because of her delay in Texas.) She was "scared by just about everything," so the impressionable young girl stood to the side until a large military policeman from her hometown recognized her. The MP called Susie's brother-in-law, also stationed at Fort Huachuca, to escort the women to the guesthouse where they were to stay until they could get permanent housing.

The women who lived at Fort Huachuca articulated the hardships more powerfully and in greater detail than their male counterparts. Susie Moore was already shaken from her experience on the train and her arrival at the fort's red-light district. Though she was immediately moved to the safety of the guesthouse, it provided her with little comfort. The house was designed to provide temporary living quarters for visitors of the men stationed at the fort. It was a converted barracks, with rows of single beds and one latrine. After falling asleep from sheer exhaustion, Susie awoke the next morning to screams. A woman had been putting shoes on her baby when she noticed a trail of bugs spilling out from his shoes and leading all the way through the guesthouse. The other women looked around and noticed more bug trails— in their sheets, on the floors, on the walls. The whole place was infested with bugs and soon echoed with the hysterical screams of the women. A handful of men came running on the double and arranged to have the place fumi- gated, but the women were determined to move out as soon as possible.

Susie and Spencer immediately went out to look for an apartment. They met a couple in Benson, Arizona, another little wilderness town, who invited them to spend the night at their efficiency apartment. Although there was only one bed everyone was accommodated—the wife slept in the middle, the husband on one side, Susie on the other, Spencer took the floor, and the couple's eight-month-old baby slept in the crib. Susie says that "military wives today don't know about roughing it; they only know a life of luxury compared to the women in Fort Huachuca, Arizona, in the 1940s."

Joseph Hairston and his wife also learned about roughing it at Fort Huachuca.

My wife and I lived in that whorehouse at the gate of the fort. One Quonset-hut type building was a beer tavern, and adjacent to that was another four-sided Quonset structure that housed the whores. It had about fifty rooms. General Almond told the owner of the huts, "You have to rent twenty-five of your rooms to my colored officers, other- wise I'll put the place off limits." So he did. Twenty-five of us moved into these rooms. And you had two cots, a hot plate, and you went down the hall to the bathroom. We had twenty-five rooms on one side of the hut, and the whores were on the other side.

Initially, when we went in, they put the men's restrooms and the women's close together. I was in the shower one day, and a woman was taking a shower. I didn't quite know how to get out of there. I wasn't a very sophisticated guy at that time anyhow. Later I told the other guys; I knocked on the door and sort of whispered the word around, and then all the men took a shower. Well, the wives wondered what was going on, and they went down and checked it out. So, then the wives made that off limits to us. They put a sign on the restroom at our end, which would rotate. It would say "Men" or "Women." It's funny to think of us living in a whorehouse!

And then we lived in Benson, which is halfway between Huachuca and Tucson. They took houses and divided them in half. We had moved up from a hot plate and two cots to a bigger hot plate. The wives had nothing to do during the day. There just wasn't anything to do. I mean, you walked down the street at Benson, and that was it. There was absolutely nothing off post, and so in the evenings we would go get our wives, and we'd walk on the post to the theater. There was always a whole drove of soldiers following you and explaining how they can do a better job with your wife than you were doing and suggesting that they would like the opportunity. That kind of put the pressure on you.

William Banks talked about the lack of officers' quarters for any kind of family-style living. "One of the problems we faced in general was the absence of officers' quarters for black families. As a matter of fact, quarters in general were pretty meager. We were well aware of the fact that this was a pretty desolate area. Some black officers did bring their wives out, but they had vehicles that would enable them to commute. There were no decent accommodations, and you just did not want to expose your family to that kind of life. Well, it was just desolate, and it just wasn't the kind of place to bring a family to."

But Joseph Hairston and Spencer Moore brought their wives, and both families ultimately found permanent living quarters in Benson. They lived in adobe buildings in a motor court setting. Susie and Spencer had a one-room apartment at the end of the motor court, with a bathroom that was shared with the couple in the adjoining apartment. Susie said:

It was a furnished efficiency, but they didn't know anything about efficiency. You had a stove with two little burners and an icebox that an ice merchant brought provisions for every day. We put a skirt around an orange crate to use beside the bed. But the bed was a big brass bed, real brass. There was a song out then they used to play, "Put Me on Your Big Brass Bed until My Face Turns Cherry Red." Well, even though the conditions were kind of crude, I have a lot of fond memories from my days there. In fact, my son was conceived there.

Susie said that all the women made the most of each day, because none of them knew when they would get the word that their husbands would be leaving. Their husbands traveled back and forth to the fort in one of the cars that two of the men owned. Spencer traded the gas ration stamps his father

sent him, from the extra allotments he was given as a doctor, for a seat in one
of the cars. Spencer also got extra rations from his friends in the Fort
Huachuca kitchen. Either the cook or the mess sergeant would signal
Spencer to stop by for "something special." Sure, it was rough living,
Spencer said, but with the special rations they were occasionally frying
steaks in butter for dinner.

There was absolutely nothing for the women to do in the way of entertainment, short of playing bridge and drinking all day, and Susie did neither.
The town was only about four blocks long, with the post office and train stop
at one end and a general store at the other. Everyday the women would wait
for the train to deliver the mail at around 2:00 p.m., and then they would go
sit under the only tree in town, read their mail, and talk. Then it was back to
the compound for more drinking and cardplaying. Susie, the youngest of the
wives living around the fort, grew up under the protective watch of the
older, more experienced, military wives. They took care of her "like a child."
She said that she had a lot to learn about life in the West.

She had never before seen snakes and Gila monsters, much less had to
defend herself against them, but she was living in a primitive setting where
the animals, reptiles, and insects ruled. She was scared of the jackrabbits,
horned toads, and tarantulas. She felt threatened by the Gila monster that
used to sit outside her window, sunning itself and staring at her while she
made breakfast. One time she had to kill a snake that was "getting ready to
come in the door." After that encounter the other women from the compound stayed with her until Spencer came home on weekends. Although
roughing it was often fun, Susie says if her protective parents had known
what the living conditions were like at Fort Huachuca, they would have
made her come back home to Indiana. "But I loved every minute of it," she
recalled. "We were just kids getting started on our own lives." She describes that time of her life as sweet and full of adventure, but surely the
strength of her character was born of the roughness of life in southeastern
Arizona.

THE COMMANDERS

The 92nd Infantry was commanded by Major General Edward Almond, former assistant division commander of the 93rd. Unfortunately, serving with
black troops did not improve Almond's outlook on the worthiness of the
black soldier. He believed that black men were fundamentally different from
white men and thus needed additional preparations and separate facilities in
order to become efficient soldiers. Almond was the brother-in-law of Army

Chief of Staff General George C. Marshall, which caused some men to question his assignment. Almond was not known for his combat or leadership
skills, yet he was given the command of an infantry division.

Many of the men believed that Almond's personal relationship with the
"upper echelons" garnered him the plum assignment of a full combat division. One man commented how Almond had "slept his way to the top," using
his wife's relation to the chief of staff as a way to get promoted. The men did
not like Almond, and they did not have confidence in his ability to command.
Almond's racial outlook prevented him from developing an attachment to
the troops, and this was never more evident than when they went into combat. Spencer Moore observed General Almond's insensitivity when the
troops were out on maneuvers. They were working on a live ammunition
problem when someone made the mistake of blowing the "all clear" signal
before the last round had hit the ground. Moore's team advanced, and a
mortar shell went off next to one of the men and seriously injured him.
Moore used the sling of his carbine as a tourniquet around the leg of the
fallen soldier.

> General Almond came up and tapped me on the shoulder with his
> stick. "Are you a doctor?" I said, "No, I ain't no damn doctor. But I'm
> not gonna let this man bleed to death." I don't know what he thought
> I was gonna do, but I wasn't going to stand around without helping
> the man. Almond was a good showman, but he didn't care for his
> troops at all.

General Almond compensated for his lack of emotion and sensitivity and
his short stature with outlandish, staged performances depicting warmth,
strength, and patriotism. Joe Stephenson described Almond as one of the
"most showy generals in the United States Army"—a man with a flair for the
extravagant display.

> I had different feelings about Almond. I saw him do things to other
> people that I thoroughly disliked, but he never did anything to me per-
> sonally where I could get angry with him. In fact, there were some ad-
> mirable things about him. I thought he was a good actor. Yeah, most
> generals are good actors. But he could really put on a show. I will never
> forget one of his performances.
> The whole division was gathered, and Almond was up on this big
> stage with something on a stand covered in cloth. We couldn't see what
> was under the cloth. He was always very, very eloquent in his speaking
> and very dramatic. So I always looked for him to do something

unusual. He loved the infantry but he could never pronounce that word infantry. "In-free" is how he said it.

So this one showtime, the artillery fired over our heads and all around and hit on a mountain in the background of the stage. Following that display Almond said, "The artillery can fire." And then the airplanes flew over. And he said, "Airplanes can fly over. They can strafe and they can bomb, but that hill," and he had a way of doing his finger real dramatic like, "will never be taken." As he said that the cloth slowly came off the thing on the stage. And there was a great big statue of an infantryman standing there with a rifle. Almond never looked around at it; he knew that performance was timed to perfection. Then he repeated, "That hill will NEVER be taken until the In-free-man has put his boots on that hill." We were all chuckling over how he said it, but I thought it was touching. I was swept away, he was so flamboyant.

Stephenson met up with General Almond on a few more occasions, and his comments add another dimension to the man.

Well, Almond was flamboyant. There's no doubt about it. I'll never forget that Sunday morning when he had us all out there sitting on some hillside. That's the first time I'd ever seen him close-up. He gave us a little talk about the artillery and all of that. Then the guns fired, and some rounds came over our heads and hit over on another hill. I was sitting there watching that hill, just sitting on the ground. I don't know what happened behind me, but Almond came from back there roaring mad. He said, "If you flinch like that when rounds come over your head then what in the hell do you think you are going to do in a real situation? Now we're going to do that again, and I don't want to see a man move."

Then he gave the signal again. It didn't bother me, really, about the rounds, because I knew the rounds weren't close, but I thought, "I'd like to look around and see who flinches." But, if I looked around he might think I flinched, so I just sat there, real still. And then I heard the rounds. Shh, boom! And then he came out and said, "Now that's the way it should be done." Hell, we were too scared to flinch. Yeah, too scared to flinch.

The men who commanded black troops were in almost all cases white officers. Most of the white officers came out of military academies or ROTC programs at universities in the South. Many of the officers, including General Almond of the 92nd, graduated from the Virginia Military Academy

(VMI). Southern schools such as the Citadel, Clemson, and Presbyterian College trained staff and line officers. One white officer from an artillery unit supporting the 92nd commented about the preponderance of officers from the VMI: "I think the only reason the VMI got picked for this job is that, in theory, they knew more about handling Negroes than anybody else, though I can't imagine why, because [Almond] just despised the ground [black soldiers] walked on." About 275 white officers served with each division, and, like their lower-ranking black counterparts, some of the officers were respected, and others were hated. A number of the white officers were content with their assignment commanding black troops, but others felt they deserved better.

Although there were exceptions, men of the 93rd were commanded by more experienced and professional white officers, whereas the 92nd was under less experienced white officers. Robert Madison was assigned to intelligence duties in the mostly white headquarters of the 370th Combat Team in the 92nd Division. He commented on the caliber of officer in the HQ: "At Fort Huachuca I was the only black officer in the headquarters, and I can tell you, the white officers who were assigned to the 92nd were not the cream of the crop, they were not top-flight. The good ones had gone with the 93rd. I didn't have any trouble with them, because I had been the only black in my [officer training] program at school. I learned to treat them on an equal basis." Fred Hurns had this to say about the white officers in the 92nd Division: "When those first white officers were assigned to our units, there was not that much intelligence there. It was the black troops who had cadred for us who gave us all of our schooling and training. Those white officers were just like overseers. Some of them didn't know anything about guns; they didn't have any training. They were all southern white men that knew nothing about how to treat black troops. They had to learn. We had to learn. It was a learning experience."

When complaints began pouring into the War Department about resentful white officers, the army conducted another survey to assess the situation. The survey revealed that the isolation of the black posts, combined with the reduced prospect of performing combat missions, contributed to the dissatisfaction of white officers. The personnel records of white officers assigned to command black soldiers were reviewed and added to the survey results. Every six months, each officer in the army was evaluated using a twelve-point scale that reviewed characteristics such as stability under pressure, judgment and common sense, leadership, force, and intelligence. White officers in black units were also evaluated for their ability to organize and foster athletic programs. Military planners learned that the majority of white officers who had been assigned to black units were rated "superior" or "excellent" on their biannual efficiency reports. These superior ratings were higher overall than white officers assigned to command new white divisions. What could not be evaluated and quantified was the white officer's ability to command black troops. No category of evaluation existed to analyze whether the officer operated with bias or prejudice.

At the beginning of the war, the army assigned only experienced officers to command black troops. These white officers had high ratings, and some of them had combat experience. Some younger officers had leadership experience from serving as commanders of black CCC units. But later, as the military continued to enlist more and more people, the ratings of both the officers and the enlisted men declined. There was a shortage of highly rated white officers, but there was also a shortage of available black officers—highly rated or otherwise. The situation for officers was always one of constant evaluation, but that situation was made tougher by the racialized aspect of the monitoring. One black enlisted man commented on conditions for officers in the segregated units: "White officers who tried to buck the system were busted and moved, those from captain down. Don't you ever think those crackers [white commanding officers] were above putting their hands on a white army officer; they weren't and they did. You can imagine where this left the colored noncommissioned officers and the enlisted men."

Hank Williams explained: "Every Saturday in the infantry you would have an inspection. That was my job. Everything had to be spit and polish. Everybody's got to be on the ball. Shaved with clean haircuts. Rifles cleaned; all your buttons in place and polished. Shoes shined and so forth. Then I would go around with my little book and mark everything that was okay and everything that needed to be fixed. Mostly, my guys gave me a good inspection. They were usually in my good graces. Our colonel liked what he saw, and so did the captain, a nice enough white guy from VMI. The captain believed in his men, and the men believed in him. When he had to leave because he got a promotion, the black men even shed tears. Now, other men would tell me about their commanding officers in the other outfits who treated them like dirt, but not my guys. They gave us a good inspection all the time."

Bill Perry also commented on his experience with army inspections, contrasting the indoor barracks inspection with the outdoor field inspection.

Most of the time we spent out in the field running problems. They worked you like a dog. Then, in the middle of all that, General Almond would come out and do an inspection. There would be about ten thousand of us out there running problems, and we had to stop and get ready for his inspection. We would polish up everything and lay it all out in the proper fashion, this piece next to that piece, all displayed

The new military on parade in Fort Huachuca.

properly on the field blanket. And then we'd wait out there in that sun for four or five hours. Finally, he would fly by in his little plane and look us over. Zoom, he'd fly over us blowing sand and debris all in our faces. That was Almond's kind of inspection.

Spencer Moore remembered General Almond inspecting the troops, up close, rather than from the air.

Almond would come down the line, inspection line, and he would say to one of our men, "Where are you from, son?" Sometimes he called him "soldier." Our guy would say something like, "Birmingham, Alabama, sir."

And the general would say, "Oh, you know Mr. So-and-so down there?" "Yes, sir; yes, sir," that soldier replied. That's how it went, because Almond liked that. But when somebody had a Yankee accent, well, Almond wasn't too keen on that, see, and he never asked those fellows anything.

Usually, officers with lower rank than General Almond did the inspections and critiqued the troops. In addition to the field inspections, ranking officers would prepare written critiques each time the units maneuvered against one another or ran problems. The men would be told their "mission" and then divided into opposing red or blue teams. They used live ammunition and other real equipment in simulated war conditions. Charles Wesly reported on the number of times the men went through maneuvers. "I don't know how many times we went through basic training at Fort Huachuca. At that time, when you finished basic training you were out of the country, but we kept doing more maneuvers and more training. One reporter who was with us, Billy Rowe, was always campaigning to send our boys out to fight."

The commanders were rarely satisfied with the maneuvers and thus kept sending the men back into the field. Major General Fred W. Miller of the 93rd Infantry critiqued one eleven-day maneuver.

> Some things were particularly commendable: concealment and night discipline were particularly good. The march of foot troops was not good. After they detrucked at Canelo store, it appears that men fell out at will. Some stated they just fell out because they were tired; others had various pains and aches. I found men sleeping all over the command posts. This must be corrected. I saw a vast difference between Sunday and Tuesday. I feel that two weeks in the field will result in a more smoothly working and coordinated staff procedure.

Joe Stephenson recalled seeing General Almond in action when the troops were out on maneuvers.

> I had done an umpire out in Huachuca, one of those little exercises. I was out for about three or four days. I knew how the exercise was supposed to go because I had already gone through it with another battalion. So early one morning I knew that the artillery was gonna fire on the hill out there at 6 a.m. A little before six I saw a jeep coming down the road with a flag on it, the general's flag. It was Almond in the jeep coming up over the hill that we were supposed to fire on. He should have turned and started coming up the canyon where we were, because that hill was gonna be fired upon. But his jeep didn't do it. The jeep went on down the road and turned and came on up that hill.
>
> I thought, "Uh-oh. We're supposed to fire where he's at, something bad's gonna happen in a minute." There was a captain standing there, along with a couple of other white officers. And some artillery officers were standing right there, too.
>
> One of them said, "I think I see the general down there." I looked up at the captain, and I heard him say, "That's all right. That's all right."
>
> I thought, "You mean they're gonna fire on the general? Well, Hell, I ain't gonna say anything about it." Pretty soon I heard the guns: boom, boom, boom! Boy, those rounds came over my head, and they just covered that hill out where Almond was coming. And I thought, "My God, they've killed the general."

And then those two white officers went over, and they were congratulating the captain. "You did a fine job, sir. Well, done." He said, "Oh, it's nothing." And then, as I looked back over to the hill area, I saw that flag on the general's jeep coming out of the dust, just coming out of the dust, going back this way and that, zigzagging toward us.

Real quick like, those two lieutenants distanced themselves from that captain. We were all standing at attention when Almond stopped his jeep—he was completely covered in dust, and that jeep was a mess. He just got out and said, "Captain, what time were you supposed to fire?" And the captain replied, "0600, sir!"

Almond looked at his watch, then he looked out there at the hill to check the visibility. He saw that we could see quite clearly out there. And he just said, "0600? All right. All right. Well, Okay." Then he got in the jeep and left. That's all he said. I don't know what might have happened to that captain later, but that's all Almond said then. He just left. But I tell you one thing, those two lieutenants didn't want to have a thing to do with it. No way, they were just standing off to the side by the time the Almond got there.

A DAY IN THE LIFE OF A HUACHUCAN SOLDIER

Black soldiers in the 93rd and 92nd Divisions spent most of their time at Fort Huachuca training for combat. The men trained in the blazing desert heat and also in the freezing cold of the surrounding mountains. Sometimes they spent as many as twenty days in the field trying to simulate actual wartime conditions. The men called this "running problems." The army used a nearby ghost town, Charleston, as a place where the men could practice street fighting and close-quarter combat. At the beginning of the war, black soldiers were training with old World War I equipment. Bill Payne described the gear:

> Besides the "Bully Woolies," we were also issued jodhpurs with wrap-leggings. And what I called the "Monkeyback" uniform, with the high-collar and the long, slit-type cap. We had the pith helmet, I can't mention the name we called it, but it was that old World War I style. And we were issued a 1911 Field Rifle.

Because no tanks were available at Fort Huachuca, one of the men in the 93rd Infantry designed a makeshift wooden model that fit on top of a jeep. This gave the men the opportunity to practice with a simulated tank. The use of secondhand equipment changed by the time the 92nd Infantry got to Fort Huachuca. By then there were real tanks, with black soldiers running problems and teaching defensive tank strategies.

The daily routine of the Huachucan doughboy included 25-mile and 65-mile tactical "hikes," training with artillery, setting up communications, practicing reconnaissance, and digging foxholes. Every soldier had to learn military nomenclature and drill regularly on reconnaissance maneuvers. The men learned how to march and pack gear and carry it in the proper manner. They practiced speed foxhole preparation and close-order drill. Frank E. Bolden observed many of the training activities that took place at Fort Huachuca and reported his findings in a regular column for the Pittsburgh *Courier*.

These Tan Yanks of the 93rd Infantry have what it takes in double quantities! They roll out of bed at the crack of dawn, enjoy a good breakfast, and prepare to take advantage of every hour of the training day. These 'cruits learn fast. They have not only been initiated into the intricacies of squad drill but are fast learning the "hocus-pocus" of rolling that eighth wonder of the military world—the pack roll and its mysterious running mate—tent pitching—army style. Only a military Houdini could master that pack roll at the first attempt. In that pack each soldier has equipment that will make him self-sustaining in the field. It is all rolled into a compact roll that can be carried on one's back without impairing Joe Recruit's mobility. Only the pure in heart can break in a pair of those GI (Government Issue) shoes. For the first few days "they ask for you" and then after the full 15 bunion rounds you can be declared the winner. After you have beaten those cowhides into submission they perform as supple as a kid glove and do you feel happy at your first victory over the perambulating convoys. There is no let up for the elements. Drills and hikes go on during the entire day regardless of the intense heat, these "streamlined Tan Yanks" are going through the paces even in the 110-degree heat. These tanned warriors plod through these desert wastes swallowing dust whistling through parched lips and dry throats and covering ground in an amazing fashion with that easy route step that enables them to go for miles without fatigue, and laboring under the load of a full field pack. They are "cooking something" for any enemy that stands in their way. They are training with a purpose and a vengeance. They are determined to make someone pay!

The men reported that the training was rigorous and the terrain inhospitable. In September 1942, three thousand men of the 93rd Infantry moved out for a four-day tactical hike through the Huachuca Mountains. The first day was comparatively easy: a 10-mile hike with approximately 60 pounds of gear strapped to the soldier's back. A "jam band" traveled with the men and set up shop at the end of the day's hike to give some relief to the soldiers. They played "Jumpin' at the Woodside" and many other dance favorites. The post newspaper wrote: "The jam band 'gave out' for hundreds of 'jive happy' soldiers." Corporal "Noody" Bowman, a talented performer in the unit, sang "Star Dust" underneath the star-filled Arizona night sky. The second and third days were filled with hiking through the mountains while practicing ambush maneuvers. The fourth day was the hardest: the men climbed over the 4,000-foot Montezuma Pass and practiced ambush maneuvers against one another. At the end of the maneuvers, as the men returned to the barracks "the band piped the boys in with a rendition of 'Noble Men'. . . . even though dead tired, they moved in unison to the beat."

Hank Williams described some typical days training with the 93rd.

Close Order Drill was a mandatory sort of thing, and hikes were mandatory. Keeping foot soldiers in mint condition, that was the idea. We would start off with a 5-mile hike in the beginning when we were recruits, simple. It's only 5 miles. The 10-mile hikes got a little tougher. Then 15-mile hikes. And eventually the biggie, the 25-mile hikes. But we were seasoned by then. When things were tight in civilian life in regards to fuel, they took our vehicles away from us. I was in a heavy weapons company, used to riding everywhere. I had a jeep, but I parked it. I could have used my jeep because of my rank, but I didn't. I marched with the men. We always rode, and all of a sudden we're not riding. We had to carry our machine guns and mortars and that sort of thing.

When we went out on a march, it was in front of the rifle company. Eventually they would catch up with us because we had such heavy equipment. The rifle companies started laughing at us, saying we were gonna fall out, we're not going to be able to make it. You know the way soldiers can be competitive like that. So we jokingly said if anybody falls out they'd get shot. After one particular 10-mile hike, on our way back my fellas decided that they wanted to show off a little bit. So they said, "No stop, Top." You understand that flavor? "No stop, Top" means no 10-minute break, and I'm the Top Kick Sergeant. They didn't want to stop for the 10-minute break.

So we moved on by the rifle companies while they were taking their 10-minute break. We overtook them. Then as we were getting near the camp area you could hear the band playing, and we broke the routine step and got into a march step. We marched in like we were all fifteen years of age and raring to go. By the time the other guys got in we were shaved and showered and sitting around waiting for them to come in. Just to show off.

Training was also rigorous for the women in the army. Madine Davis Lane explained how nurses' training was based on the training for male soldiers. The first order of business for any woman in the military, as for male recruits, was understanding military rank and hierarchy. The women had to learn to instantly identify an officer's insignia and salute in the proper fashion. After that most basic training, the women were taught map-reading skills. "They'd start with the basic map, nothing but the lumps and bumps that indicated mountain streams and things like that. Then we kept building up the map by adding in what other things we could identify around us. They knew that when we went to war we might not be able to get a complete map of an area where we would need to be, and they feared that we might be separated from our unit. So they taught us how to find our way around and create our own maps."

Soon after the classroom training, the women went out into the field and trained in the heat and dust of the desert. Lane said:

> Before we went overseas, we had to go over to the rifle range and learn how to roll on our belly and not raise our head up and get shot. They had live ammunition shooting over us. First they taught us how to do it by taking us through the course. They said, "If you raise your head up out there, you'll find there is live ammunition. You'll get your head blown off. So don't look around for your friend; don't do anything." They taught us how to go under barbed wire by turning on our backs. What to do in a ditch. How to lower ourselves into the ditch and come up in case we had that kind of terrain. We drilled on all that, and it was the same kind of training as the men.

The post papers, *The Blue Helmet* for the 93rd Infantry Division and *The Buffalo* for the 92nd, reported on the training and other activities of the new divisions. When the 93rd was stationed at Fort Huachuca more than twenty thousand papers were distributed on the fort each Friday, making the circulation the second highest in the state, surpassed only by the (Phoenix) *Arizona Republic*, which at the time had a circulation of about thirty-five thousand. The back page of every issue of *The Blue Helmet* was dedicated to war news, with maps and other information concerning both the European and the Pacific theaters of war. Jokes were used as fillers; for example: "What's the difference between a Japanese and girdle? None, they both creep up on you and it takes a good YANK to keep 'em down." Morale-building stories and cartoons were scattered throughout the paper, but news about Fort Huachuca's soldiers and the division's activities received the most coverage. The men could read about their comrades out on maneuvers in the nearby mountains. They could get up-to-date, albeit heavily censored, war news, and they could read special columns written by black journalists. They could also see which units in the division were passing or failing inspection.

"MILITARY INTELLIGENCE"

To be inducted into the army, each man had to take a written examination, the Army General Classification Test (AGCT). The results were then used to determine the man's military operations specialty (MOS). To be eligible for Officer Candidate School, each candidate had to receive a score of at least 110 on the AGCT and, in addition, receive a recommendation from his white commanding officer. Ted McCullough talked about his experience with the exam.

> One thing that burned me at the induction center was there were white officers giving the tests and they were telling our fellas, "This doesn't mean anything. It's just army stuff they got you going through." So I tried whispering to the fellas, "This test means everything!" It irked me that the officers were lying like that.

The AGCT was not supposed to be an intelligence test. The Army Officer Training Manual described the AGCT as "a quick and reasonably dependable measurement of an enlisted man's *working level* and *ability to learn*." In World War I, the army had administered the "Alpha and Beta general intelligence exams," but by World War II it had developed the new AGCT and suspended the old intelligence exam. But the AGCT discriminated against men with minimal schooling and those with little or no exposure to world events. In the training manual for white officers assigned to black troops, the army chastised its officer trainees for interpreting the AGCT as an indicator of racial differences. But the test results were often interpreted in a racialized way. Despite its stated policy, the army treated the AGCT results as being indicative of "native intelligence" and thus did not readily recommend black men to OCS. Among those taking the test, only 5 percent of black enlisted men received a 110 on the test, compared to 45 percent of white enlisted men, presumably because of educational inadequacies.

The army resented being pressured to recommend more blacks, citing low AGCT scores as an inhibiting factor for recruitment to OCS or even placement of enlisted men in combat units. The induction standard called for men to be able to read and write at the fourth-grade level. The army expected the men to have a "reasonable amount of education" in order to be of value to the more complex, modern war machine of World War II. To explain the high number of black rejections at induction centers, the army said:

> Since 1940 induction standards have changed at different times. Men who were once rejected might later be reexamined and accepted. This is markedly true of illiterates. They could be inducted only in limited numbers prior to 1 June 1943. After this date all restrictions on the number of illiterates who could be inducted were lifted, with the result that many previously rejected illiterates are now in the army.

After literacy was eliminated as a requirement for induction, the army crafted new "psychological tests directed at discovering levels of native capacity." The army also established Service Training Units (STUs), where men without the benefit of a high school education could go to improve their performance in basic training and also their reading and writing abilities.

Ezell Jackson had firsthand experience in an STU. Although Jackson's educational experiences were humble by anyone's standards, he was assigned to teach new recruits how to read and write. Jackson was born in a log cabin in northern Spartanburg County, South Carolina, in an area called "Little Africa." He said: "The whole area around there for miles and miles was owned by blacks. We raised cotton, corn, and a little tobacco, and peanuts. Everything we ate we grew there." Jackson worked on a farm until he was sixteen, when he ran away from home. His education up to that point was based around the farm schedule. "You would only go to school for three months and not every day. Because if there was something that needed to be done around the farm and the weather was good, you had to come out of that school and work on the farm."

Jackson returned to high school when he was twenty-six years old because he wanted to learn to read and write and do things for himself. Even though he was ten years older than the rest of the students, he finished high school and even went to college for one year. He married while in college and did not have the money to support a family, so he took a job as a butler and chauffeur for a prominent South Carolina family. After a few years of that work, and while he was working at a bakery, Jackson was drafted.

They drafted me when they said they weren't taking fathers. I had two children, and they still drafted me. And I had a job at the bakery so that I wouldn't get drafted. We were making bread for an army camp and you weren't supposed to get drafted if you had one of those jobs. It seemed like such a crazy army to me. After I took my test [the AGCT] they assigned me to the STU to help the guys learn how to read and write.

Joe Stephenson also noticed the high degree of illiteracy among the men of his company.

I was shocked because I had not experienced anything like that in North Carolina where I came from. Five of us went down on the train together. I was a college graduate, and the other four were high school graduates. Most of the soldiers in my company came from Mississippi, Alabama, and other areas in the Deep South. They were very poorly educated. I was angry when I saw what the country had done to them. Some of those guys would bring me letters to read and write for them; we were kind of a cadre for them. I was glad to do it, proud to do it, because I had advantages that they never had.

Jackson was proud to be involved in teaching, but he noted that some men used the STU as a way to get out of the army. "Some of them could read and write, but they would pretend they couldn't so they might get sent back home. I worked with them, but some of them, I couldn't do a thing with." There have always been goldbricks in the army, as many of the men noted.

The army had its official training units, but the men formed their own unofficial educational groups to assist one another with the rigors of army life. In the official training units, over two thousand men attended literacy classes taught by both enlisted men and officers. There is no estimate on the number of men who attended the unofficial educational groups. Both the official and unofficial forms of education were designed to improve the men's ability to perform their military duties, and both were aimed toward compensating for low AGCT scores. Test scores were scaled into one of five categories, with the highest value placed on the first two categories of classification and less value on those men who scored in the middle and below. The army deemed men scoring in the last two categories to be unworthy of military service.

In the all-white units there was also illiteracy, as well as low scores on the AGCT. The difference, as Joe Stephenson pointed out, is that the percentages were more evenly distributed in the white units. There were more white units for low-scoring individuals to be transferred to, and they could be evenly distributed: thus no white units had a disproportionally high concentration of low-scoring individuals. This was not the case in the black units: because there were fewer units, each one had to absorb a higher proportion of low-scoring individuals. Stephenson said:

> The white troops were different. They had a large number of illiterates too as far as numbers are concerned, but not percentages. Their percentage of illiteracy was much lower, even though overall they had more illiterate people total. But in a white unit, you can hide the illiterates. You can take that small percentage of illiterates and scatter them around and pretend they never existed. Put them in the boiler room, anywhere. But we couldn't do that in all-black units; we couldn't hide those people too many places. So we had to deal with it, and it takes leadership among other things.

In the 92nd Division, the majority of the enlisted men scored in the lowest two categories, which confirmed the racial prejudices of some of the white officers. Many black officers, however, recognized other ways in which the men were skilled and worked to capitalize on their assets. Joe Stephenson said:

> I didn't care about their AGCT score. I had the feeling that most of the company had low scores. But I made those men believe they had been especially picked for my platoon because they were different. The weapons were different, and I had to have smart people and different people to handle those weapons. And they believed in me, trusted me. They weren't really any different from the other platoons.
> Now I never spoke to them about patriotism. "We've got to learn to do this, to learn to shoot, because of the flag or the country." I never said that; I talked to them about self-preservation. You will either kill him, or he will kill you. And that's the way the men felt about it. My men always fired well. They always made high scores on all the firing tests, or performance type of tests, that anyone threw at them. Whether it was the mortar or the machine gun, they were extremely good at what they did. I didn't care about their AGCT scores. The only thing I cared about was them learning to shoot those guns. And they did it and did it well.

Wade McCree of the 92nd Division also commented on the AGCT scores of his fellow Buffalo Soldiers. He said that one of his jobs was to teach reading and writing to the men who scored in the lower categories. His two years of law school at Harvard obviously contributed to the reservoir of knowledge he could tap when teaching the men in his unit. McCree noted the irony of a government that had no difficulty drafting black servicemen from the South but was incapable of building adequate schools in their communities. Still, the low test scores did not make McCree look down on the men he taught.

Even the illiterates were quite skilled in many particulars. In terms of skills required for infantry service they excelled. Almost all were familiar with firearms. Some were absolutely fantastic shots. They were to a great extent familiar with the outdoors, and infantry warfare is an outdoor activity, so they fitted in very well there.

SPECIAL DAYS: FINDING FUN AT THE FORT

While most of a soldier's time was devoted to combat training, special occasions like dances at the enlisted men's and officers clubs, holiday celebrations, and military parades enlivened the regular course of events. Madine Davis Lane described life at Fort Huachuca after the nurses had completed their basic training.

Hot and lively nights, then I would get up and play tennis in the morning or go horseback riding. Then I went on duty and came off in the evening to play tennis again. And back to the club to dance from nine until two in the morning. Every Saturday night a band played at the club, but during the week we danced to the jukebox. Also, many of the top black performing artists of the day came through Fort Huachuca at that time. We saw the Mills Brothers, because John Mills was a soldier out there. Thayard Nicholas was a soldier there, so naturally we saw the Nicholas Brothers perform.

Ernestine Hughes also described the off-hours life of a female soldier: "Soldiers and WACs are dancing to the mellow strains of the post's famous orchestras; others are bowling, skating, seeing movies, or settled down to games of cards, or parked on the desert's edge, romancing under the Huachucan moon."

Because Fort Huachuca was so isolated, the army attempted to create and maintain a totally self-sufficient entertainment and recreational calendar of events. A 1943 post newsletter reported:

There is a special challenge to the Special Services Division to create an all-out program of recreation, education, and entertainment. A hundred miles from any large center of population, twenty-five miles from the main line railroad, even if gasoline and tire rationing were not a major factor there would be little object in hauling thousands of soldiers to the small neighboring communities . . . without the facilities to entertain them. A broad program has been instituted to develop local musical and theatrical talent and a constructive program of competitive sports. All programs are designed for one purpose—to maintain a top degree of morale.

The Special Services branch maintained a full calendar of events for the soldiers. The men and women could participate in badminton or tennis, baseball, softball, swimming, and even horseshoe-pitching.

Before the Special Services division instituted entertainment programs, finding something to do was the main activity of the Huachucan soldier. When those first recruits got to the base, there were few leisure establishments and even fewer women. The men drank and relieved their boredom at the Halfway House, a bar located just outside the back gate of the fort. It was also referred to as the "Bloody Bucket," because at least once a month someone got into a fight at the bar. Felix Goodwin was in that first group of soldiers stationed at Fort Huachuca before the building boom. He said: "The soldiers would leave the Halfway House at 10:15 and run all the way back to the barracks, which were almost to the mountains, about 5 miles inside the fort. They were doing 9-minute miles to get back by bed check."

Hank Williams also remembers some escapades at the Halfway House in those early days. "One day a bunch of us from Cleveland planned a big party down there just for something to do." The men from Cleveland formed a social organization called "The Huachucans," with Williams in charge of entertainment. Because of the lack of women, the men arranged for one fellow from L Company to don a red dress and dance for the entertainment of the other men. So they sent to Tucson for a special dress. Everyone was busy making preparations for the party when they received orders to leave the fort on a training maneuver. They packed up and marched out, but when they discovered they were going to be on an overnight bivouac, the men were severely disappointed—they would miss the party! Williams took immediate action. Without even getting permission from his commanding officer, Williams went over to regimental headquarters and asked to speak to the adjutant general (AG). He told the AG about the party and the disappointment of the men, and he described all the plans that would have to be scrapped.

Williams said the AG consulted with the colonel and they advised him: "Move on out. Get some trucks to get up there and bring those men back down from the operation. Morale is more important than what we're doing." Perhaps the commanders were following an old army adage attributed to General Pershing: "Give me a thousand soldiers occasionally entertained to ten thousand soldiers without entertainment." Membership in "The Huachucans" increased after men from other companies realized that the group had enough influence to have an overnight maneuver cancelled. (Although "booze and broads" were the underlying organizational concepts of the organization when they first gathered at the fort, today in Cleveland, Ohio, the club provides leadership to junior ROTC boys and girls interested in the military and has women veterans as members.)

When more men accumulated at the post the entertainment organizations escalated their activities. Recruiting women to attend dance parties and other special events on the base was part of the job of the United Service Organizations (USO). Women ran the two USO clubs at Fort Huachuca and contributed to the war effort by organizing entertainment for the soldiers stationed in the deserts of Arizona. When the second of the two USO clubs opened for entertainment and dining, seven opening nights were scheduled so that all of the men could participate in the events. Until September 1942, Shirley Graham, later to become the wife of W. E. B. Du Bois, worked at the Fort Huachuca USO planning and scheduling events. The clubs were always busy with dances and fashion shows, whist tournaments, and pool and Ping-Pong games.

Music was a big part of life at Fort Huachuca. The USO provided occasional professional entertainment, including musical performances by Lena Horne, Dinah Shore, Louis Armstrong, Duke Ellington, and Kay Kyser. Lena Horne performed so many times that the men of the 92nd dubbed her the "Sweetheart of the Division." The post commander also named the outdoor theater in her honor. For a special performance in September 1942 Horne accompanied other cast members of the popular musical *Cabin in the Sky*. She sang "I've Got a Gal in Kalamazoo" and "You Are My Thrill," which must have thrilled her audience of some ten thousand soldiers. Horne had a nephew stationed at the fort, and she also had a special spot in her heart for the eighteen thousand-plus black soldiers stationed at the base. Whether she performed for the 92nd or the 93rd, the men considered it a special assignment to escort her around the fort. Fulfilling his additional duties as a special services officer, Joseph Hairston occasionally escorted her. He said she was the most gracious person he had ever met, and he had the pleasure of remaking her acquaintance in the civil rights marches in Washington, D.C., in the 1960s.

During the war years, Horne performed with an assembly of stars who called themselves the Hollywood Victory Committee. Reporting on one Sunday performance, the post paper wrote:

> The Hollywood Victory Committee headed by Clarence Muse gave a variety show that was received with roars of applause. Hattie Morrison's "boogie-woogie" piano got a stamp of approval. Chinkie Grimes was

called again and again for encores of her red-hot dancing and singing. Two of our enlisted men made this a well-rounded show: Corporal Effert "Noody" Bowman and Rico Harrison sang "This Love of Mine." Clarence Muse closed the show with "Ol' Man River."

According to the paper, the variety show also included one-man comedy acts such as Sunshine Sammy, Mantan Moreland, and Monte Hawley.

Musical entertainment did not always need to be imported—both the 92nd and the 93rd Divisions, along with various regiments within the divisions, maintained bands that were a source of pride for many soldiers.

Lena Horne, star of motion pictures, theater, and
radio-television, at Fort Huachuca, August 22, 1943.
(U.S. Army photo, courtesy of Fort Huachuca Museum)

Division headquarters sent out recruiters to enlist well-known band members and other musical performers. One talented couple, Mercedes and Joe Jordan, were stationed at Fort Huachuca, working for the Special Services Division. Mercedes was known for her songwriting, popularized by the swing bands of both Jimmy Dorsey and Jimmy Lunceford. Joe was Fort Huachuca's Special Services music director. Joe recruited Lawrence Whisonant, the "Singing Sergeant," to perform numbers from his role as Porgy in the Broadway production of *Porgy and Bess*. The 92nd's divisional band, the "Bouncing Buffaloes," was particularly admired for the "tone color" of its dance orchestra. Frank E. Bolden wrote in his regular column that "there is more musical and dramatic talent in this Division than has ever before been collected under a military tent."

William Banks was one of the many talented individuals in the 92nd Division. He was part of a comedy and music act called the "Swing Four," which performed for the amusement of the other men. By all reports they were well received when they performed. Each divisional band could break down into smaller orchestra, swing, or jam bands. Other popular entertainers included the 368th Swingeroos, consisting of members from the 368th Battalion. They were booked most Saturday nights, at either the Savoy (also called the Field House), the USO clubs, or at one of the two officers clubs at Fort Huachuca.

The Special Services newsletter regularly printed a guide to the upcoming USO entertainment, imaginatively describing the evening events. "The 368th and 369th Infantry Battalion Bands vie for first place in popularity, either is a good bet for the many dances and parties given on the post," one article reported.

> The whole Division has taken the "Deep River Boys" to its heart. The 368th orchestra gives out with some "pick up" acts. Pvt. Lawrence Neely emcees, and Billy Kyle at the piano steals the show for a thunderous moment of applause. They're warmed up now. The jam session is on. 1,200 hearty voices cheer as Billy Kyle's piano thunders the "Bivouac Bounce." Sgt. Bob Taylor's old trumpet blares out "Nona, Nona, Nona," Corporal Cooper's bass fiddle mourns while Kenneth Sanders drums the tom-toms. A break in the beat and Corporal Frazier's xylophone comes in on a jitterbug tempo. Funnyman Harris does a hilarious bit of pantomime and "Deep River Ray" Branch takes over at the piano. The old clock strikes ten and the evening's fun is over.

The newsletter used the colorful lingo of the day to report on events at "deah ol' Hoochee," including such phrases as "solid sender that is a bender";

"that's no jive, five by five"; "hepsters"; "jitterbugs jitting"; "a jam that will end all jams"; "jump of the season"; and "root and toot."

In addition to popular music, division headquarters provided other types of entertainment for the men stationed at the fort. Every Sunday evening from 7 until 9 o'clock the games and jitterbug music were put aside for what the Special Services newsletter called "The Hour of Charm"—one hour of classical music played on records. Cultural and sports figures such as Langston Hughes, Sugar Ray Robinson, and Joe Louis ("The Brown Bomber") regularly appeared at the fort. Also, to boost morale the army recruited visual artists and asked them to portray black men fighting in the war effort. Sergeant Lew Davis of Tucson, Arizona, joined the 93rd Division at Huachuca and immediately began repainting the traditional images seen on war posters with ones that included black faces. His most striking poster depicts a black soldier with the caption "History will judge us by our deeds."

The library provided another diversion for the soldiers stationed at Fort Huachuca. Seventy magazines and newspapers, updated regularly, were available to read on the premises. In the archives several photographs depict studious black soldiers enjoying the quiet peace of the library. But reading the wrong material could get a soldier into trouble, as Clarence Adams discovered. "I drew the book from the Service Club Library to read," he wrote to the Baltimore *Afro-American*.

> I had finished up my work for the day and was just about ready to leave when the company executive officer walked in the office. He picked up the book and began looking through it; finally he came to this poem: "Mulatto" by Langston Hughes. He cursed and used all kinds of vile language about the author. "Take that damn book back where you got it and I don't want to ever see anything like that around the company. The wrong person might get a hold of it and it might cause some trouble."

One of Bill Payne's memories about life at Fort Huachuca is of a special Christmas dinner celebration. He remembers it so well because he was given a commemorative three-color menu that was specially printed for the occasion, and he still has it among his military memorabilia. The rank and name of each member of the unit were listed right after the main dish— roast turkey with sage dressing. Jehu Hunter also remembers the Christmas celebrations, because all of the officers, black and white, had to greet General Almond and wish him "Merry Christmas." The men were instructed to put some sentiment into their Christmas wishes, and Hunter says he always managed to put just the right emphasis on his greetings to the general. For Christmas 1942, the division entertainment featured bandleader Noble

Sissle, who had served in Europe with the 369th Regiment during World War I. The performance was broadcast live over NBC radio. Later, when Sissle more informally played the Field House, a recreation center for black

"To my loving mother, from her son," Bill Payne
and buddy at Fort Huachuca. (Photo by Roland Dix)

soldiers, a special system was designed to pipe the music into the white officers' Lakeside Club.

Competitive sports provided another type of entertainment. On the newly built-up post, the Rube Foster Memorial Baseball Field had room for ten thousand spectators, and there were twenty-five more baseball fields for the fort's hundred or so teams. The soldiers could play basketball or volleyball at one of the many courts on the post. There were six football fields where any of the fort's seven football teams could gather to play. White southern officers with strong college-sports experience were recruited to coach football for the regimental teams. When Lieutenant McGrath, former New York Giants player, came to Fort Huachuca, he participated in all types of sports, including track and field. Lee Quarterman and Captain Roy, both of the 93rd Division and formerly football stars of Presbyterian College in South Carolina, coached teams for the division. The 369th Infantry team dubbed their football team "The Hellcats," a tribute to their World War I moniker. They routinely played against "The Hornets," the 368th Infantry's regimental football team. On New Year's Day 1943, the Hellcats and the Hornets met on the field in the first ever "Desert Bowl" competition.

Other special events included numerous military parades in the local towns. When Tucson requested some soldiers for the annual Armistice Day parade in November, General Almond sent 1,200 men from the infantry and from specialty detachments like the band and medical units. Almond watched from the reviewing stand as his men were joined by white troops from an Arizona airbase. The parade started with a memorial "Taps" commemorating the World War I peace treaty. Then nine B-24 bombers flew over the formation of soldiers, cannons, and machine guns. The 92nd Division was escorted by its mascot, a live bison named "Buffalo Bill." Normally, Bill lived out on the range on the base, but Almond never missed an opportunity to show off all the assets of the division. The 93rd Division was also sent to various Arizona towns to parade its military might, and occasionally its mascot, Myrtle, a thirty-four-year-old mule, tagged along with the men. She had served with General Pershing during the Pancho Villa raids in the Huachuca Mountains, but mostly, like Bill, Myrtle stayed out on the range. The men and their mascots marched in Flag Day parades and Fourth of July events in neighboring towns such as Bisbee and Douglas.

THE "NOT SO SPECIAL" ACTIVITIES

Not all of the recreation at Fort Huachuca was of the wholesome type sponsored by division headquarters. A cluster of Quonset huts just out-

side the gates of the fort where prostitutes plied their trade provided perhaps the main recreational outlet for the GIs. It was nicknamed the
"Hook" because "anybody who went there was going to get hooked by
something—the clap, a knife blade, or if he was lucky, just a tough black
fist," remarked Nelson Peery. Mr. Fry, a local townsman, rented the
makeshift huts to the one hundred or so prostitutes and pimps who were
drawn to the area by the easy market of eighteen thousand potential customers. Because more than $100,000 was paid out to the soldiers every
payday, the post naturally attracted prostitutes, drug peddlers, bootleg-
gers, and other unsavory types. The army countered with its more virtu-
ous USO and officers clubs, but the Hook flourished anyway. Bootleg
whiskey sold for $7.00 per pint; between paydays a soldier could "put a
quarter on the pint" and get a swig of homemade brew. In 1943 some
black businessmen from Chicago decided to invest in the construction of
an amusement center to be located just outside the main gate of the fort.
The post commander, Colonel Hardy, sanctioned the green-domed center known as the "Green Top."

The army was well aware of the problem of prostitution at military establishments. In fact, the Federal Security Agency was charged with the task of
closing prostitution centers around army bases. Responding to a complaint
about a rise in venereal disease, Eliot Ness, director of social protection at
the Federal Security Agency, wrote: "For over a year this office has been
working with the army and the U.S. Public Health Service to bring about the
closing of houses of prostitution and red-light districts and to facilitate the
elimination of all forms of prostitution. This activity was necessitated because of the large amount of venereal disease directly traceable to prostitution." Venereal disease was a by-product of prostitution, and Fort Huachuca
had its share of victims. In 1943, the rate of venereal disease was 368 cases
out of 1,000 soldiers, and by November 1944 the rate had dropped to 157 in
1,000 because the army was actively engaged in reducing the disease.

Jim Williams was stationed at Fort Huachuca as part of a medical battalion. He said he had very little free time because he worked almost nonstop
at the Hook. He said they

> set-up a prophylactic station where all the prostitutes were located.
> We kept it stocked with personnel and medicine. It was a rule that if
> you visited one of the prostitutes you had to go through the pro-
> station. If you didn't, and you came up with a disease, then you could
> be subject to a summary court-martial.

Williams said the medical staff kept pictures of the different prostitutes
posted in the dispensary. Ted McCullough said most men avoided

venereal disease court-martials, but he recalled a dressing down they received from a strict first sergeant nicknamed "Little Hitler." "It could be
embarrassing, but 'Little Hitler' would say to us: 'Tell me who you've been
with, I'll tell you what you've got.' He knew what he was talking about."
Ultimately, Fort Huachuca's commanders decided to attack the prostitution problem more directly. Colonel Hardy had the difficult task of erad-
icating prostitution at the Hook. He proposed three possible solutions:
(1) segregate the women and provide preventative health treatment;
(2) ignore the problem—the original "don't ask, don't tell" approach; or
(3) establish the Hook as "off limits" and apply disciplinary measures to
individual soldiers caught there. Hardy picked solution number three.
This "built up attendance at football games and the theater" but did not
eliminate prostitution near the base.

Besides the investigative skills of Eliot Ness at the Federal Security Agency,
J. Edgar Hoover's men at the Federal Bureau of Investigation (FBI) looked
into the illicit activities at Fort Huachuca. What sparked the FBI investigation
was an allegation that hospital officials were somehow connected to the alcohol and narcotics traffic that made it to the Hook. There was also an investigation into the alleged investors of the Green Top, as well as investigations into
prostitution rings running out of both areas. The FBI report could not sub-
stantiate any involvement between post officials and the illegal activities just
outside the gate. They did discover inappropriate solicitations by agents of a
Chicago insurance company—apparently in violation of a War Department directive. The company was allowed to solicit insurance on the post when other
companies were prohibited entry. Investigators concluded that the post commander was in collusion with the insurance company. After a reprimand in the
post commander's personnel file, life went on pretty much as usual at the fort.
The special and not-so-special activities continued as before.

Although the army attempted to limit troop entertainment to wholesome
activities, the soldiers at Fort Huachuca constantly sought out less savory di-
versions. Bill Perry talked about the weekends at the fort.

> Some of the guys like me would sleep all weekend long. I was tired.
> But a lot of the guys were drinkers. Drinkers and gamblers. On payday
> they'd gamble in the barracks until they had to report to work on Mon-
> day morning. You had a hard time getting into the latrines on payday
> weekend, because some guys would be set up in there with their blan-
> kets spread on the floor throwing dice and what-all. They'd be in the
> latrine because it was the only place with a light left on. But if you had
> to go in there to actually use the latrine, they would cuss you out and
> tell you in very colorful language that you better not disturb the game.

Joe Stephenson talked about some questionable activities in the barracks.

> One of our guys, Blondie, was from Chicago, and Al Capone was his
> role model. He was always getting into trouble at Huachuca. He hit
> the captain and got sent to jail once, and he used to get marijuana and
> smoke it. So did some of the other guys. Sometimes I could smell
> something funny coming from down their way. They would be sitting
> in the dark smoking that stuff. One guy was a musician. He used to dry
> out his marijuana on the top of his helmet. He would braid it through-
> out the netting and then wear it all day while we were out on maneu-
> vers. He'd use it like camouflage.

Whether they planned activities or the army attempted to entertain them,
there were too few recreational opportunities for so many men. "When men
are stuck out literally a hundred miles from nowhere, only so much baseball
or basketball can be played. Tempers flared and fights resulted," noted
Richard Carter. It is just a question of numbers and opportunities before soldiers find trouble, and that was certainly the situation at Fort Huachuca during World War II. Everyone stationed there in both the early and later war
years learned the danger of putting so many soldiers in one place with not
enough to do. Hank Williams says "The Huachucans" planned parties at locations close to the base to keep the men from traveling to Mexico, where
they were more likely to get arrested. If soldiers got into trouble and were
detained by local police in Mexico, the military police at the base were supposed to be notified to handle the matter. Robert Madison said he went to
Nogales, Mexico, one weekend, looking for something to do, but one of his
friends was nearly put in jail, and the guys had to spend all their time trying
to get out of town. One soldier was murdered around the post bowling alley,
apparently killed by a man wielding a bowling pin. A local civilian was murdered with an ax when a soldier suspected the man of having an affair with
his wife. Many other similar tales can be found in the Huachuca archives.
On weekends, the guardhouse on post and the jails in the surrounding towns
would fill with soldiers who had little else to do but get into trouble.

Madine Davis Lane said occasionally she would "travel to Tucson, but
sometimes there would be problems because too many soldiers were overcrowding the clubs. Even if they weren't doing anything they would get dis-
persed because the locals didn't want that many black soldiers in one place."
Reuben Horner was from Tucson, so he knew where to go when he left Fort
Huachuca. Still, he said there were few social functions or locations for
blacks to go to in Tucson. On several occasions, Horner and eight of his
friends, the "Beau Brummel Club," took over a building on Main Street in

Tucson and held formal dance parties with live acts, including Louis Armstrong. But these sorts of special activities were unusual for the bulk of the population stationed at the fort.

Trouble was brewing in all of the areas to which black soldiers had access. Several major melees involving black soldiers occurred in Mexico and Arizona, resulting in near-permanent off limits designations for Phoenix, Bisbee, and Nogales. Many of the melees were described by local papers as "race riots," presumably because black people were gathered in groups, fighting with and occasionally shooting at white people. In fact, one of the first "riots" involved black soldiers fighting with black MPs. It started on a Thanksgiving weekend, allegedly as an argument between a man and a woman, which then escalated into a "minor war that raged over twenty-eight blocks of East Phoenix." Approximately one hundred men of the 364th Infantry unit on leave in the East Phoenix area refused to disperse when ordered to do so by the MPs. The *Arizona Republic* reported: "Some soldiers broke into the armory and stole rifles, and machine guns. For a few minutes gunfire filled the air." The army brought in an armored personnel carrier to pick up suspects and then conducted a house-to-house search. The tank-like vehicle would park in front of a house and yell for the men to come out. If there was no reply, they would shoot into the house with a .50-caliber machine gun. Two men were killed, and twelve were seriously wounded before the fighting was over. Sixteen men were court-martialed and given fifty-year sentences.

Although they were never together, Bill Payne, Howard Hickerson, and Nelson Peery regularly rode army transport trucks into nearby Nogales and Agua Prieta, Mexico. Each said that within Mexico, there was slightly less discrimination against black soldiers. Hickerson commented that Mexico was a place where a soldier could go to "kick up his heels." Bill Perry commented wryly: "I could go to towns in Mexico, but I couldn't go to towns in the United States. I went to Tucson twice and then they cut it off. At one point, the whole state of Arizona was off limits." Nelson Peery said he liked the nearby western mining town of Bisbee for entertainment, but when a black soldier visiting there was told "we don't serve niggers," the ensuing melee caused the army to declare the town off limits.

Following the Bisbee incident, relations between the white officers and black enlisted men deteriorated. One white officer was hit in the head with a shovel when he was asleep in his tent, and a car of white officers was stoned as they drove off the base. Officers and men of the 93rd Infantry clashed in the streets and bars of Nogales, Mexico. The Associated Negro Press reported: "Information trickled out of camp that several white officers including one colonel have been severely beaten up or killed in altercations with enlisted personnel. The officers are said to stand far behind the lines during firing practice with live ammunition because they fear a sharpshooter might train his sights upon them and revenge mistreatment." Richard Carter analyzed the situation.

> Here was a big sprawling camp containing somewhere between seventeen thousand to twenty thousand black men with a small percentage of white officers who enforced the strictest segregation possible between themselves and the black officers. Their only contact was strictly in relation to military activities; social contact was out. How they would possibly function together in combat was a question that had to pass through many a black officer's mind, not to mention the minds of the enlisted men. Fights were a regular occurrence on the post.

The Inspector General of the Army also noted the poor relations between white and black officers at Fort Huachuca. He sent out Brigadier General Benjamin O. Davis Sr., the nation's first black general, to report on the situation.

> There appears to be very little contact between the colored and white officers, even for the discussion of, and conversation pertaining to, professional subjects. The chaplains expressed themselves as feeling that the white officers were all too prejudiced to be fair. Efforts should be made by higher commanders to bring about a closer professional contact between colored and white officers.

Another story illustrates the sorry state of relations between white and black officers at the fort. Reuben Horner was at a meeting of battalion officers for the 92nd Infantry when he was instructed by a ranking white officer, "Boy, run up to the captain and tell him we're waiting on his officers." Horner was stunned to be addressed in that manner, and he became even more aggravated when the major said to him, "Boy, get going!" Horner did not budge. Instead he replied: "Sir, are you addressing me? I was commissioned a second lieutenant in the United States Army, and as far as I know that has not changed." The major said: "Oh, don't start that. I call all of my junior officers 'boy.'" That may have been the case, but not all of his junior officers got reassigned to low-level jobs like Horner when they complained about the name-calling. After that incident, Horner was always assigned weekend duty, which prevented him from visiting his wife in Tucson. He was also assigned to trash duty, investigating all of the garbage at the base to make sure no one was throwing out government-issue items. This type of treatment left Horner "quite bitter and rebellious, in a hidden or underground type of way."

General Davis was sent several more times to Fort Huachuca to look over the troops and determine the sources of unrest. Many black soldiers, enlisted men, and officers were in the guardhouse pending court-martial charges for various offenses. Joe Hairston described a significant event that worried the commanding officers.

> At one point, there were about thirty [black] officers in the guardhouse for various indiscretions, most of them resulting from racist treatment. Every day when the officers came outside for their exercise, they would be in full dress uniforms, and they would march in formation around the confines of the area. They marched with such dignity, you know, straight ahead, soldier-like. They were making a strong statement about the injustices on the post.

The investigation by General Davis revealed the resentment many soldiers felt toward General Almond. Apparently they were beginning to act on their feelings. When General Almond took to the stage for one of his planned performances, many soldiers jeered and booed him. There were even rumors among the men that Almond had been shot at by a sniper. The chief of the War Intelligence Division, Colonel F. V. Fitzgerald, received word from "inside sources" that black soldiers were concealing arms. Many of the men confirmed that they did indeed appropriate guns and ammunition while stationed at Fort Huachuca. Bill Perry assisted the supply sergeant responsible for the weapons count in one unit of the 92nd Division. He said: "Some of the guys were returning from the rifle range with leftover ammunition, and people were beginning to get shot. So we had to set up an arsenal in one of the squad rooms in the barracks." Every night Perry counted all the ammunition and all of the M-1 rifles, .45-caliber pistols, machine guns, and 60-mm. mortars. He filled out a certification form for all of the weapons and after locking the arsenal with three locks took the report to the officer of the day. Things were heating up at Fort Huachuca.

When General Davis made a formal inspection of the conditions on the base, he also held informal discussions with the black officers. One black officer commented: "They thought when he got up there in front of us with that star of his, he would make our eyes shine with pride at his accomplishments. But that just meant he had accepted the practices that had been imposed on black officers at the time." Davis did recognize the low morale and high tension of the black soldiers on the base, and he attributed the problems to Almond's mismanagement in his final report.

> General Almond has, in the opinion of the Inspector General, overlooked the human element in the training of the division. Great stress

has been placed upon the mechanical perfection in the execution of training missions. Apparently not enough consideration has been given to the maintenance of a racial understanding between white and colored officers and men. The execution of ceremonies with smartness and precision and the perfunctory performance of military duties is taken as an indication of high morale. This is not true with the colored soldier. He can be driven to perform without necessarily having a high morale. Due to long suffering and working under conditions highly distasteful to him, he has developed, as a defense mechanism, the ability to present a calm outward appearance.

Although Davis brought attention to the plight of black officers and black enlisted men stationed at Fort Huachuca, he was attacked by some of the men as an "Uncle Tom." On his way into the informal gathering of officers, Davis was approached by a man who was wearing a handkerchief on his head, the symbolic representation of slave men. The man said: "General, from one handkerchief head to another, we greet you." The military police quickly removed the man, and Davis continued his investigation. Then, in an address he made to the rest of the assembled men, Davis said:

You're in the army now. You do what you're told. Never mind the background or the feelings that these white officers have for you. You toe the line.

He continued, saying that he was the "same color, but not the same kind" as the other officers. Some of the men supported the "protest" of the man wearing the handkerchief, but others said they were embarrassed by it and ashamed. Yet, for most of the black soldiers on the base, the visits by Davis were empty gestures by an army unwilling to recognize them as human beings with real grievances.

STATESIDE

LOUISIANA MANEUVERS

In April 1943, seventy-two railcars transported the soldiers of the 93rd Infantry Division to Louisiana for additional training. Just about the time that the soldiers at Fort Huachuca were feeling overtrained and underutilized, the army shipped the eighteen thousand men deep into the South for additional training. The 92nd Infantry had been training at four separate facilities and then moved in to Huachuca when the 93rd went on maneuvers to Louisiana. Ultimately, the 92nd traveled to Louisiana for three months of war game maneuvering, but again, not until the 93rd had moved on. After a year in the dry deserts and mountains of Arizona, the men had to get used to camping in the swampy backwoods of western Louisiana.

The terrain was unfamiliar to most of the men. Charles Wesly said that Louisiana was the only place he had ever walked on a sponge. "They had some curly grass that acted like a sponge so that when you walked down a hill or something, the grass held you up, but the water would just come up over your shoe. You would just sink into the mush." Jehu Hunter also recalled the swamps of Louisiana.

There was always plenty of mud that you had to keep trying to get off your boots and your equipment. You would try to put some sand on it so it wouldn't be so gooey, but it was a mess. We had to wade through these creeks and rivers just loaded with cottonmouth moccasins and armadillos, too. That water was stagnant, and you smelled bad when you got out of there. You smelled bad, your clothes smelled bad, you were covered in sludge. I don't know what was the worst.

Even those soldiers accustomed to the snakes and scorpions of Arizona complained bitterly about the number of critters crawling out of the swamps around their new encampment. Feral pigs, armadillos, snakes of numerous sorts and sizes, and swamp rats were common residents. The soldiers were always on the go, moving from one swamp to the next and living in tents with no permanent encampment. They were in a perpetual battle with the elements. They had to keep constant vigil on their equipment to keep it free from corrosive elements. And there were always chiggers, crickets, raccoons, and many other unwelcome creatures trying to camp with them.

The soldiers had to contend with the animosity of the locals, the inhospitable terrain of bayou country, and some very unfriendly wildlife. Many said they eventually adjusted to the snakes and armadillos, but the razorback hogs that would come running through the camp were a constant source of trouble. Jehu Hunter described the feral animals.

Louisiana was overrun with hogs, those razorback hogs. They had that sharp spine and those long legs. The males had tusks. They would run wild and just tear through the camp, coming in even where the people were. They'd come in troops with the male leading and the female and the little ones following in back. They wanted to get to our food waste, but the kitchen guys always had to take care to bury everything. It was a very efficient way of handling things, because it kept the hogs from getting in there and rooting around. But still they would come running in to the camp with the male leading, challenging you.

Lawrence Johnson had a close encounter with the wild hogs. He said that he was alone when a group of them approached him.

I tried to shoo them away, but they wouldn't back up. Usually animals are more afraid of you, and they'll run if you shoo them. But those hogs didn't run. They were tall with skinny legs, and they had tusks. I tried to maneuver my way around them, but I fell backward on my back onto the ground, and one hog straddled me. I was young and pretty fast, so I started rolling back and forth until I could get that hog off of me. I rolled right out from under that hog and luckily did not get harmed.

Edward Price described the way that some of the soldiers treated the situation. "We had soldiers from all parts of the country out there who knew how to do all kinds of things. They'd kill those hogs and then barbecue them." But sometimes the hogs were not wild; they were the property of a local farmer. The men had been instructed not to kill any of the animals—wild or otherwise—for fear of angering the local population. Bill Perry said:

> Sometimes we would run across a civilian's farm. There were a couple of times that the men would bandit the pigs. They'd say it had come after them or something. That caused a problem with the farmers, because they would be complaining about their property loss and so forth.

Ultimately, what kept the men from barbecuing everything they could lay their hands on was the penalty of being charged with the cost of replacing the farm animals. Perry said: "I don't think they ever charged anyone with a 'Statement of Charges,' but it was like if you lost some of your equipment or something, theoretically they could charge you and take that out of your pay." Perry said he felt the threat of such charges kept the barbecuing to a minimum.

The men also had to adjust to living within the constraints of Jim Crow Louisiana, with its not-so-neighborly locals. Bill Perry succinctly captured the sentiment of most of the men when they traveled into the Louisiana maneuver area: "The terrain is different down there. And the people are different. Unfortunately, we ran into both, and we had problems." Howard Hickerson described his first lesson in "southern hospitality."

> There were all kinds of stories about soldiers getting refused service while we were in Louisiana. One time the word passed down that some little country store owner had refused service to one of our guys. The store was by itself at the crossroads of this nowhere place that we had to drive by with our convoy of trucks. Well, after we heard about them not serving us, it was just kind of silently agreed that we'd make them know we didn't appreciate it.
>
> One afternoon as the trucks were coming back to camp, one driver took the corner just a little bit wide—you know those were *big* vehicles—and zip, there goes a bit off the porch of that little store. Then the next truck followed and zip, there goes a little bit more of that porch. Pretty soon: zip, zip, zip. That porch was all torn up, and there was dirt kicked up all over that store. And our guys were saying: "Oh, sorry. These trucks make wide turns."

WAR GAMES

When the 93rd moved to Louisiana, the division's chief of staff noted several technical problems in their transportation. His report of the movement critiqued the manner in which the equipment was loaded and reloaded onto trains. He launched his sharpest criticism against the commanding officers, citing their failure to teach the men how to properly prepare for troop movement. A closer look at the loading problems and traveling slowdowns reveals other interpretations. Some of the soldiers were ordered to sleep outdoors because the loading took longer than expected. They had insufficient clothing and blankets to sleep on the ground, so they broke into the post exchange (PX) to "requisition" some blankets. Forty of the men were arrested and sentenced to several months of labor detail.

When other men of the 93rd heard about the court-martial, they became resentful and slowed down all of their jobs. Howard Hickerson was on the train going from Fort Huachuca to Merryville, Louisiana. "I had a special assignment typing up a court-martial transcript," Hickerson recalled.

> I got to stay in this real nice officers' section because of my work. Every time they asked me if I was finished typing up the notes I'd say: "Oh, not just yet, sir. I just have a little more to do." Well, I'm no fool. I stretched that thing out all the way to Louisiana.

Despite the loading mistakes and slowdowns, the men detrained without error at Merryville, just across the Sabine River from Texas.

The maneuvers were meant to train the soldiers how to react in jungle warfare, and the training took advantage of the many wet days and swampy conditions. For three months they trained and ran problems in the bayous and backwoods of Beauregard and Natchitoches Parishes, from the little towns around DeRidder and Leesville all the way up to the Shreveport area. Bill Perry had been training in the remote areas of Arkansas and Arizona, yet when he came to Louisiana he said he experienced "culture shock." He recalled: "I went to Lake Charles once, and I thought it was supposed to be a big city. Hell, they still had dirt streets in the downtown area. I realized right then that America is a big place." Edward Price was also shocked when he first got to Louisiana.

> It rained down there a lot, and it was just a big swamp. Everything you did was in the field. You slept, ate, and did everything in the field. There were snakes and wild hogs, and it doesn't make you too comfortable when you're camping out with all that wildlife out there. It was the worst place in the world.

The black units of the 93rd Division were maneuvering against an all-white division, the 85th Infantry, all throughout the hot and humid areas of western Louisiana. This meant that about forty thousand men with weapons were moving through the swamps and woods of Louisiana. Normally, in war game maneuvers, the competing divisions swapped officers to act as umpires. Because the 93rd contained black officers, and the white soldiers in the 85th were prejudiced against having a black man critique or evaluate them, the commanders organized different rules. In an attempt to prevent officers from getting caught in "racial friction," the War Department carefully assigned umpires to the games. The commanding officers decided to use black officers only within black units. They would be allowed to grade and evaluate only their own troops. Still, there were not enough black officers, so white officers from the other division were swapped for some of the white officers in the 93rd.

Units of men marched into an area as either an attacking or a defensive group and then maneuvered against the other division in the area. Planes flew over the area, throwing out sacks of flour and announcing to the soldiers that were hit: "If this was a bomb, you would be dead." Spencer Moore recalled how an ice cream truck came out to his maneuver area so often they had to camouflage the truck because it kept getting hit with flour. It was such an easy target, with all the soldiers swarming around for

In the field on maneuvers. (Photo by Spencer Moore)

ice cream, that the opposing team simply took advantage and "bombed" the truck and the soldiers.

Bill Perry explained the regularities and irregularities of war games.

> Usually on maneuvers you aren't given ammunition. You get red flags and blue flags and umpires. It's like a football game with the umpires deciding what things are going to happen out there. The idea is to give the commander the experience of moving large bodies of troops. Theoretically to give the guys some symbolic experience of being in the field. You do go out to a firing range at times and use ammunition, but it's all controlled. They fire over your head while you're scrambling or something. But nobody is supposed to have ammunition after that part. Well, at night you can hear guns going off. I don't care what is supposed to happen. You get that many men out there, and somebody's going to have some ammunition. You could hear them firing all over the place at night.

The war games were tough and relentless. Nelson Peery described the morning regimen while out on maneuvers. "We crawled out of our pup tents, scratching at the red bugs, stretching out the stiffness of a restless night on the damp, cold Louisiana ground. First stop was lining up at the slit trenches that served as a latrine. Next, line up for a helmet of water. A cupful to brush the teeth and rinse the mouth. The rest to wash from the top down. Next line up before the big kettles where Black Jack ladled out the slop. The smell of GI coffee, dehydrated eggs, and potatoes all mixed in with waking up at 4:30 was enough to make a soldier puke." Ted McCullough also remembered the Louisiana maneuvers as particularly distasteful. "We were there during the rainy season, and the snakes must have enjoyed that weather because they were everywhere. In the river, but also in everything else. They came into my pup tent with me."

ENCOUNTERS WITH THE LOCALS

After a year of rigorous training at Fort Huachuca, the men were feeling restless and discontented. They were suspicious of all the training, and many wondered why they were not being sent into combat overseas. The grueling training activities, combined with the isolation and the men's youth, created a sense of commonality among them. Nelson Peery summed up the feeling: "We were no longer a conglomeration of men; we were soldiers in a military organization. We sensed the growth of our consciousness, unity, and strength, a unified consciousness." The growing consciousness of the men, along with their newly acquired military skills, posed a threat to the local population. Eighteen thousand armed black men running over the rural countryside was a bitter pill for many old-school Louisiana folks to swallow. Many of the black soldiers were involved in hostile encounters, including several armed clashes. Fred Hurns said he wished he could do something about the racism in the little southern towns, but he knew "one soldier could not do anything about a town that's been like that forever." Yet he noted that some of the soldiers were able to resist the prevailing discrimination and even to fight back in their own way. Journalist Roi Ottley wrote about tensions between black soldiers and white civilians in the South. He noted that the newly trained black soldier was well aware of his rights, and because he wore the uniform of the United States Army, his self-respect was high. But Ottley also noted: "To some Southerners such a man is a dangerous 'nigger' who must be made to 'know his place' with violence and terror if necessary."

Many of the soldiers had never been in the South and were thus unfamiliar with the long-standing peculiarities of behavior many whites expected of blacks. Nelson Peery learned how he was supposed to act from his commanding officer, a native of Mississippi. The commander explained:

Now men, we in the South, and we in the army. You all know that. Some things you all don't like. You all know the score. Ah done et your ass out about disobeyin' me before. You do it down heah, and Ah'm gonna get you a court-martial.

Fred Hurns got his lesson in southern mannerisms from his grandmother and mother, both who had lived in the South. "They told me that if I was ever shipped to the South, I better act differently so I would not get into trouble. They said, 'stay on your side of the street, and if a white person is coming down your side of the street, then go on over to the other side.' So I did just like they advised me." Despite the advice from loving family and commanding officers, black soldiers ran into a multitude of problems in Louisiana.

When Howard Hickerson encountered Louisiana-style prejudice, he was without the benefit of sage advice from his commanding officer or any family members. Hickerson had been informed about the off limits sections of town, but his superiors had not clearly spelled out the ramifications of entering an off limits location.

My friends and I went over to this little town in a jeep. I guess it was a weekend or something. We went into one of those small parts of town. We were having fun, this and that, and we thought, this area's so small, let's just go on across over there and get some booze. And just like you see in the pictures, this big, fat sheriff with a little ol' police car and a rifle came up and said, "Hey, what you doing over here?"

"We're just going to get something at the store, sir."

And he said, "Oh, no. You can't get nothing at that store. Go on back to your side of town." Then, he threatened to arrest us! "I'll put you all in jail over here if you don't get on back across the street. And you can tell the rest of those niggers I'll put them in jail if they don't stay in their part of town."

Hickerson said that when a soldier strayed into the areas designated as off limits, the white sheriffs would be right there, ready to arrest him. "In those areas you weren't a soldier, you was a nigger, and they made no bones about telling you that."

At different times, but with nearly the same outcome, Nelson Peery and Lawrence Johnson ran into southern racism in one of the small stores in the backwoods around Many, Louisiana. Johnson described an incident where a shopkeeper demanded that black soldiers go to the back door of the store in order to get waited on. Johnson said the men refused to go to the back. They told the proprietor that if he would not serve them in the front they would just take what they wanted. When he refused to accommodate them, they just helped themselves. In Peery's encounter, he too noted the way the group acted as one cohesive unit when they confronted the Jim Crow system at a little country store. He stressed the orderliness of the ten or twelve soldiers, each waiting his turn to get to the counter. Then, one of the men tore down the sign that said "colored," and the store owner said: "That's the law. If you're not gonna act right, you get outta my store." Spontaneously, the rest of the men reacted by stuffing their pockets with items in the store. Within minutes the shelves were cleared, and the soldiers were leaving with a warning to the shopkeeper: "You damned peck—we're the fucking, fighting 93rd. When we leave the 92nd is coming in. You better get used to it." It is astonishing that one white shopkeeper among a group of armed black customers would believe himself so superior as to be beyond reproach. Did the locals believe the soldiers would just shuffle out without a comment?

Things were bad in the southern countryside, but they were just as bad or worse on southern military bases. The men expected to be served at military establishments because they were wearing the uniform of the U.S. Army, but they learned that southern ways prevailed over military procedures at many camps. At the PX at Camp Claiborne, Louisiana, the white proprietor became so agitated with a group of black soldiers that he singled out one

man and hit him on the head with a hammer. The government report denied
that the soldier was injured, but it noted that after the incident, more than
one hundred black soldiers came in and harassed the owner. Other black soldiers complained of service problems in the PX.

Howard Hickerson remembered:

We were around DeRidder, Louisiana, and there was a small air force
base there. It was a hot, humid July day, and we had to go to the base
to wash our vehicles. We'd rinse them off, then bring them around to
our area, about half a mile away, and put them back in line. We were
a convoy of about thirty or forty trucks and vehicles. We got almost up
to the front of the wash line when it turned 12 o'clock, and zip, everything closed up for lunch. So we went over to this canteen in the PX
for a Coke and hamburger. About five of us—me and a couple of guys
from Mississippi and Alabama—got up to the counter and there was
this Caucasian girl behind the counter waiting on people.

She went past us and waited on the white soldiers beside us. Then
she went over to the other side of us and waited on another bunch of
white soldiers. And she kept passing us by. So the other guys with me,
they recognized what was happening. And they said, "Come on, Hick.
Let's go." And I said, "No, let's get our Coke." They said, "Naw, come
on now. Let's just go."

She passed by again, and I said, "Hey! We want to get a Coke." She
said, "What do you mean?" I repeated, "We want to get a Coke."

She just looked at us and said, "You know your PX ain't open yet.
The PX for you niggers is around the corner, and it don't open till after
12." Well, that was kind of hard to swallow. This was a U.S. military
base, and we could not get served because it was all segregated and
everything.

Well, it just got me so mad, I went back to my truck and jockeyed it
out of the line and drove straight back to the base—dirty truck and all.
And when I got back to camp, the commanding officer wanted to
know why my vehicle wasn't washed. He knew something was up because I was fuming. He took me into his tent and gave me a cold beer
and said, "Okay. Now what happened out there?" I told him about the
Coke and what the waitress said and how mad it made me and all. And
he said, "Hickerson, you're not from the South. This is just the way
things is down here. You just gotta get used to it. Now go on and get
your truck back over there to be washed."

I was still mad, and there was no amount of talking that was going
to get me to go back there. But you don't defy your commanding

officer's orders, especially if he is giving you a beer and being nice. A soldier can get court-martialed for less than defying direct orders. After the beer took hold, I thought to myself, "Well, I don't want to go to jail over this." So I calmed down and got some buckets of water and hand-washed my truck.

"RACIAL FRICTION"

Between 1942 and 1943, black combat divisions maneuvered throughout the western part of Louisiana, and black soldiers were stationed at military camps throughout the state. Reports of "racial friction" flowed into the War Department from Camps Claiborne, Livingston, and Plauche, which were located near Alexandria, Louisiana. The situation was so bad at Camp Claiborne that Eleanor Roosevelt wrote to Army Chief of Staff General George C. Marshall asking for an explanation of what was going on there. She sent along an excerpt from a letter she had received from a white officer at the camp, who wrote about the racial friction on the post. General Marshall responded in writing to her letter.

> It is unfortunate that the young officer arrived at the Camp when conditions were such that a discouraging impression was obtained by him. A thorough investigation has been made at Camp Claiborne. It was found that some of the personnel were influenced by a Negro soldier who is an ex-criminal and was able to excite a group to acts of violence. He and his immediate followers have been tried by court-martials and sentenced. As a result of our investigation some officers have been found not suited to command colored troops and have been transferred from that station and a new camp commander has been assigned.

Mrs. Roosevelt must have been satisfied with Marshall's reply because she did not ask for further clarification.

The investigators at Camp Claiborne had relied on a familiar strategy: round up the usual suspects, blame outside agitators, and then convict and transfer a few people. The camp's white officers were not rebuked or tried, they were just reassigned to new camps without black personnel. Even more interesting, the investigators' report goes into greater detail than General Marshall's soft-pedaling of the incident. The investigators inspected several bases in the South where black troops were stationed and found that morale and discipline among the thirteen thousand black soldiers at Camp Claiborne were the "worst of any camp visited. Racial relations have been bad for a long period."

> Which condition culminated in a riot 8 August 1944. The immediate
> cause of the riot was a rumor that a Negro soldier had been hanged
> by civilians. Negro soldiers were attempting to get guns and ammu
> nition to take matters in their own hands. The principal cause for
> this situation was lack of strong command; failure to build up and
> maintain discipline. Contributory causes included the assembly of a
> large mass of Negro soldiers in this camp and at others in this vicin
> ity; the lack of facilities in the nearby city of Alexandria for the large
> number of Negro troops, the fear of civilians of the area due to
> crimes committed by Negro soldiers and the fear of soldiers by the
> civilian population.

These details were left out of General Marshall's reply to Mrs. Roosevelt.

The unrest at Camp Claiborne was not simply an explosion of anger
loosely attributed to a lynching rumor, with the crowd led to action by "an
ex-criminal." The government report attributed the start of the rioting to the
fact that a black soldier had "confessed to raping two [white] women." That
soldier was in custody; there is no mention in the report of other soldiers inciting groups to riot. The report details many more causes for the unrest
than General Marshall indicated to Mrs. Roosevelt. The two-day uproar was
marked by many antagonistic incidents between black soldiers and the local
population. Groups of angry soldiers amassed at the PX and harassed the
staff. Soldiers "threw bottles and other missiles, damaged the building and
fixtures and stole merchandise. The manager at another Post Exchange said
he was robbed of cash and bus tickets."

In nearby Camp Plauche, black soldiers "scattered merchandise on the
floor, refused to admit anyone not in fatigues, and then proceeded to dance
and perpetrate similar depredations." The next month at Camp Claiborne, a
"white lieutenant shot and killed a Negro private after the private threatened
three officers with an axe." These government reports and investigations,
shocking as they are, still do not fully reveal the extent of the racial friction
at military camps in Louisiana. Clearly, deep antagonisms and armed incidents occurred throughout the area.

Joseph Hairston was in Alexandria, Louisiana, during the riot of August
8th. He tells a complex story, one "you won't find much in the books about."
Yes, he said, there was a government investigation into the cause of the riot.
But, according to Hairston, the official records do not tell the full story

because none of the investigators were on the scene at the time. With the immediacy of a firsthand account, Hairston recalled:

> Lee Street in Alexandria was the center of the black community. It was a long block with no cross streets. It was the equivalent of about two or three regular city blocks. There were juke joints shoulder to shoulder down there. On the weekends it was the only place the black soldiers from Camp Livingston, Camp Polk, and Camp Lee could go. All the troops would come into this area, and they would be like maggots.
>
> One time a soldier got drunk, and the black MPs took him into custody. A couple of white MPs came in and tried to take him from the black MPs. Because they were intruding on the black MPs, the crowd just chased the white MPs out of the area. They came back with reinforcements about a half-hour later, and the black soldiers chased them out again. I got to the end of that long street, and by that time the white civilian police had arrived.
>
> One white policeman pushed me in the chest and said, "Get out of my way, nigger." Then, as I was moving out of the way, they just opened fire, point-blank into the crowd. It was just a barrage of gunfire into the crowd. They were shoulder-to-shoulder, marching abreast of each other and shooting into the crowd. We were all unarmed; in fact, we weren't allowed to go to town with weapons. Nobody knows how many people were hurt or killed. They investigated it, but we never heard about the final report.

Many of the black soldiers were uneasy in Louisiana, whether camping in the woods and swamps on maneuvers or stationed at permanent posts. Black members of the Women's Army Corps (WACs) were unhappy in Louisiana, too. The army noted the number of women who asked for transfers or medical-hardship releases in order to transfer out of the base at Camp Claiborne. The morale of the women was also at a notable low, the report warned. Camp Claiborne was treeless and unattractive, whereas Camp Livingston was more "hospitable with pine trees and a few recreational facilities." However, Joseph Hairston, who was stationed at Camp Livingston, did not find it particularly hospitable.

Shortly after construction to build the camp began, the contractors stopped working on the site because they encountered too many snakes. They brought in a special crew to clean out the snakes, waited a few days, and then built the camp on snake homeland. Life at Livingston may have been better than at Claiborne, but the living was uneasy at both camps. About 2,700 of the soldiers at Livingston were black, and they were perceived as a problem by the camp's white soldiers as well as by the citizens of nearby towns. Hairston recalled his first brush with Louisiana-style discrimination.

> I got off the train on my way to the camp, and there were a couple of locals just standing on the platform. One said to the other, "That looks like a bunch of them goddamn northern niggers. We'll have to show them how we do things around here." That's an exact quote, and that was my first real exposure to the South.

Government records are filled with reports of "racial friction," including one account of black soldiers exploding a gas grenade in a movie theater presumably because of being required to sit in the "crow's nest," the segregated section upstairs. Just as tent life for the maneuvering troops was filled with hardships and racial friction, so too was life on the neighboring bases. Like at Huachuca, getting on and off the bases was a problem for black soldiers, made more difficult because they had to wait for the few Jim Crow cars and buses. The men retaliated in many ways. Black soldiers stopped a bus at Camp Livingston, beat up the driver, and fired their rifles. In the nearby town of Alexandria, three hundred black soldiers caused a ruckus when they were told to wait for the segregated car at the railroad depot. Farther up the road in Shreveport, the public safety commissioner attacked a black soldier because the soldier said, "All white girls in California like Negro men." The commissioner became so incensed that he threatened to shoot the soldier and the black MP who was there to keep the peace.

Louisiana folk did not know how to react to a black man in uniform, as many reports of the day testify. The men were abused and antagonized by the local population. White women accused black soldiers of "accosting" them when the men interacted with them. Any organizing by black men led to accusations of radical militancy. To add to the terror, black churches were burned by undiscovered assailants.

SWEET LAND OF LIBERTY

Ironically, during the 1940s, as the nation unified to fight enemies abroad, relations at home between white and black Americans deteriorated. Attitudes from Washington set the tone of the national dilemma, but prejudice and racial fears were internalized and acted upon by individuals throughout the nation. There is no way to measure the impact on racial attitudes of Attorney General Francis Biddle's statement, repeated in a 1943 *Harper's* magazine article, that "Negroes should be chained to their places of abode as were the serfs in the medieval days." Because he was not dismissed or reprimanded for his remark, many white Americans could feel comfortable with their own racial prejudices. Conflicts over jobs, housing, and military service, as well as individual acts of discrimination, pitted many blacks and whites against one another. The situation on military reservations mirrored what was going on in civilian communities across the nation: race relations worsened.

Active militancy emerged among the black population during the war years. Walter White, executive secretary of the National Association for the Advancement of Colored People (NAACP), warned that the black population was unwilling to accept conditions of earlier periods. "Only now [1942] is official Washington beginning to realize that it has a quite different Negro to deal with than it had in 1917. There were protests then against discrimination and segregation, but they lacked effectiveness because Negroes were not well organized, nor were Americans of both races as aware or as vocal about the ideals for which we are purportedly fighting." Some writers and speakers called the period "a harvest of disorder"; others labeled it "the bloody summer of 1943," but the unrest among blacks began before that summer and stretched out beyond the end of the war. Roi Ottley, a prominent wartime journalist, reported an increase in black militancy and warned: "Black men have become noisy, aggressive, and sometimes defiant. There is considerable doubt in the minds of the Negro civilian and military populations, which seriously hampers the war effort, particularly among those who are unable to *lift their eyes to the hills*." Segregation and discrimination in civilian and military communities stressed black and white relations to their breaking point. Racial violence around military camps and reservations alarmed government officials and kept both black and white populations in a constant state of tension.

But not all relations between whites and blacks were hostile. There were many soldiers who said that some of the white officers treated them fairly. Clyde Whitted's commanding officer reflected the paternalistic attitudes of the day, but Whitted remembers him kindly. Whitted was worried about his wife's health. She was about to give birth, but she was having some problems. She was in North Carolina, and he was not. Her last letter expressed worries, and Whitted could not stop thinking about her. He told his company commander that it was hard for him to concentrate on his duties knowing the situation at home. The captain asked Whitted if he were granted leave, would he go AWOL (absent without leave) after that. Whitted responded: "Certainly, not!" Then the captain asked if he had enough money to make it home. When Whitted said he did, the captain told him to gather his things because his leave papers would be ready in fifteen minutes.

Fred Hurns also tells a story of a white commander, at Camp Van Dorn, Mississippi, who looked out for the black enlisted men stationed at the base. He said one time the artillery unit got into a "little trouble," and the civilian police put a few black troops in jail. "The commanding officer went over there and demanded that they turn them loose. And he told them that if they didn't turn them loose that he'd come back with his artillery and blow that little town off the map. Well, they let those men go."

Despite the best intentions of some white officers, racial tensions on U.S. military bases sometimes erupted into violence. Camp Van Dorn was a flash point for racial friction during the war years. When black and white soldiers were fighting on the base one participant observed: "The result was small fights that grew into big fights that mushroomed into a full-scale riot. I had seen white hatred many times, but that night I saw stark black hatred. Some of the blacks who had never had the chance to swing on a white were making up for lost time; they were getting rid of hostility."

Blacks and whites met in combat-style formation, and a white colonel ordered his men to lock and load—in other words, prepare to fire on the black troops. Showing more mettle than their colonel, "the white men refused to fire on the [black soldiers]. To sum it up, white enlisted personnel showed more understanding than all the big brains on that post; it could have been a bloody mess."

Many black soldiers were committed to militantly resisting acts of discrimination. Militancy is very difficult in a military environment, where all behavior is controlled and resistance is not tolerated. Group or individual acts of resistance—any sort of direct insubordination—can get a soldier court-martialed, thrown out of the army, or even jailed. Still, many of the black soldiers were unwilling to accommodate racist attitudes or being called "boy" or "nigger." A story told by Nelson Peery in his autobiography *Black Fire: The Making of an American Revolutionary*, particularly illustrates this point.

A white major insulted the men of the 369th Infantry unit during a routine rifle training class. As the officer was going over the use of a semiautomatic weapon, he referred to one of the soldiers as "boy." The men in the company were incensed and indignant; they decided to strike by refusing to answer formation calls until the major offered an apology. Word spread of the strike, and none of the enlisted men followed any direct orders to mess, formation, or any other duties. The major sent a lower-ranking officer, Lieutenant Quarterman, to warn the striking men that what they were doing was mutiny, punishable by death in wartime. Despite this threat, the men still held out for the major's apology. After a few more refusals to formation, Quarterman offered the men an apology on behalf of the major. Peery wrote: "We knew we had won a terrific victory as incomplete as it was. A bunch of goddamned recruits defied the Jim Crow army and won."

Military archives contain many similar stories of resistance. The men also remember specific incidents that never made it into the military records. Although this next story is in the archives, only the action, not its cause, was recorded. Allen Thompson remembers:

> We were in tank training at Fort Knox when all of the sudden they told us they were going to put us into a trucking company. So we refused to eat. We did not go to the mess hall. We did it as a whole unit. There were a couple of lawyers in the group, and they got us organized. We just did not eat. And we said that we wanted to be trained as tankers and used as tankers, that was our demand. We did not want to be truck drivers or port battalion or loaders. We wanted to be tankers. Finally, they saw it our way. We even got black cooks because we complained that the white guys didn't know how to cook for us.

Soldiers are trained to be disciplined individuals who follow orders given by their officers. What is significant about the number of armed incidents, or otherwise full-scale hand-to-hand riots, is the individual manner in which each soldier decided to strike back. The army normally discharges a soldier for acts of defiance or disobedience. Many of the black soldiers protesting segregation, whether through civil disobedience, work stoppages, or armed rebellion, were court-martialed during World War II. But significantly, many incidents were simply put down or resolved without anyone coming to trial. Black soldiers, with voices too loud to ignore, but in numbers too large to prosecute, were willing to confront Jim Crow.

Military officials noted the increase in "racial incidents." In confidential summary reports circulated among the commanders, numerous armed conflicts on military bases were reported. In California, several racialized incidents around military camps alarmed the public and produced a reaction within the political arena. In Vallejo, black and white navy men clashed several times over issues of inadequate recreational facilities and other discriminatory practices. At Camp Stoneman in Pittsburg, California, approximately two hundred black soldiers engaged in civil disobedience until military police with machine guns herded them back to camp. At Camp Beale, nine hundred black soldiers threw rocks and beer bottles in a "racial incident." At Port Hueneme, approximately one thousand black soldiers in an engineer company went on a hunger strike to protest the rotation and promotion of white men over blacks. And in the little town of Auburn, a fight broke out in a cafe when a white soldier threw a cup of coffee in a black soldier's face and said, "You black sons of bitches should not be in here."

Perhaps the most significant soldier strike occurred at Port Chicago, approximately 30 miles northeast of San Francisco, California, a military base where bombs and other munitions were loaded on U.S. Navy ships. In July 1944, a mysterious explosion killed more than three hundred men, two-thirds of them black. While the cause of the explosion has never been determined, one survivor commented:

> Everyone began to get careless. There was a race to get the ammunition loaded quickly. A "split bomb" had been loaded and unloaded three or four times. My theory is that it was left on board and then it rolled around and blew up.

Another survivor commented that nobody knew what they were doing; the soldiers had received no formal training in the handling of explosives. The men worked up to sixteen hours a day unloading 1,000-pound bombs from railcars and then loading them into ship hulls. Many of the officers in charge made bets with each other about the amount of explosives that could be loaded in a day, and they prodded their men to meet the quota. After the explosion, 258 men refused to load another ship because of safety concerns. Fifty men were tried, convicted of mutiny, and discharged from the service. Their sentence has never been commuted, although many advocates are working to have the work stoppage understood as an act of protest rather than a mutiny.

Even before the start of World War II "disturbing reports were tumbling out of the army camps" wrote Roi Ottley. Those reports cited "race riots," stabbings, and black soldiers going AWOL. Of course, not all of these incidents were acts of racial defiance. Army life is tough, as many soldiers—black and white—discovered. Some men went AWOL because they did not want to serve anymore. Some black men were fed up with the racism, but others just got caught off base on unapproved leaves of absence.

Felix Goodwin came across quite a few "deserters" in New York and New Jersey, where he ran a military police unit.

> If the deserters were apprehended by civilian police, the army paid a $50 reward, but if we picked them up, they wouldn't give us [the military police] a dime. So we worked out this deal where we let the civilian police know who had deserted and where they might be located. On weekends the civilian police and some off-duty MPs would go out

picking up deserters; it was almost like rabbit hunting. Sometimes they could pick up as many as twenty deserters in one weekend.

On Monday morning the civilian police would come by and get their vouchers and then divide up the money among all the participants. He kept $25 and split the rest up into little envelopes he would put on the desks of the MPs. It was a very lucrative thing, because at times there was as much as $1,000 for a weekend's work. Finally, Mayor LaGuardia [of New York] got word of his cops getting money from the military, and he was mad that the money wasn't going into the city coffers or something. Well, that stopped that little racket right then and there.

It is unclear how many soldiers went AWOL over racial discrimination, but the records indicate that many soldiers reacted to individual acts of discrimination as well as to institutional racism. When asked if the army discriminated against him, Donald McNeil commented that the "separation of races upon entering the service and returning to the states" was the worst part of his military experience. Deton Brooks told a reporter that his unit was isolated in one section of the camps, "as if by contact we'd give our white brothers the 'black plague.'" Again, not all white soldiers actively discriminated against black soldiers. But the rules of the system—military policy—promoted a separation of and distance between black and white soldiers. Soldiers are naturally divided by rank, but they were also unnaturally divided by color.

One white officer in charge of a black battalion wrote in his diary: "It is a dirty shame the way the white American soldiers treat our boys [black soldiers]. The only solution would be to send our battalion away from any town." Allen Thompson had another way of dealing with white racists. He told a story about a time when he was out on maneuvers in Tennessee.

One of our fellas made a mistake and hit a telephone pole with his tank. Well, it just brought out the whole town. It was about 2 in the morning. One old guy was just looking at us and then at the tanks, going back and forth. Finally, he says: "My God, I didn't know they had niggers in tanks." He was just so taken back. We thought it was funny. We laughed right at him. He was so ignorant, and we just laughed at ignorance.

Racism was not just a southern phenomenon. It existed in every corner of the United States. When Spencer Moore was on maneuvers in Massachusetts and New Hampshire, he said that some children had never before seen a black man, much less a black soldier. "They'd wet their fingers and touch your skin and then look at their fingers. Like it was going to rub off or some-

STATESIDE

105

thing. We thought it was amusing." Lester Duane Simons commented about serving in New Jersey: "Fort Dix might have been above the Mason–Dixon Line, but it was strictly an accident of geography. We not only had cracker civilians to contend with, but cracker soldier boys who were stationed there. Dix had several race riots—I'm referring to the big incidents, not to the almost daily name-calling and fisticuffs between black and white soldiers." Roi Ottley confirmed the racialized strife at Fort Dix. He reported on an escalation of tensions at the base that resulted in a gun battle between black and white soldiers. Three men were killed, and five were wounded.

> A Negro lunged for the MP's pistol, but only ripped the holster and then ran into the tavern. The MP commanded him to halt, and fired a warning shot. This was the signal for a fusillade of rifle shots from the Negro barracks. White and Negro soldiers began pouring out of the barracks and the tavern. A battle began from opposite sides of the highway.

When Felix Goodwin was first shipped to the North, he encountered white soldiers who did not welcome his arrival. He remembers that when he arrived at Indiantown Gap, Pennsylvania, the rest of the unit was white and mostly Jewish. He was a senior master sergeant, which would have put him in command of some of the lower-ranking whites.

> For some reason, my record did not have the 'C' beside my name, identifying me as "colored." When I reported in to the major, and he took a look at me, he was shocked. He kept asking me, "Are you sure you're Felix Goodwin?" None of them could accept a black sergeant major.
>
> One day I said to the colonel, "Sir, since everyone around here is Jewish why can't you accept me?" Well, that was the wrong thing to say, and they were all over me. They sent me back up to the barracks, and I laid around without anything to do for about a month. I mean absolutely nothing. They wanted me to mess up so they could bust me.

White soldiers' resentment toward their black comrades-in-arms sometimes turned violent. After watching the movie *Wuthering Heights* at the black theater on base in Camp Shenago, Pennsylvania, several black soldiers were surrounded by six truckloads of white soldiers with guns. Dempsey Travis explained:

> [They] cut the street off. The lights went out, and they started firing. Firing, firing, firing, just shooting into the goddamn crowd. Everybody

started scrambling like hell. . . . I put my hand on my leg, and I could feel something warm running down my pants. [This Red Cross worker] threw a flashlight on my friend and said, "He'll make it. Niggers don't die when you shoot them in the head. . . ."

In the ambulance, one of the drivers said, "Where I come from we shoot niggers like we shoot rabbits." This stayed with me. This sound of two men talking about two disabled black soldiers. Shot not by the enemy but by Americans.

According to the army's confidential reports, routine inspections sometimes located secretly buried ammunition. Many black soldiers at military camps all across America began to secure and hide ammunition in preparation for racial warfare. At times black soldiers purposefully attacked the system of segregation, starting first with reasoned actions and at times resorting to armed violence. For example, at Camp Patrick Henry in Virginia, black soldiers entered a service club filled with white paratroopers. After a round of insults and some punches, a full-scale riot ensued. In preparation for the struggle, black soldiers had broken into a weapons storehouse and appropriated Thompson submachine guns and miscellaneous rifles. The government report noted that all of the paratroopers were unarmed, and one was killed. It does not explain how one black soldier got shot in the leg. There is also nothing in the report that explains why the black soldiers felt the need to procure weapons and certainly nothing that describes the whites as anything other than victims.

But Allen Thompson was there, and he remembers the events differently.

When we got to Camp Patrick Henry, I saw it brewing. I could smell trouble, and I could see it too. When we went in for our indoctrination, the paratroopers on that base were antagonistic. They would gesture. They had shroud knives, the kind you use to cut your shroud when you drop in a parachute. They patted them, and they made gestures with those knives. We were told when we got there we could go anyplace on the post, because we are in the United States Army and all that. It was the post commander talking. "You are not confined to any area. You can go anywhere you want to." Well, that wasn't the case.

Some of our men had gone to the PX and were escorted out or run away from the area. The PX in our area was mixed, white and black soldiers. But the problem began because some white girls were overly friendly with the black soldiers, and the white paratroopers didn't like it. I was in the PX that night with a couple of sergeants, and I said, "Let's get out of here. I see some problems." So we got out.

The next night I was in charge of quarters, and, oh, about fifty of those paratroopers came down the road in front of our barracks. They were making a lot of racket. I said, "What do you fellas want?"

"Well, your boys are trying to emulate paratroopers," they said. "They have their pants stuck down in their combat boots like us, and we feel that you all are trying to emulate paratroopers."

I said, "Well, these men are authorized for combat boots." And I told them to get back to their unit because they had no business over here. They left, but the next night about two hundred of them came back.

That night they said, "We're gonna kill some niggers tonight." Well, some shooting started. I don't know what side started it. But I do know that my company commander was supposed to have been knocked down, and the key to the armory was taken. And guns were taken out. And we had a small gunfight. It lasted about a hot minute. Because when the shots rang out and people fell, those guys cleared out in about two seconds. One of my men in the company got shot in the foot. One of theirs got killed. So they more or less quarantined the company, and there was a large investigation.

They took us in one by one and questioned us. They didn't have any evidence. None of the guns had fingerprints; nobody remembered nothing. But they busted the staff sergeant in my company, said that he had taken the key from the company commander. They couldn't figure out how my gun had been fired, and I said, "I don't know either."

We heard that paratrooper unit had jumped on every black unit that had come through. They found some excuse to jump on the black units, and they had never been stopped. One officer said, "Your outfit was the first to stop them." Yeah, my bunch of boys in the 758th Tank Battalion were crazy, I tell you. We had fellas from Chicago, New York, Detroit, Cleveland, Philadelphia, all, mostly, city boys, big city boys.

Bill Perry was also at Camp Patrick Henry in Virginia before his unit was shipped overseas. The situation had not improved. White soldiers did not like black soldiers at the camp, and they showed it. They particularly disliked black men in close proximity to white women. Perry described another armed battle.

They had a system in the theater where the white women ticket-takers made you put your money on the counter, and they would rake it in. They didn't want you to touch them by putting the money in their hands. One of them made a mistake with the change, and of course, an argument ensued.

So then somebody called the MPs, and they flooded the place. There was a black captain there trying to settle the thing, but that wasn't working. So the MPs announced: "We're closing this PX down now," and somebody in the rear said: "Well, then close the mother-fucker." All of a sudden it looked like on cue, everybody just left there. It looked like somebody had just vacuumed everybody out of the PX.

Everybody left there, and they went across the street. And when the MPs came out, there were BARs [Browning automatic rifles] and machine guns and people laying up on the road with rifles and everything. The MPs called the regimental commander, and he came down there and got the issue quieted down. I tell you, the MPs never came back in our area again. For the next two weeks, we had one of our own guys detailed to act as the military police, and we were not bothered again.

These examples of militant fighting back are certainly not descriptive of all black units, but many black soldiers individually reacted to acts of discrimination in a physical, retaliatory manner. As expected, discrimination against black soldiers was more prevalent in the South than in other areas of the nation. Allen Thompson described an incident in Tennessee.

I had to use a little force to get some men fed on the train when we were loading up in Tennessee. I went to get some hamburgers at this store, and I went through the front door with my machine gun strapped on my shoulder. I got about a dozen burgers and brought them back to the train, and the men finished those off so I went back for more. This time when I ordered the burgers the guy says, "You got to go around the back."

I said, "I was just in here and you gave them to me then. Why do I have to go around to the back door?" He was just mumbling and pointing to the back, so finally I said, "I'll tell you what. If you don't give me these GD hamburgers right now, I'm going to shoot this place up." And I took the gun off my shoulder. You know, I got those hamburgers and right quick, too.

At Drew Field, Florida, approximately 350 black soldiers rioted when they were not served fast enough by two white food attendants. They threw bottles, broke windows, and disrupted the base's service club. At Fort Jackson, South Carolina, black soldiers swimming in their own segregated pond were attacked by white soldiers, and fights immediately broke out. One soldier said:

Truckloads of colored soldiers shortly arrived. The fracas was broken up by the commanding officer, but a regiment of white Georgia National

Guardsmen marched to the place and took up battle formation. They had two machine guns and opened fire. Negro soldiers returned the fire. Fortunately, no one was seriously hurt.

Sometimes the rioting was more than blacks resisting whites. In Tennessee, when black soldiers were prevented from traveling by rail with a white soldier, all of the men—white and black—rioted. The official report said the men were "rowdy, used profanity and molested white women." They were charged with disorderly conduct and carrying concealed weapons.

Black soldiers did not always defy orders or respond in an aggressive manner. Sometimes they used military rules to press their point. At Freeman Field in Seymour, Indiana, sixty-one black officers organized a protest against the inadequate facilities at their officers club, which they called "Uncle Tom's Cabin." Small groups of black officers entered the field's all-white officers club and requested service in a nonabrasive, nonviolent manner. Like the training the officers had received, the mission was well planned, and each individual was well briefed. The men carried out their protest in an orderly manner. As punishment, sixty of the black officers were restricted to their quarters and the mess hall while a mutiny trial was convened. Each officer received a reprimand in his permanent file; one officer was court-martialed and convicted.

The War Department had made it clear that it would not interfere in local practices of segregation, whether on military bases or in local communities; nor would it interfere when national railroad companies or bus companies segregated soldiers. During the war, many government agencies received complaints about problems with the transport of soldiers. These complaints, in the form of letters, came from both sides of the segregation–integration argument. Some letters said soldiers were disregarding local segregation policies, whereas others said segregation was unfair to black soldiers. One citizen in Clearwater, Florida, wrote to the War Department after observing a black soldier on a Pullman sleeping car who did not observe the "customary proprieties" by closing the curtains of his berth. A War Department official sent his regrets and assured the writer that, had the incident been reported to the military police on the train, the necessary corrective measures would have been taken.

Military police were under War Department orders to keep the peace, and this often meant enforcing local segregation policies. If no one complained, the MPs stood to the side as peacekeepers. When whites complained of improprieties, MPs generally acquiesced and took corrective action in order to prevent an incident. When blacks complained about unfair treatment, the MPs were slower to respond, if they responded at all. For example, new black recruits in transit from California to Arizona complained to the MPs that white recruits were being fed first. All of the black soldiers were segregated into one car of a twelve-car transport train. They noticed that occupants of nearly every other car had been fed before them. Several black soldiers complained to the MPs. They were told to sit and wait. After the MPs refused to correct the situation, one of the men, who had been a Pullman porter before his induction took action, pulled the emergency cord and stopped the train. One passenger reported:

> We were out in the middle of nowhere, and when he pulled the cord that train just went chick-a, chick, ker-plunk. And it stopped. The brakes locked up, and the MPs came on the double to our car. They could tell which car had pulled the emergency brake. They put a guard on each of us—an MP with a rifle and gut-buster. They said whoever did this was going to be found and court-martialed. Of course nobody knew who did it. But I'll tell you one thing, they fed us. Oh, yes. They fed us, and then they continued in that rotation system of feeding the others. The next morning we were fed in order— not first, but not last.

When government and other military officials enforced racial segregation policies, they did so with impunity. Segregation was practiced in society, and the military lived by the values of society. Within the War Department military planners worried about the high level of discontent within black communities, but no agency considered abandoning segregation as a method of ameliorating the situation. Yet the War Department was getting pressure from every corner, from organized groups and from individual critics. Black complainants were asked to be patient and nonmilitant about integration, whereas whites who were resistant to change were appeased with a soft-pedal approach.

One black draftee wrote to Elmer Davis of the Office of Facts and Figures (OFF), complaining about discrimination and prejudice in the army. Enclosed in his letter was a warning that he would take action against acts of discrimination. The response from Davis informed him that nothing would be gained by threats of violence. Davis admonished him: "You will contribute a great deal to the future of America and your own people if you can temper your chagrin with the realization that the causes of today's troubles are too deeply inbred in too many of our people to be dealt with summarily." But when Davis received a letter from an attorney and self-identified Ku Klux Klan member, Horace C. Wilkinson, describing integration as a "menace to national security and our local way of life," the writer was not asked to temper his chagrin. Wilkinson railed: "A Herculean effort is being made to break down and destroy segregation and with it many of the most cherished institutions in the South." Though Davis was quick to respond to black critics, he constructed no correspondence to Wilkinson when he complained. A flurry of commentaries and memos flew between numerous government offices, but no direct action was taken because Davis said that "OFF was a policy organization and cogitated in the hopes of persuading someone else to accept the results of its cogitations." The government asked black critics to be moderate and patient, but no such demands were put on whites.

The unrest around military bases was mirrored in the civilian community. During the war years, hostilities erupted between whites and blacks in several civilian communities around the nation. In Detroit, for example, race relations deteriorated to the point where active conflicts and riots intermittently broke out. Housing issues incited rebellious actions in several cities. War industries attracted new migrants to communities ill-prepared to house them. One government report noted: "A sporting goods store [in Chicago] which normally sells hunting season ammunition to two or three Negroes reported that this year shot gun, high powered rifle, and .22-caliber ammunition was purchased by approximately 200 Negroes. There is no report of a corresponding increase in Negro duck hunters." Also in Chicago, some white Italians formed gangs to protect themselves from the threat of newly arrived black war workers. In Texas, irate whites shot and killed a black rice worker, supposedly because he had been drinking on the wrong side of town. The Houston *Informer* reported:

> Wilpitz [the black rice hand] broke loose and holed up in a toilet. The cops got 25 to 30 residents with high-powered rifles and shot up the outhouse. One woman saw his body and said that his stomach had been torn away by bullets. It was tied up with rags to prevent the stomach from wasting on the ground.

Walter White noted the similarity between crumbling race relations in the armed forces and the deterioration of race relations among civilians. In his opinion, the breakdown in black–white relations occurred partially because the government was infusing the black soldier with the notion that his fight against fascism would bring him freedom in the future.

Civilians and soldiers engaged in violent reprisals all across the country. Throughout the soldier grapevine, among the black population, and within numerous government agencies, an increased level of militancy was noted among black soldiers. The militancy was fueled by the discrimination they faced within the segregated facilities on the military compounds and by the racism they encountered on a daily basis. One soldier wrote to a government agency:

> A crisis is nearing in racial affairs here in America because the younger Negro knows no slavery liké his forefathers and he refuses to accept any. The type of Negro that these white race baiters have to cope with in the future are fellows like me, 20 years of age. We won't be the passive type, we may even start the riots, but not when we are soldiers. It will be after the war when we return to civilian life that we'll try methods other than waiting or trust in a political party's ideals.

Nelson Peery believed that the war would give black citizens a chance to be free. He said the War Department needed soldiers—even black soldiers. He advised his militant comrades to become indispensable and then "force race changes after the war."

CONTROL OF INFORMATION: PROPAGANDA AND CENSORSHIP

The Office of War Information (OWI), Office of Censorship (OC), and the Office of Facts and Figures (OFF), along with the Justice Department and War Department, were involved in controlling information they deemed detrimental to the war effort. The Code of Wartime Practices required that all newspapers refrain from printing any information regarding the general character or movement of military troops for fear the enemy would use troop locations and activities to their advantage. Destinations, troop strength, the racial makeup of a military unit, and troop locations were all restricted information. Both the black and white press were asked to comply voluntarily with the government's censorship code.

The code presented a difficult hurdle for journalists of the black press to overcome as they were constantly censored for writing stories about the government's use or nonuse of black soldiers in the war effort. The code did not explicitly restrain publication of information regarding "race relations," but the government was hesitant to allow newspapers to print any stories of race friction that might feed into the propaganda machine of the enemy. News about race relations was not explicitly part of the censorship code, but government agencies invoked the code in numerous instances throughout the war, and thus many articles about black troops were kept out of the newspapers. When Walter White of the NAACP heard that news about the relationship between white and black soldiers was being censored, he demanded an explanation from the OC. The director, Byron Price, told White that no policy to suppress news was in effect, but "overzealous employees" might be censoring articles in error. When pressured, government officials allowed the press to print articles reporting on the state of race relations.

Still, very little information about racial unrest in and around U.S. military bases appeared in either civilian or military newspapers, because military planners and government officials felt there was good reason to suppress and control such information. According to the government's confidential reports, in the summer of 1943 the number of "race riots" throughout the United States increased. Numerous spontaneous rebellions erupted. Blacks on military bases and in civilian communities, as well as in the workplace, more frequently responded to prejudice by fighting back. Not every dispute between whites and blacks qualified as a race riot, but as one soldier commented, "when a common brawl was reported between two men, one white, the other colored, a race riot or race friction was reported." Government agencies were concerned that a national press report of an increase in race riots would in turn incite rebellion on military bases. The uneasy relations between white and black soldiers on military reservations would erupt in a fireball of rioting that would engulf everyone. Thus, government agencies frantically gathered information, controlled stories, and asked numerous groups to censor material that might provide a motive for future riots.

Certainly the easiest group for the government to control was the black soldier community. Its members were held on reservations away from the public and funneled information that was government-approved. *Life* magazine was asked by the OWI to suppress an article and photos about racial unrest during the summer of 1943. When *Life* editors asked what censorship code the government was invoking, OWI censors backed off. "It will look as if we are drawing color lines, that we are intolerant, brutal and unfriendly and that there are permanent barriers." The OWI rescinded its request for suppression, and *Life* magazine subsequently published its article about race riots in the inner cities of America. However, the OWI openly controlled many other channels of information provided to black soldiers.

Censorship extended to soldiers writing both official and unofficial correspondence. Howard Hickerson, Signal Corps member of the 93rd Division, received a course in censorship training in order to help the government control information while the men were overseas. He said:

> All the letters were censored. That was part of my job in communications. If there was something in the letter like "we're at such and such location and we are moving out tomorrow," then we'd have to cut it

out, you know, censor it. Then we would put the letter back together, put a stamp on it "Censored," and move on to the next one.

But not all information could be controlled. An unofficial "soldier grapevine" reported stories of riots and national unrest on military bases and in civilian communities. When an especially violent riot broke out in Harlem in the summer of 1943 over the shooting of a black soldier, the OC stopped distribution of the story to the soldiers. However, because black soldiers acting as military police were on the scene, the story could not be totally suppressed. News of the event was not deleted in letters that passed between soldiers and their families; thus the riot news was discussed among black soldiers. Many black veterans said the unofficial grapevine—a news outlet no government could control—was the chief instrument of their consciousness-building during World War II.

In an attempt to understand why such a high level of unrest existed within the black population, several government agencies tracked stories in the black press. Numerous government officials commented that the black press was in the business of inciting discontent and crisis rather than merely reporting on the condition of race relations. In the OWI, several employees were assigned the mission of detecting and reporting seditious articles in the black press. Each week, the Analysis Branch of the OWI clipped and reviewed articles from all of the black papers. Analysts designated each article as "favorable," "unfavorable," or "neutral." The analyst then tallied the number of articles in each category and provided a summary report that was circulated throughout the War Department. Government analysts warned that the black press was "flagrantly abusing its privilege" and was in fact creating unrest with its "extremist tenor." Milton Starr of the OWI summarized the sentiment within many government agencies when he commented that the black population was a "large, apathetic and seditious minded group." Critics inside the government argued that much of the material in the black press violated the tenets of honest journalism. It is not surprising therefore that government policy sought to control information in the black press either by feeding propaganda through news services or by instituting special wartime censorship powers.

Government analysts tracked and studied black soldiers with a fervor never before exhibited during war or peacetime. Staff from the War Department, OWI, OFF, and OC compiled statistics and graphed data on black soldiers with regularity and vigor. Each month, staffers compared the number of promotions of white officers with the number for black officers. They also reviewed many of the nation's newspapers and prepared summaries of the racial incidents that had gotten into print. War Department analysts prepared reports with summary categories that included "racial incidents," "provocation by whites," "sex," "communist attitudes," "weapons," and "army criticism." If trouble erupted when white men "dated" black women, the incident was added to the "racial incident" category. Black men engaged in any sort of a relationship with a white woman were tallied in the "sex" category. Complaints about segregation in the army were added into the "army criticism" category. The number of racialized incidents tallied in each report was staggering.

The OWI was the largest controller of information, though many agencies dabbled in propaganda and suppression of materials. It did not want its employees to confuse their job duties with a campaign to improve conditions for black Americans. The stated OWI policy was to get black Americans to support and take part in the war effort, not to solve "the Negro problem." Employees of the OWI were asked by the director, George Barnes, to "use methods that will bring the quickest, most positive results . . . [which means] filling the Negro with information about his stake in the war, in effect, a direct and powerful Negro propaganda effort as distinct from a crusade for Negro rights." In an effort to increase morale and garner support for the war effort, government officials spoke at public meetings and encouraged articles in the press about the need to fight for democracy and against fascism. Citizens were bombarded with information that called on them to work their hardest; overcome their prejudice; band together as a nation; and, of course, buy war bonds. All of these activities would ensure that democracy would thrive.

Some citizens recognized the jingoistic speeches as unhealthy propaganda and wrote to government officials criticizing the campaign. Caroline Blake complained about a speech delivered at an Urban League function she attended. She wrote:

Your speech as representative of the government was most discouraging. It was tragically unrealistic. Patriotism and loyalty cannot be built up and held by the mere saying that it exists. The colored people are not wholeheartedly supporting the war effort and they are unconvinced that they have a stake in the cause of democracies. You in our government must not disregard that restive one-tenth of our population.

Constantly bombarded with wartime propaganda, blacks were being told World War II was a fight for freedom and against tyranny and oppression.

We have to fight! To fight on the sea, on foreign shores, and at home! The challenge in all its cold-bloodedness has been thrown in our face.

> We must put away party strife, petty bickerings, close up ranks, and all face one way. This fight must be won! We are fighting for our lives, as free men and as a nation.

Also, the black soldier heard from black leaders that an Axis victory "would mean actual slavery for men and women of all races all over the world." So how could they be expected to sit still for tyranny and oppression at home?

There was considerable disagreement among black Americans as to whether or not the war would bring them any gains as individuals. Newspapers provided a forum for the numerous voices of black citizens across the nation. Arguments raged between pro- and anti-integrationists in the seventy or so papers of the black press. Most of the integrationist papers—the Baltimore *Afro-American*, the Pittsburgh *Courier*, and the *Atlanta Daily*, to name a few—were located in metropolitan areas. Also, the radical papers that promoted a nonconciliatory voice of discontent were located in urban centers. Both opinions prevailed in the press during the war years, and many citizens debated the merits of service in a segregationist military. The "restive one-tenth" was not always supportive of the war effort, and this caused the Analysis Branch of the OWI to keep a constant watch on a variety of publications produced by and about black Americans. One of the newspapers, the *San Francisco Reporter*, was monitored because a black columnist, Private Thomas Fleming, wrote articles that attacked the War Department's series of propaganda films "Why We Fight." In one column, Fleming accused the War Department of "trying to force such drivel down the throats of Negroes who are asked to get out and make the supreme sacrifice so that some plant that manufactures sewing machines in New Jersey can continue to operate."

There was also great skepticism among black soldiers that any of the so-called black leaders spoke for them. Nelson Peery criticized the black leadership that emerged within the government and the black press at the beginning of the war. He wrote: "Self-appointed black leaders, and those appointed by the white political structure, appeared as if by magic." He was not alone in his criticism. Rienzi Lemus, a black veteran of the Philippine Wars, commented to the OFF that too much importance was being placed on the words of the so-called race leaders.

> None of the colored leaders who have been in your office speak for a large number of the people. There is nowhere any Negro group norm. One-tenth of the nation's constituency cannot be grouped as a race and governed in the abstract. That is axiomatic.

Lemus called attention to the nation as an aggregation of individuals—all Americans. He distrusted the modern day "pseudo-social science" that made all black people one race and all white people another. For Lemus the problem was the misconception that only one black viewpoint existed, the one expressed by black leaders in government: "There isn't any national Negro viewpoint, any more than there is a universal white point of view."

GOING AWAY TO SCHOOL

Because of the cost of maintaining separate training facilities, the army decided at the beginning of the war to integrate its Officer Candidate School (OCS). It was the army's first experiment with integration, and by all accounts it was a success. This experiment with integrated training was constantly monitored by the army. The ninety-day OCS for black and white infantry officers was located at Fort Benning, Georgia, around the civilian town of Columbus. Where large groups of black soldiers were stationed together, they could form their own island community, removed somewhat from the racist hot spots surrounding them. But when the men were sent to OCS they were in small groups of four or five and generally left to fend for themselves. The training was equally tough for both black and white candidates.

Bill Payne said he experienced the same torture as the white guys who were in OCS. They would run double-time between classes. They would practice their "voice-in-command" in the nearby woods, shouting commands at all hours of the day and night. All of the candidates would undergo hours of continuous harassment from commanding officers bent on "busting them out" of the school. In Payne's class there were approximately two hundred white and six black candidates. One of the six black candidates did not make it to graduation. Almost half of the white candidates met the same fate.

Another officer candidate described his OCS class, which had six hundred white candidates and six blacks.

> We were housed in the typical barracks, but instead of being in the large area with the whites, we were given private dwellings at the end of the building. With the exception of this, we ate at the same mess, attended the same classes, and even used the same latrines. Three hundred of the total class were punched out; three of the blacks included. I'll say the officers there were tough on everybody, so I cannot call them unfair.

Even though the commanding officers meted out equal harassment to white and black officer candidates, the latter had the additional stress of rampant, southern-style discrimination. Payne once read a sign on a fence that said "Nigger read this and run. If you can't read it, run anyway." Away from the military base, soldiers were called "Niggers," "Snow Balls," and "the Black African Army." One black officer candidate, who was refused service at the lunchroom on base, looked on as white soldiers and white prisoners-of-war were served. He wrote an angry letter to the military paper *Yank*, in which he complained about not being treated as a true American soldier. Of the three hundred letters he received in reply, two hundred were from white soldiers from the South, proud of their heritage but "ashamed to learn that so many of our own people are playing Hitler's game."

Payne commented that all stories of discrimination did not end with blacks being victimized. Refused seating at the movie house at Fort Benning, he said it made him proud that several of his white OCS classmates walked out with him in protest. He said: "That made me feel good. I paid my money, and I didn't know you had to sit in the back. I was a soldier, but they even had those kinds of discriminatory practices on base, not just in the surrounding towns."

Each black candidate at OCS had his own experience of the army's experiment with integrated training. Jehu Hunter described his class. "At first when I was at OCS, we had about thirteen black guys—we made up a platoon," he recalled.

> We had our own hut. The other three platoons were all-white and they had their own area. After the fifth-week board exam, there were only three African Americans in the hut, and all the rest of the platoons had big holes in them, too. That's when a lot of the guys wash out. Well, it was kind of interesting when the captain put us all together in the same hut. Initially, things were kind of chilly, but we all had to work together in order to keep from washing out.

Joe Stephenson's experience at OCS was different.

> When I got sent to OCS, I was one of only two black candidates. They moved us into a barracks with five black candidates from the previous class. Those guys gave us some tips and pointers about what to do and what to look for. So there was only seven of us in a barracks that was supposed to house forty men. Over in the barracks where we should have been, it was loud and noisy, with a bunch of rebels in there—you know, rednecks. Those guys told us to eat in the kitchen instead of the

dining hall with them. But the first sergeant didn't go for that at all. As time went on, attitudes changed.

After the other five graduated, it was just the two of us left in the barracks. We were spending a lot of time studying, and we kept getting high 90s on all our exams. The grades were posted, so everyone could see. And those rebels kept wondering what we were doing to get such good scores. Well, our secret was, we were living quietly over there, and we worked.

They formed a little committee and demanded that we be moved into the barracks with them. They thought we had it too good over there; we were too comfortable. So we had to move. Move to where we should have been in the first place. Then we were studying together and tutoring the white guys.

School began for Jim Williams the day he left home for OCS. At a train stop in Richmond, Virginia, Williams unknowingly "broke the rules" that governed the rest stop. He was proudly wearing his new insignia—the OCS patch—as he took his leave of the train and entered the men's room in the train station.

I heard this: "Hey, boy. We've got a place for you over there." And I ignored it. I didn't know who the man was talking to. He said, "I'm talking to you, nigger." Boy, every ounce of blood just drained out of my body. He started to turn like he was gonna come to me, and I didn't turn. I figured if he's coming over I'm gonna stick his head right in the urinal.

Right then another man's voice said to me: "Sergeant, get over here." When I turned his way I noticed he was a major. He asked me, "What's your name?" and I told him, and he said, "Where's your outfit?" I told him that, too. And he said, "I see you have the OCS patch on." And I said, "Yes, sir, that's where I'm going now."

He said, "Now are you gonna let an incident like this spoil your chances for becoming an officer?" I said, "No, sir." He said, "Well, you get back on your train and go on now. And good luck to you."

As I went out I noticed he had been drying his hands, and he had torn the paper towel to shreds, and the vein in his head was standing out. And that other guy must have noticed how angry the major was, because he walked out quickly. He was mad, but I think that guy knew if he said one more thing that major would have killed him in there. The major told me, "You're gonna face more incidents like this, and you're supposed to know how to handle them." And I never forgot that. I never forgot that.

Bill Payne learned a few lessons before he ever got to OCS.

I left Fort Huachuca by train going to Fort Benning in Georgia. And I arrived first in El Paso, Texas, with about an eight-hour layover. I had never been out in a southern town, alone like that, you know, by myself. I was from Cleveland. And I felt very strange. I stood on one street corner for about six hours. I was afraid to move. I didn't know who to talk to or what to say to anyone.

Then I caught the train to New Orleans, and I wanted to see the town. It was about 3 o'clock in the morning, and I figured no one would be about. I started strolling around the town to see what I could. Then I was accosted by the police who told me, "You better get your butt back to the train station." Fortunately, I was in uniform so the MPs quickly took over the situation.

Harold Montgomery's story of traveling to OCS is a little unusual. He wanted to travel with his wife, so she got dressed up in uniform—Buffalo shoulder patch and all—and impersonated a young soldier. Montgomery told his wife to keep her head down and let him do all the talking. When the MPs looked her over at one military stop, Montgomery explained, "That's my kid brother, and we just happened to get in the same unit. He's young."

Many of the new officer candidates traveled by themselves and experienced racialized interactions with the locals. Dennett Harrod's experience is typical.

I was in Atlanta trying to catch the train to Columbus, Georgia. I asked the ticket clerk where I could catch the train, and he wouldn't even talk to me. He just looked at me and went back into his office. When the porter came over to me, I asked him, "What's wrong with him? Is his tongue tied?" And I said it loud enough for him to hear it in that back office. I had my pistol on me, and I was certain we were going to start the Civil War all over again right there. The porter was quick to tell me where to catch the train after that.

Much of the training at OCS was intended to "bust" the candidate out of the course—this was especially true for black soldiers, who had to overcome expectations that they would not do well. To even be considered for OCS, a soldier needed the recommendation of his commanding officer. To qualify he had to receive a score of at least 110 on a placement exam. A six-member board of officers reviewed the test scores and the recommendations. Even if a black soldier made it past these two hurdles, he still had to wait for an open slot—the War Department's quota system limited the total number of black officers. In the last quarter of 1942, more than four hundred black soldiers submitted applications for OCS, but only two hundred of them were approved. Spencer Moore wanted to go to OCS.

> I was a twenty-year-old buck sergeant, and I was a good soldier. I could shoot, I could salute, and I knew the manual backward and forward. Still I couldn't get a promotion. So I decided to try for OCS.

Moore just squeaked in, as the age requirement (twenty-one) was lowered two months before his birthday. Moore, and all the other soldiers who finished the three-month OCS course, were called "Ninety-Day Wonders." This term separated them from officers who had completed a two- or four-year Reserve Officer Training Candidate (ROTC) program in college.

Even if the men finished the ninety-day program, they were not assured of an officer's commission when they got out. They could only be assigned to command black troops, and those positions were limited. General Benjamin O. Davis Sr. questioned the army's policies on black promotion—specifically the policy that restricted the number of positions available for new black candidates. In a 1943 memorandum to the Inspector General, Davis wrote that the "special policy" for the promotion of black officers effectively set them outside of normal military procedures. The policy was demoralizing for the black officer because it created a separate and lesser status for them. There was the white officer and then there was "the other," the black officer. Both were wearing the same uniform and making the same sacrifices. Davis clearly articulated the problems with the policy, but he stopped short of recommending that black officers be integrated into white troops as commanders. He simply asked for a reconsideration of the promotion policy for black officers, because "in all fairness and in the light of the principles upon which our country is founded there should be but one promotion policy applicable to all officers." He wanted the slots white officers held in the all-black divisions to be opened up for the newly trained black officers. Even though the approach Davis was suggesting was merely incremental, the Inspector General did not concur with the premise or the recommendations in Davis's report. Even when the Inspector General looked at the outcome of the existing policy—the disparity between blacks who were available for officer's commissions and those who got them—he would not accept Davis's critique. The Inspector General replied: "I believe it was never the intention of the War Department to render higher grades impossible of attainment by Negro officers."

Going to OCS was sometimes a mixed blessing. Some soldiers wanted the promotion, whereas others were not interested in the problems of management. When Fred Hurns was told he scored high enough to go to OCS, he gave it serious thought but ultimately rejected the idea.

> I had moved up in rank to a staff sergeant, and I didn't have anything but paperwork and stuff like that to do. So I said, "Now why should I be an officer and wind up getting back into the Infantry? This is the best job in the world, being a medical supply sergeant." My biggest job was keeping up with medical supplies."

Felix Goodwin said he felt the same way. He noted that all of the men who were sent to OCS went on to command infantry troops, and he was just not interested in "going to the front." But Joe Stephenson was ready for OCS. When he was in high school, one of his teachers, a World War I veteran, made the students practice marching and military formation. Noting his preparedness, Stephenson's company commander recommended that he go to an OCS preparation course. The commander also promised to promote Stephenson to the rank of corporal when he returned from the course. Unfortunately, when Stephenson got back to his company, everyone had moved on.

> I was ready to take my rightful place, but the company commander was gone and nobody could remember any promises made. The first sergeant was still there, but when I asked him, he said: "I don't re-member a thing." So I did not get a promotion then. Ultimately, I went on to Benning, but I had to repeat the whole thing I had done in the preparatory course.

The entire process of getting recommended and going to OCS was difficult, as Thomas McKinney noted. "In most cases your officers were not interested in you bettering yourself, whether that was educational or with OCS. They felt they could control you better if they just kept you where you were at."

The infantry trained its officers at Fort Benning, Georgia. However, there were other places where officers were trained in the United States. For instance, Jim Williams went to OCS in Camp Barclay, Texas. He was in Medical Administration School, learning the management skills necessary for officers in the medical corps. He said Camp Barclay was where "everybody wore ten-gallon hats and boots with spurs, and everybody called you 'boy.' The sheriff's deputies did not care that you wore the OCS patch on your shirt. If you were black, you didn't belong, so get out." Between classes, everyone ran to the PX to get something to eat or drink. Williams always tried to get to the head of the line, but no matter where he was, the white waitresses still served all the white soldiers before him. When he complained, he was confined to his barracks for a week.

There were about twenty other black men in Williams's class, and, remarkably, they were all integrated into mixed squads.

> There were five people to a squad. In mine, we had a Japanese American, two whites, one Jew, and me. That was an odd squad. When we tried to go out together, we'd get stopped and split up. The sheriff told the Japanese guy, "You get back to camp," and he let the white guys go on ahead. Then he said to me, "You know where you belong. Get on the other side of town." We had to comply even though we didn't like it.

Although as Joe Stephenson noted most of the men at OCS were "conscientious about studying and unconcerned about recreating," the soldiers needed relief from the daily grind of the classroom. But getting into the local town was a problem for the black candidates. Robert Madison described the way a soldier had to get into Columbus, Georgia, outside of Fort Benning. "The only way you can get in there was with a taxi cab. And the taxi cab driver would not take a black soldier and white soldiers together." Madison, like many other black candidates, had to wait for a special bus to transport them to the "black part of town."

Jehu Hunter said that most candidates were on the "squeemy side about going into Columbus, because the white MPs would pick you up on the slightest pretense and put you in jail. And then your OCS career was out the window." The men wore a patch that designated them as officer candidates, but Hunter said that meant nothing to the white MPs. "They would find some transgression to put you in jail in Columbus." As a result of this fear, most of the candidates stayed in the barracks and studied. Charles Wesly said they were "dog-tired after a full day of school" and did not miss out on anything by staying in the barracks.

SHIP THEM TO "WEST HELL"

There was a growing restlessness among the men of the 93rd Infantry Division that was noticed even by the military hierarchy. One report noted:

> Colored troops have been in training over a year and a half. They are bored, overtrained, domesticated, and subject to any bad influence upon their emotions. It is recommended that every effort be made to

move these troops to some other locality, preferably in the direction of their ultimate destination. New surroundings would quiet their restlessness.

Although extra manpower was desperately needed overseas, the 93rd was not immediately sent to help. Military planners instead sent them in June 1943 to the Desert Training Center on the California–Arizona–Nevada border. After three months of training in the humid swamps of Louisiana, the men now faced summer in the Mojave Desert. The training center included vast tracks of uninhabited land dotted here and there with a few lonely towns. The soldiers called the area "West Hell." Ted McCullough recalled his first impression:

> I remember that place. Camp Clipper. When we jumped off the truck we sank down into powdered sand. There was nothing green in there but some of the troops. Everything else was brown from that hot sun.

For the next six months the men lived in a tent encampment rather than on a real post and repeated many of the same exercises they performed in Louisiana.

For the desert war game maneuvers, the 93rd opposed an all-white division commanded by General George S. Patton. The men faced endless days of reconnoitering in the blazing, dry heat of the desert. There was no running water and no electricity. Each soldier was given about one canteen of water per day to sip during the hiking and running exercises through the desert. The war games were rough and included one simulation that almost proved fatal. Bill Payne explained the exercise, which included chasing flags and "capturing" enemy prisoners. On one flag-chasing mission his men were duly captured and placed in a makeshift prison camp. Unfortunately, the strategic planners—all of them white officers—forgot about the "prisoners" and left them without food or water for three days. Payne said the experience was worse than anything he experienced in combat in the South Pacific or later in Vietnam.

Moving the 93rd Division out of the Deep South did not end acts of discrimination against its men. Donald McNeil complained about an incident where black soldiers were ordered to pick up paper plates and other trash at a railroad right-of-way after a train carrying white soldiers went by. Another soldier from the division's 369th Infantry Regiment confirmed the mistreatment. "While the other guys were sacking out," he said, "[the black troops] would be picking up paper or policing the area." He likened the mistreatment to the old system of "white master and black subject." Regimental

bands provided entertainment for the men while they were in the encampment, but the commanding general sent word "not to allow white women to
dance with any of the entertainers" or with any of the black soldiers.

The men, sweltering in the Mojave Desert, were proud soldiers, trying to
keep up morale, but they were constantly reminded of their second-class status. When the nearby civilian communities complained that too many blacks
were coming into the area, military officials cordoned off the areas and declared them off limits. What particularly angered black soldiers about the off
limits designation was that often it applied only to them—white soldiers
were free to frequent the areas. Some of the black soldiers slipped out to the
off limits areas, but the local restaurant owners and storekeepers would not
serve them. The locals knew the black soldiers were not supposed to be out
of the camp, and they threatened to report the men to their commanders.
Black soldiers questioned the policy that allowed whites to move about while
they were restricted. One commander responded: "The order should apply
to whites and blacks, but the military commander's first obligation is to the
members of his command, and at the same time he is under an obvious responsibility to observe the expressed wishes of civilians resident in the area."
This obvious act of discrimination angered many of the soldiers, and there
were the usual grumblings and miscellaneous acts of retaliation.

Black soldiers began to bury or otherwise hide weapons and ammunition
in the desert. Nelson Peery and his fellow soldiers came across an abandoned water-cooled machine gun. They buried it at the base of the Clipper
Mountains, noting its location so they could later retrieve it. The situation
never got out of hand, Peery said, so the men never retrieved the machine
gun. "It may still be out there in the desert."

Dissatisfaction rose to the surface as the men watched white soldiers
training in the desert and then moving immediately overseas into combat.
Because the black troops stayed behind to train—always more and more
training—an attitude of resentment filled their daily exercises. Some of the
commanders were concerned with the "racial unrest" and attempted to find
ways to improve the situation. During a field exercise, a white soldier approached Peery to ask questions about the racial situation.

We were out there maneuvering against this all-white division, so
when I saw a guy come in crawling, perfectly low to the ground, I figured it was one of the guys from that division. He didn't have anything
that showed his rank or unit. He asked how I was being treated and
what I thought about the relationship between the white and black soldiers. He also asked how I felt about my division. We spoke pretty
frankly to one another, and then I introduced myself to him. He shook

hands and said: "Nice to meet you, soldier. I'm General Lehman."
Hell, he was the commanding general of the 93rd!

Lehman and other high-ranking commanders contacted the War Department about the rising discontent among the black troops and asked that
the soldiers be sent into combat. Many commanders concurred with General S. G. Henry's analysis: "If the Negro soldiers were given more opportunity to participate in actual combat, it would result in an improvement of
racial relations."

The War Department was inundated with requests to get the men into
combat. Amidst all the consternation, the 93rd was sent to the San Francisco
Bay Area to await shipment to the Pacific theater of war. The 92nd moved
from the Louisiana maneuvers area, reconnoitered at Fort Huachuca, and
finally departed for Italy. When the 92nd returned to Fort Huachuca, the
men reconnected with their wives and loved ones who had stayed behind.
Everyone knew it was just a short time until the men got shipped overseas,
so the reunion was bittersweet.

Susie Moore recalled her last days at the fort. She explained how only four
of the wives were left at the efficiency apartments in Benson, Arizona, because the rest of the women had been sent home on earlier schedules. The
last day the men had to spend with their wives was an emotion-filled one.
Everyone got up at about 5 o'clock in the morning and gathered together

Fred Hurns and friends relaxing after maneuvers, Fort Huachuca.

outside in the motor court area. Susie said it was just like a scene from the movies, with a spectacular sunrise and the warm light of early morning flooding the desert landscape. Most of the wives were crying, but Susie remembers that she was dry-eyed, holding herself back. Still, she was enormously worried. Spencer teased her. "Don't worry about me," he said. "I'll be back. You know the bad penny always comes back." The other husbands were comforting her, telling her they would bring him back safely. It was the last time the men and women who made a life out of the hardscrabble conditions of the segregated army in Arizona would all gather together. The wives who had cooked, played cards, drank, cried, and comforted one another were sending their men off to an unknown and dangerous situation. The men walked down the dirt road, four abreast, heading toward their destiny. "The fellas never looked back to say good-bye," Susie recalled. It was the end of stateside military life for the men and women of the 92nd and 93rd Infantry Divisions.

THE "GOOD FIGHT"

COMBAT OR NOT?

"All colored officers report to Colonel Wood's tent!" That call echoed through our area, and shortly thereafter a large number of our officers assembled. There he was, sitting on the ground with his legs folded under him like he was some kind of Indian chief. He said: "My name is Colonel Sterling A. Wood, and I understand colored people. I had a plantation in the South. So I know your needs. Now, I know there has been much discussion in the colored newspapers as to whether this division will see combat. I was talking to the chief of staff, General Marshall, and he agreed with me that colored troops would very likely see combat in this war. Why is this? Because 10 percent of the population of this country are colored people, so it is only fair that in this war 10 percent of the casualties should be colored. Therefore, you will be trained, and you will be sent where the fighting is the thickest." And that's when I knew we were going to be sent into combat. All because of some percentage nonsense.

Fifty-five years later, Charles Hanson still remembers "that little pep-talk." In 1944, his unit was deemed fit for combat, so they were shipped out to Italy to meet a quota. Cullen McKissock dubbed the policy "false liberalism." The number of black servicemen in the army never reached the goal of 10 percent, and, fortunately, their fatalities never reached that goal either. Ultimately, approximately fifty thousand black infantry soldiers were assigned to combat operations during World War II. Hanson's comrade, William Banks, was among those combat soldiers. Whereas Hanson understood his role as primarily fulfilling the "percentage nonsense," Banks assumed that combat was part of their overall mission as infantrymen:

> I assumed from the beginning of our training that we would be sent into combat. That was part of our mission as infantry soldiers. We were part of a unit, the American army, which was part of the Allied forces. We had the mission of seeking out and destroying the Axis forces.

Actually, both men were correct in their assessment of why they were sent into combat.

Black soldiers were assigned to theaters of war overseas as part of the military goal of representative participation, *and* they had always been trained with the idea of sending them into war when they completed the training. Most military planners never felt the black troops were prepared enough for combat, so they kept sending the men for another round of training. "Right after the desert training, I got a short leave home, and when I came back to the unit they didn't know where I was supposed to go," recalled Charles Wesly. "Everybody had packed up, taken the tents down, and there was my stuff just sitting in a pile in the desert. The word was we were going to ship overseas. Everybody was surprised."

Donald McNeil expressed the sentiment of many men. He said: "After fourteen months still in the states, I was feeling overtrained and getting nowhere. Tired of the routine. Finally, the division was alerted to go overseas, but we thought it was just another move to another state for more maneuvers or guarding dams." It was only after pressure groups and individuals assailed the government with demands for equal service that military planners relented and assigned black soldiers to combat zones. They were sent into combat in numbers no higher than their percentage of the population, with the expectation that they would take 10 percent of the casualties.

The issue of sending black soldiers into combat was heating up on the home front during the war years. Black soldiers were commonly assigned to units that specialized in engineering, supply and service tasks, and other types of noncombat jobs. Although these tasks were necessary and vital, the men of the 92nd and the 93rd had trained for infantry combat and wanted to be used in that role. In other words, the men wanted to be used as soldiers rather than laborers. However, the two black combat divisions, and the miscellaneous infantry regiments that were trained for combat, were still stateside at the beginning of 1944. Black soldiers were either on guard duty at American posts or still undergoing training. Numerous groups and outspoken individuals, including civil rights groups such as the NAACP and the Urban League, church organizations, individual black servicemen, and even some of President Roosevelt's close advisers, called for black soldiers to be sent into combat so that democracy at home and abroad could be achieved. This "Double V" campaign for victory at home and abroad inspired many Americans, black and white.

The Double V campaign received extensive press coverage. In the minds of many Americans, military service equaled full citizenship. Pastor Jernagin, director of the Fraternal Council of Negro Churches, an organization with more than six million members, appealed to Roosevelt's sense of justice in the following letter.

> Negro troops are begging for combat. . . . This war is producing a large number of mental casualties among Negro servicemen. Their dignity and humanity are outraged and insulted. These casualties are produced by our own military who insist upon relegating the Negro troops to second-class service when they are prepared for first-class service. Our men who are prepared for combat want contact with the enemy. Will you give them that chance? Speak boldly to the military officials concerning the plight of Negro servicemen as you have so often done on behalf of the down-trodden nations of the world.

In fact, as pressure from outside was building, within the military a new type of thinking began to emerge. Military planners noted that nonwhite and nearly illiterate soldiers were in combat at the European front fighting for the Allied forces. African soldiers fighting for colonial governments had dispelled the myth that the black man was incapable of combat. Russia had conscripted so many of her men that literacy was no longer a prerequisite for combat service. This evidence went against standard American military thinking that white skin and literacy (measured by the AGCT, the Army General Classification Test) were requirements for good combat soldiers. The military hierarchy could no longer rely on standard racial stereotypes, which said that black men were suited only for physical labor in hot climates, whereas white men could perform any functions in any climate. These stereotypes had, in the past, prevented black American soldiers from being sent into combat, but perhaps the time to reassess them had finally come. Despite the evidence coming from Europe of nonwhite soldiers performing heroically, the War Department continued to commission additional studies and reports to assess whether black troops should be sent into

combat. One strongly worded report called on the War Department to assign black men into an "integrated part of the total war effort" in order "to
establish a firm conviction that they have a stake in the common effort."
Still, military planners sought more opinions about and examples of successful utilization of nonwhite troops.

Although the Allied forces committed semiliterate Russians and black
Senegalese to combat, as well as the "darker" colonial troops from the
Caribbean and the Indian subcontinent, in most war zones the theater commanders were reluctant to send black American troops into combat. Few
government or military leaders anywhere around the world wanted black
troops assigned to their region. The War Department received requests
from government officials in Panama and Trinidad to station only white
troops in their regions. In Africa, the Liberian government made the same
request. Colonial officials were concerned that well-paid black American
soldiers would mingle with the not-so-well-paid "dark" locals and that both
groups would then unite against the local white authorities. In the Alaska
territory, authorities also asked Washington to send black soldiers elsewhere.
They claimed the cold weather would inhibit the men's productivity. This
ridiculous claim did not even address why white Americans would be better
suited for work in subzero temperatures. The Australian Embassy did not
even dissemble about climatic conditions; it simply asked Washington to
honor its "White Australia" immigration policy and send black troops to
some other region. As more whites-only requests poured in, Secretary of
War Henry L. Stimson became increasingly agitated about the spuriousness
of the claims. He especially did not like taking orders from other governments. Stimson commented that black labor had built the Panama Canal,
and he dismissed the other ridiculous requests. Thus began the commitment
of black troops to combat theaters.

Before the 93rd Infantry Division was assigned to a combat zone, its officers were briefed on how to deal with black soldiers once they got overseas.
Some of the junior officers, like Second Lieutenant Bill Payne, were black,
but they were required to attend the meeting. At the end of the meeting, a
higher-ranking white officer handed Payne a pamphlet called *The Negro Soldier* and asked him to read it. Payne threw the pamphlet to the floor and
said, "I'm one of them!" In the mindset of War Department officials, the
black soldier was an anomaly to be studied and managed. He was not considered on par with the white soldier except in exceptional and individual instances. The black soldier was generally considered in terms of group behavior. The category of "Negro" was thought to be scientifically meaningful,
and individuals making up this "natural grouping" could be analyzed and
their behavior predicted. Although black men had enlisted or were recruited

from all regions of the United States, and came into the service with a variety of backgrounds and social classes, the army tried to understand them only as a single cohesive entity. Military archives abound with studies, reports, articles, and memoranda that discuss the "the black soldier" as a distinct racial category with predictable actions and behavior.

The ideas promoted in the War Department's printed materials were not always reflected in the beliefs of white military personnel who came into contact with black soldiers. There appeared to be many conflicting ideas about what governed the behavior of black soldiers. For instance, the army portrayed the black soldier as anxious to get into battle with Hitler to stop "the worst form of slavery" ever known on Earth. In this case, the black man was portrayed as aggressive and patriotic—fiercely loyal to the notions of freedom and other American ideals. In another scenario, black soldiers were viewed as aggressive but not patriotic—they were suspected of harboring deep-seated resentment against whites. Some military authorities even thought that if given ammunition, black soldiers would fire upon white soldiers—a fear not without some substantiation.

The white officer training manual *Leadership and the Negro Soldier* warned against the tendency of black men to shirk work and engage in rumor-mongering. An entire section of the manual, "Rumors and the Negro Soldier," was devoted to controlling the tendency of black men to gossip. The black soldier was portrayed as shiftless and lazy, but supposedly he could be scientifically managed with the proper propaganda. The scenario with the most currency portrayed the black soldier as cowardly—he would run from combat if put in the line of fire, or "melt away." One black soldier who was fed up with comments about the so-called cowardice of black men said: "I find this hard to believe, since the average cracker is scared to death to tangle with a black man on a man-to-man deal." Military planners, white officers, and government officials generally believed that all black soldiers could be relied on to behave alike. They were just never sure whether black soldiers would be aggressive or cowardly, patriotic or shiftless, so they kept the men under constant surveillance and engaged in predictions about their potential behavior.

It is important to note again that the army of the 1940s reflected the manners and mores of most of American society. It was common practice to categorize people by "racial" differences. Even the black press was not immune. For example, many reporters in the seventy or so black newspapers played down stories about cowardice among black troops and their "melting away" in combat situations. If they mentioned that type of story at all, it was mainly to discredit it. But black reporters engaged in another type of mythologizing—the future of the "race" would be brighter if black soldiers were allowed to fight. Articles and pictures of fierce black soldiers fill the pages of the black wartime press.

Journalist Frank E. Bolden, who traveled with the 93rd Division, wrote a weekly column in the post paper called "From the Grapevine." Shortly after the division was constituted at Fort Huachuca, Bolden wrote, "I sometimes wonder if the men who are serving in this combat unit are aware of the great responsibility that rests upon their shoulders . . . the magnitude of responsibility and the opportunities that this Colored army unit affords." The message was clear: If the individual black soldier bungled his opportunity in the army, he could in fact be ruining the future of his race. The black soldier was the hope of the future, and he had better "straighten up and fly right," as the popular expression of the day advised. Bolden admonished the soldier to stay away from those "crystal ball gazers who know nothing about everything and everything about nothing, who pass out those intellectual cocktails that leaves one drunk with discontent."

"PAPA'S ON HIS WAY TO CROSS THE SEVEN SEAS"

Finally, after almost two years of stateside training, the 93rd Infantry Division received notice to ship out. Some black soldiers were skeptical when they got word to prepare for shipment overseas. Donald McNeil recalled that they "were all numb with silence; we thought that we were just going to some garrison for duty." Because of their last round of desert training in the Mojave Desert, many of the men thought they were being sent to Africa. Howard Hickerson said: "We thought we were going to be sent to North Africa, because Rommel was kicking the hell out of the Americans over there." That was not the case. When they shipped out of Fort Mason in San Francisco, the men discovered they were headed for jungle warfare in the rain forests of the Pacific islands.

The Pacific was split into two theaters of operation: Admiral Chester Nimitz controlled the navy in the northern theater, and General Douglas MacArthur commanded the army in the South Pacific. One of only a few officials to take an integrationist stand, MacArthur assured the War Department that he would not refuse the assignment of black troops to his theater of command. MacArthur commented to General Marshall that he would take the "higher perspective and viewpoint," thereby attempting to contain any sort of "racial friction." When NAACP chairman Walter White traveled to the Pacific, MacArthur committed himself further with this strong statement: "Any man who says that another man's fighting ability can be measured by color is wrong." MacArthur was well aware that a general's cachet and personal power is directly proportional to the number of troops and re-gions under his control, so perhaps his statement was motivated more by politics than by liberal ideology. Still, boldly stated opinions, combined with the desire of both Stimson and Marshall to assign black troops to different combat zones around the world, signaled a change in military thinking.

Assigning men to a combat zone did not mean sending them into combat, as the men of the 93rd rapidly discovered. It also did not mean keeping the division together as a unit. In San Francisco, the men were broken up into smaller units before shipping out, never to be assembled into full-division strength again. No matter the underlying policy, only segments of the 93rd were sent into combat, and those individuals who were in combat situations served mostly in small patrols. The 93rd never engaged in any division-sized operations.

There were some soldiers, however, who were not ready for combat. After all the training and time on the job, Hank Williams fell ill with a recurring eye ailment. He wanted to be with his outfit, which was preparing to go to the Pacific, but the doctors felt that he needed to be hospitalized. Still, the army was able to utilize his leadership skills even while he was assigned to the hospital. Williams was the ranking noncommissioned officer and had been given the command of about two hundred men who were deemed unfit for combat. When he got to the unit, housed in a tar-paper colored bar-racks, called the "black barracks," he was greeted with: "Welcome to the Sick, Lame, and Lazy, Sergeant." All of the men were suffering some kind of ailment and needed to be processed out of the troop lists getting ready for overseas command. Williams said: "I wanted to be with my guys. I didn't leave them earlier when I could have cadred a new outfit. I knew there were men in my company who were depending on me. I think I was a good sol-dier, and I knew how to take care of my people." Still, Williams was left be-hind to heal his infirmity while the rest of the 93rd was sent off to war.

In San Francisco, the men got on ships and passed under the Golden Gate Bridge, bidding farewell to American soil and not knowing when, or if, they would see it again. Howard Hickerson described the processing of shipping out.

> When we shipped out of Camp Clipper, in the Mojave Desert, that was the last time the whole division was together. We shipped out in different units according to what they could ship you out on and where you were going. We shipped out in stages. We came by rail to Camp Stoneman in Pittsburg, California, then they had ferry boats to take us to Fort Mason in San Francisco and from there onto a troop ship and off to the South Pacific.

They used everything for troop ships at the time. Ours was a Liberty ship. The holds for cargo in this ship were converted into these personnel carriers. There were three or four holds with five hundred people in each, five deep, sleeping in hammocks, like tiers. It took us fifteen days on the way out. We didn't have an escort. We were just a lone ship out there, and we were kinda nervous.

Bill Payne also traveled through the Pacific unescorted, but his accommodations were a bit more upscale than Hickerson's. Payne and the entire 369th Regiment of the 93rd Division were traveling on the *Lurline*, the queen of the Matson shipping line. He said it was the best ship of the day—a big luxury liner. Although also unescorted and therefore exposed to attack by submarines, the *Lurline* was a fast ship and relatively safe, so the men were told. Payne said he felt like he was on a cruise, but that feeling quickly died away as his unit unloaded at Guadalcanal, at the southern tip of the Solomon Islands.

"WELCOME TO THE WAR"

In January 1944 the 93rd Division landed on Guadalcanal in stages and immediately started a process of acclimation. Even though the major battles had ended on Guadalcanal, the island, considered the doorstep to Australia, was still susceptible to a Japanese counteroffensive. The mission of the 93rd was to protect the island from Japanese landings by air, land, or sea. Also, there were "pockets of Japanese soldiers still remaining on the island who were giving us trouble," commented Hickerson. During the first few weeks after their arrival, units of the 93rd established a camp and assisted in port operations. They also underwent a few rough weeks of jungle training, including scouting, patrolling, perimeter defense, and weapons training.

Almost immediately, complaints started circulating among the men about their assignment to laundry service, truck detail, and port operations. According to one soldier:

When we landed at Guadalcanal, we were immediately put to work unloading ships. Now I don't know what MacArthur's racial policies were, but I do know that all men landing in the area were put to work stevedoring. There were two reasons: no place in the U.S. has the climate of the South Pacific; acclimatization was necessary. Also, there was a shortage of men to unload ships. I will say black combat troops

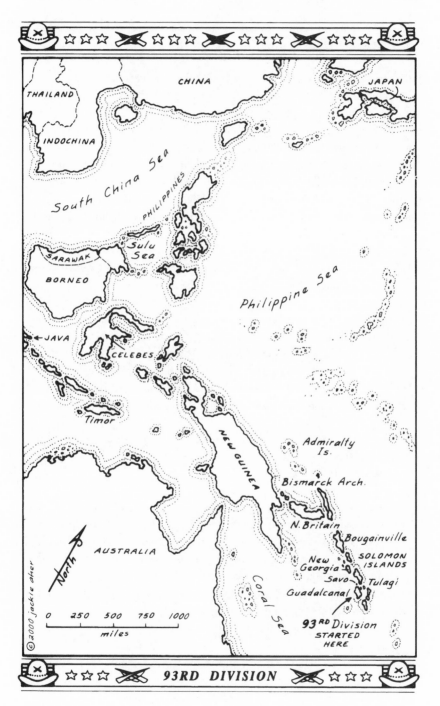

THAILAND
CHINA
JAPAN
INDOCHINA
South China Sea
PHILIPPINES
SARAWAK
Sulu
Sea
BORNEO
Philippine Sea
JAVA
CELEBES
Timor
NEW GUINEA
Admiralty
Is.
Bismarck Arch.
N. Britain
Bougainville
AUSTRALIA
New
Georgia
SOLOMON
ISLANDS
Savo
Tulagi
Guadalcanal
Coral Sea
93RD Division
STARTED
HERE
North
© 2000 jackie aher
0   250   500   750   1000
miles

93RD DIVISION

did a lot more stevedoring than whites, and I'm sure we became accli-
mated as quickly as they did.

Other soldiers were less kind about the military's policy of assigning them to
labor details. Bill Stevens heard they were assigned to stevedoring under the
guise of keeping physically fit. "If totin' that barge and liftin' that bale was a
physical fitness program, then the 93rd should have been in superb physical
condition compared to similar white units."

Although the 93rd's landing on Guadalcanal has never been immortal-
ized in film or in folklore, for the individual soldier the experience was life-
forming. Donald McNeil and Howard Hickerson stayed on Guadalcanal
until June 1944, unloading ships and performing training exercises.
McNeil noted the beauty of the island, but also the thickness of the jungle,
the mosquitoes, and the flies. Hickerson was horrified by the number of
dead bodies they were assigned to bury. Nelson Peery most clearly conveyed the harshness of the area.

> Acclimation in Guadalcanal after months in the desert was a physical
> and psychological shock. Acclimation meant endless maneuvering
> through the humid, stinking jungles. We learned to live with the
> hordes of mosquitoes and green flies, fat from the corpses that still rot-
> ted, half covered by the mud and slime. We unlearned the tactics of
> desert warfare and learned squad control and combat in the jungle.

After getting over the initial shock of dead bodies and life in the tropics,
a number of the men were able to fashion a somewhat regular lifestyle. Bill
Payne described the adaptation.

> We got to Guadalcanal during the hot part of the day. When we landed
> we were ushered to an area, a big open field, and we had to pitch our
> pup tent. There were a lot of weeds and reeds, and it was infested with
> mosquitoes. They were everywhere. So we were issued Atabrine and
> mosquito repellent to use. After we were there for a while, we man-
> aged to put up larger tents that could hold eight to ten people. And
> these were housed down on the beach.
>
> Someone had enough foresight to build a movie theater where we
> could go and watch movies. It was the forerunner of today's drive-in
> movie. I remember watching a movie in the rain. I had my pith hel-
> met, my poncho, and my boots. So I just hunkered down and watched
> the movie in the rain. I had no problem whatsoever seeing the movie.
> But, I'll tell you it was a pretty good storm, because when I got back

to my tent it was laying on the ground! I had stayed through the movie—all the way through that tropical storm.

The men arrived in the rainy season, which runs from December through April. At some point of nearly every day, the sky would let loose with a full-speed cloudburst of rain that could suddenly change directions and shoot sideways. The well-equipped soldier traveled with a bar of soap and, during a rainstorm, would strip down to his skivvies for a spontaneous shower. Of course, he had to be careful where he showered: not around the crocodiles that lurked in the mangrove swamps or atop a den of snakes. Food became damp and moldy from the daily torrent. Howard Hickerson recalled his own acclimation process.

> The South Pacific is always hot and always wet. The islands, wherever you were, different ones, rain and rain, and hot humidity. Maybe it would rain for three days, and then it would be hot and damp for three days. So your clothes were always wet and smelly. Anytime you sent a letter it was damp or moldy. Your cigarettes would be half-soaked.

Weapons regularly misfired because of the rain or the intense humidity. In addition to the fear and uncertainty of wartime living, jungle-rot and malaria affected many soldiers.

"PRAISE THE LORD AND PASS THE AMMUNITION"

The 93rd Division was parceled out to numerous islands in the South Pacific. The volcanic mountains, island rain forests, coral atolls, and blue-green waters of the South Pacific became theaters of war rather than areas of serenity and beauty. The 93rd moved through the Solomon Islands, the Slot; fought on the islands of New Guinea and New Georgia; and headed up toward the Philippine Islands. Sometimes they formed a complete regiment of three thousand men. At other times, the men were in battalion formations of one thousand. Most of their daily maneuvers were done in small patrols. The island jungles defined the manner of war: soldiers maneuvered through dense, wet, and nearly impenetrable forests. When large groups of troops landed on beaches, Japanese soldiers fired with impunity from protective caves. Bill Payne recalled:

> The terrain was really tricky. A flat stretch of beach maybe one hundred to two hundred yards, then all of the sudden you've got these sheer

cliffs. The height! Up there the Japanese had caves and guns all along the coastline. What amazed me is how the Americans could go in and take an island with that kind of situation. When we got there, all the Japanese had been pushed to the interior or the far side of the island.

Still, at any time of the day or night, the men were subject to fire from antipersonnel artillery, phosphorous grenades, or jellied-gasoline bombs. Soldiers who went out in small groups on patrol or reconnaissance faced every kind of booby trap, from trip-wire hand grenades to tree-stump "surprise" traps. As they approached the enemy, some men witnessed barbarities such as a dead man hanging from a tree with his body parts strewn about. The major battles with the enemy were over. But the men had to deal with the psychological impact of being in a war zone filled with pockets of enemy soldiers intent on fighting to the death.

Segments of the division were used in "mopping-up" operations and perimeter maintenance. After frontline troops secured an area on one of the islands, elements of the 93rd landed and held the area by establishing secure perimeters and setting up airbases and communications. While most of the time spent "mopping-up" was not as active as frontline combat, soldiers in the 93rd experienced bombing attacks, mortar fire, rifle fire, and bayonet attacks in their role as occupation troops. They were on foreign soil, armed and trained to defend themselves against an enemy that was intent on killing them. This was combat. Certainly it was not of the same type as the invasion of Guadalcanal or the D-Day invasion on the beaches of Normandy, but the men of the 93rd encountered the enemy on a regular basis in some fierce situations. Even service workers such as engineering battalions commonly encountered enemy fire. One army engineer recalled an assignment to build a road through the mud and muck of the jungle for tanks and other armored vehicles to pass. Army engineers are generally not thought of as combat troops, yet he had to stop working every few minutes to fire off a couple of rounds at the Japanese snipers who were shooting at the men from the safety of the bush a few hundred yards away from the road. Perimeter control and guarding are less "active" than combat "at the front," but both situations involve combat actions.

MacArthur's aim was to retake the islands of the Pacific from the Japanese, especially the Philippines, which had fallen in the five months following Pearl Harbor. The men of the 93rd moved from island to island. Howard Hickerson described the policy known as "island hopping."

We would stay on an island for a while, then move on. After we established that Australia was safe, then we concentrated on going to the

Philippines. Get it free. We were going up the Slot, the Solomon Islands. We'd free all these small islands all the way up. We just wanted the islands in order to get an airstrip on them. We were on five or six islands. I can't even name them—some were so small. We would land on them, and the engineers would come in and clear a path, flatten a strip out for an airstrip. We needed a lot of airstrips so we could hop up to the Philippines with those little short-range bombers we had. We would land on an island, establish a base. Boom, and then move on. Bypass some, boom and move. Get another island and another airstrip, boom, boom.

Nelson Peery wrote to his mother about the difficulties of warfare and life on the move. "Lord, it's been a long haul from Guadalcanal to Morotai," he wrote.

Our job has been to hold the island of Halmahara, which is twelve miles from here and crawling with 37,000 Japanese soldiers. Their job is to retake the island. Sometimes their suicide units would break through, and off we'd go again. It's really nasty business hunting them down like dogs and killing them.

Soldiers of the 93rd on the Lookout. (Used with permission of U.S. Army, Signal Corps Photo)

Out on patrol one night, Peery's friend Lonnie was killed by a Japanese sharpshooter. Peery said there was no scream, no blood. The bullet that hit Lonnie's heart ended his life instantly. For Peery, this death was not at all like the dramatic representations of war he had seen at the movies. Peery was shocked to near immobility. He was horrified at the quickness, stunned by the finality. Moving through the haze of his shock, Peery then responded to the attack with all of his military training. He located Lonnie's attacker and thrust a bayonet into his chest, killing his enemy.

Peery said a soldier does not really get accustomed to killing, especially if the action takes place at close range. The soldier is always on-edge, anticipating the next attack, hoping to live through another day and another encounter. For the men of the 93rd Division, stationed on numerous islands in small configurations, enemy attacks came regularly. From small firefights to aerial bombings, the men were reminded of the ferocity of the Japanese soldier. Even in World War II, many Japanese soldiers still followed the traditional code of warfare termed *bushido*—death before dishonor. Bill Stevens described what fighting the Japanese was like.

> Let us just talk about the Japanese or the little "monkey men." They were a colored people, so the big bad American marines were going to kick their asses properly. In reality, the Japanese were excellent soldiers. They had been fighting in the Pacific for a long time, swallowing up bits and pieces. They had occupied islands and were prepared to be there a long time. Our marines stormed the beaches of those islands, and the Japanese beat the shit out of our legendary marines. That inferior breed happened to be superb contact fighters, besides not missing a trick in the book and inventing some new ones. They had all kinds of booby traps. Every trail, every bush, every tree could prove to be disastrous.

In many instances, the Japanese held strategic advantages over the units of the 93rd. They had the high ground, and they knew the terrain. They also relied on psychological warfare to press the advantage. For instance, when the Japanese found out that some unseasoned black troops were in the vicinity, they waited until the quiet of the night and then shattered the silence with the roar and flash of heavy artillery. Disrupting the soldiers' sleep kept the men jumpy and on-edge. In the volcanic hellhole of Biak Island, off the coast of New Guinea, one soldier in the 93rd Division reported on the state of affairs.

> Scrub typhus was prevalent. The food was bad. It was the rear end of the world in all ways. Our forces were trying to evacuate this island,

but the Japanese were quite active and aggressive. We ran patrols and experienced our first casualties there. The Japanese kept us awake with mortar fire at night. We had been on some rough patrols together. On one, we crossed a river, and two of the fellows lost their shoes. Those men didn't complain, and they kept up. We found an old abandoned army dump, and there were some shoes, damp and fungus-covered, but those fellows put on those shoes without a word.

Vincent Tubbs, a reporter for the Baltimore *Afro-American*, described another hot firefight. "The tactical advantages held by the enemy made the encounter one of the worst since the division's arrival here. . . . [They had] superior machine gun and mortar firepower against our two Browning automatic [rifles] and Thompson submachine guns, plus cunning and secure camouflage . . . yet more than 20 Japanese died. . . . Our men shot their way out."

Bill Payne summarized his feelings about the Japanese enemy.

Like many other American troops, I did not have much respect for the Japanese soldier. They were tough fighters; don't get me wrong. They were really tough fighters because they could maneuver through the jungle and the trees and the caves far better than we could. They had gun emplacements dug in between the banyan tree roots. And they had to be routed out of these caves, which was nearly impossible. However, their imagination was limited.

They took orders and followed them, and that was it. They followed orders to the letter, and at the end of that order, that was it. There was no individual thinking. Our troops were trained to think for themselves. If they got into a situation, they could find a way to get out. We were taught to follow orders of course, but we were also taught to go beyond that from time to time.

The rigors of combat took a mental toll on the men of the 93rd. Many of their patrol missions were grueling and downright horrifying. Every day in a two-month period Walter Green led a combat patrol of men from his company. Several men were killed, and many others were wounded in numerous firefights with small bands of Japanese soldiers. The men were fatigued, and there was no relief in sight. Finally, the men rebelled on their last patrol. Green remembered that mission.

We were ordered to find what was left of our recon patrol and bring them back. All communication had been cut off. This time, half of our

company was going, the white captain and exec, and two black lieutenants. We went well prepared for trouble, heavy weapons, grenades,
the works. Our orders were to find them and get them back. It was a
real rugged trip through the jungle, always on guard against an ambush. You more or less had to stick to the trail, because it was practically impossible to cut your way through the surrounding jungle. We
had to go through several bamboo forests.

It was a day and a half before we reached them. We found their bodies, stripped of everything. The bodies were bloated and covered with
flies. We were ordered to bring the bodies back. We had no equipment
for doing this. The men rebelled on this and sat down. They did not
want to touch these putrefied bodies. One enlisted man had been a
mortician, and he helped us make litters to carry them and cover them.
We sprayed the remains with sulfur powder. We managed to get them
back, but we were afraid every step of the way.

Communications and command problems plagued the small patrol units.
Howard Hickerson described some of the problems he encountered with an
inexperienced commander. "We came from one island to another in the
Marianas and were told that the new place was secured—free of the
enemy—in this perimeter," recalled Hickerson.

A junior officer got a map and some instructions to take a crew up
this road and look around. The senior officers were already ahead in
the established region. When we started out it was kinda late, about
dark and raining. He had us set in there for the night. We set up the
little tents and opened a can of field chow. Water was leaking on me
while I was eating this ration of food. It was a mess. Meantime, the
junior officer had read the map wrong. The Japanese were in the
area, and they just opened fire on us. Luckily it was small-caliber
fire, and we were too far away. But they ripped up the area there for
a bit. We pulled back, and then the next day we found out we were
in the wrong place.

Charles Wesly also remembered being sent out on a patrol that was poorly
planned. His unit was given a map with a trail clearly marked and told to go
out and reconnoiter the area. "So when I got the unit together, we went out
about 200 yards on this trail, and there we were right in a trash dump," said
Wesly. "I mean it was pathetic, that type of command."

Sometimes the men on patrol encountered people other than the Japanese
enemy. Each island was populated with several native tribes. It was never clear

to the soldiers whether the local inhabitants were friendly or unfriendly. Most of the soldiers just tried to steer clear of them. Numerous tribes that spoke a variety of languages inhabited the islands in the South Pacific. Even up to World War II, many of the islands were still unexplored by the colonial powers. An outsider knew very little about the lifestyle of the local inhabitants, and the locals knew even less about any of the heavily armed outsiders. When soldiers of the 93rd encountered the "wig-men" of New Guinea, resplendent in their large headgear, the "mud-men," who wore masks and covered their bodies with mud, or the brightly colored "henna-men," both the soldiers and the natives registered shock. The soldiers felt no kinship with the natives and looked on warily as the tribesmen moved on.

Bill Payne described one such encounter.

> The last patrol I made was on an island off the northern coast of Biak. We were on a little landing craft, and we made our way up this river. We had to drop off another patrol along the shoreline, and then my group continued on through this winding snake-like river. The boat got stuck about halfway through. We couldn't maneuver. So we sat there overnight waiting for the tide.
>
> During the night we were awakened by a loud noise—a gunshot fired by one of our guys. And the first thing in my mind was: "Get that damn Jap!" I looked to make sure my men were secure and all right, and then we looked off in the distance, and there was a light moving through the jungle, through the trees. We couldn't figure out what it was, and here we were straddled across the river, vulnerable. When we looked again we realized it was a native canoe coming down the river. Going from one island to the other. They saw us and they were backing up the river like mad, trying to get away from us. Finally they found a way around, but it sure shocked the both of us.

"WE'RE ALL IN THIS TOGETHER"

When the 93rd moved in behind white troops in mop-up work or as occupation troops, friction sometimes developed between the two groups of soldiers. Several regiments of the 93rd followed behind the "Dixie Division," the all-white 31st Infantry Unit, and over time the relationship soured. The Dixie Division initially had high praise for black troops because an all-black amphibious unit assisted them in a difficult beach landing. "As the Dixie Division attempted to land on a flat stretch of beach, Japanese soldiers entrenched in caves and cliffs laid on a barrage of fire,"

Bill Payne recalled. "The 'Duck Unit' came in under fire and extracted many of the Dixie Division's soldiers."

But relations worsened when units of the 93rd and the Dixie Division were stationed together on the Philippine Islands. Many of the white soldiers were angered by the attention black soldiers showed the local girls. Friction turned into all-out warfare, according to Walter Green. He said: "Our men had been overseas nineteen months without seeing any women to speak of, so when the guys hit the Philippines they went hog wild. The Dixie Division couldn't stand the Filipino girls going for the Negro soldiers. After several days there were small battles." Ultimately, the small battles turned into a major melee, with large groups of soldiers from both divisions involved in armed conflicts. "It took the colonels of every battalion from both divisions to get their men and bring the situation under control. They were real busy running up and down that road to keep down outright war."

Black soldiers serving in the South Pacific were segregated, in contact with only a few white officers and only occasionally in contact with white divisions. This did not prevent some blacks and whites from developing friendships, nor did it always mean antagonized encounters. Sometimes blacks and whites got a chance to learn more about each other. Sometimes what they learned confirmed their prejudices, but at other times, different attitudes prevailed. Nelson Peery recognized that some white men could be good soldiers and command black troops without prejudice. "It's a funny fact but a white guy as an individual is okay, a clear thinker and a good soldier. But collectively they can become a cruel, mean mob," he commented in a letter to his mother. Peery talked about one nice guy, Colonel Frank LaRue, who was so well liked that several of the black enlisted men named their children "LaRue" in his honor—a high honor indeed for a white commanding officer in a segregated army.

Walter Green talked about his commanding officers in the 93rd, identifying most of the relationships as "farcical." He said: "The very guy who would make your life miserable in the States was your best buddy over there. I never quite figured it out. Oh, we accepted the friendship offered, but we never forgot that one day we would be going home and not to take this bit for real." Ted McCullough was also critical about the relationships in his unit. He noted that the white officers were always getting transferred out or promoted, but the black officers remained at their rank until a general order promoting everyone was issued. Still, no black officer outranked a white officer, and this situation and the prejudice that surrounded it angered many black soldiers. McCullough commented: "I got better treatment than a lot of our black officers maybe because I was a platoon sergeant, but still they treated me like I was the enemy, like a Japanese. Seeing the way the white officers treated the black officers, well, I thought I could just as well shoot them as I could a Japanese."

Charles Wesly concurred with the criticism.

> They got so many complaints from the black officers about not getting promoted that MacArthur finally sent a special investigation team to our unit. We told them that if given an opportunity to get out of the 93rd, there wouldn't be a black officer in the division the next day. So they set up this jungle school where you could go and qualify for a promotion. I never will forget that. A guy from California, Arnett Hartsfield, and I finished one-two in the class. So naturally we wanted to know where the promotion was. The explanation we got was "a representative number didn't pass, so everybody would have to take the course over again." I said to heck with that; I don't need a promotion. I began to get a little belligerent, and my military career went downhill from there. I got the reputation of being a renegade.

The relationship between white and black soldiers was complicated by the authority that white officers had over black enlisted men and over lower-ranking black officers. One officer commented in his diary that his men resented the fact that he was dictating the whole show.

> They feel that because I am white and they are colored that I am taking advantage of them. That is one thing I won't be able to knock out of their heads. Before I die I must help stamp out this crazy idea that the white man has about his superiority over the colored man. In no concrete way has he ever demonstrated it.

While the officer did build strong relationships with his men, he constantly worried that his motives were being misinterpreted. When white officers were promoted and then replaced by new white officers, black enlisted men had to begin again the dance of racialized relations.

Black officers could never be transferred out of the 93rd because it was the only division overseas that used black officers. But they could be reassigned within the division, something Peery learned firsthand. He was quite fond of a black officer in his unit, but the man was moved to another regiment and replaced by a white officer from Georgia. Peery said the new officer had two strikes against him—his race and the fact that he was replacing one of the best officers in the unit. Eventually the new white officer was able to win over the men. Peery said it was funny how southerners had a way of becoming really nice guys overseas.

Ted McCullough recalled an incident during which a white soldier tagged along on an otherwise all-black combat patrol and irritated the other men by throwing garbage along the trail.

> I had the platoon, and we had black officers in command with this lone white fellow with us. I didn't know who he was or what he was doing with us. He wasn't saying a word, just hanging back by himself. At one point when he was in the rear I said, "Hey, fella. Keep up now. I don't want you lagging behind. That's how we lose guys. I'm in the back, and I don't want nobody behind me." He just looked at me and moved up. But then he threw a package of cookies down, and I had to take him up on that.
>
> I said, "Now fella, we are out here to kill the Japs, not feed them." I told him to pick it up—and I told him in language I won't use here. He got the gist of it, though. He got the cookies, opened the pack, dug a little hole with his spade, and dropped them in there. Then he stirred it up with the spade and mixed sand with the cookies. I said, "Okay, now that pack of cookies is no good to the Japs. They are following us out here trying to exist and picking up what we throw away. It's guys like you that keep them going on." The other guys in the platoon started laughing, and we all kept moving ahead.
>
> The next day we continued our patrol, and in fact, we captured a Japanese colonel and killed some of the others in their camp. After that we took all the good things that they had. You know like compasses and little generators, rifles, pistols, flags, swords, stuff like that. We made quite a killing, literally. There's two ways to look at that. Anyway, the next time I saw that white fella was on the beach where we were waiting for transport back to the base. He had eagles on his collar—a full colonel, apparently the chief of staff of the division. He said to all of us, but looking straight at me, "I want every one of those souvenirs you got put on this shelf right now." Well, after that trip I figured I'd been in that company long enough, so I put in papers to transfer.

While some individual soldiers could overcome racial stereotyping and forge friendships, relationships between blacks and whites in the military were hindered by many institutional constraints. Assignment to the 93rd Division limited the advancement of both black and white officers. Black officers could not be assigned to command any white person, and they could not be transferred to any of the other divisions in the Pacific. White officers were constrained by the lack of high-profile assignments. Because black troops were not being utilized as frontline combat soldiers, their white commanders also lacked opportunities for field promotions.

One white company commander, Captain Lee Quarterman, repeatedly requested combat assignment as a possible means of advancement. His army efficiency ratings consistently noted that he was personable, of high morale caliber, and efficient. But the army refused to activate his all-black unit for frontline combat duty. He had a cushy headquarters job pushing papers around, but wanted to be commanding troops in the field. Despite more than eight years of preparation in the United States and two years of service overseas, Quarterman was advised to stay put, do his job, and forgo any hope of commanding troops in the field. In the last months of the Pacific war, Quarterman was promoted out of the office and distinguished himself with a Bronze Star throughout several combat patrol assignments on the island of Biak. But he was never sent to the front line—and for this his daughter is eternally grateful.

Soldiers must maintain high morale if they are to perform courageously in battle and act with discipline. Several incidents gravely affected the morale of the men in the 93rd Division, to the detriment of their service capabilities. Charles Wesly described a situation that unnerved the men in his unit. "We had one guy, a regimental commander, move in, and he must have thought he was moving onto a plantation," recalled Wesly.

> He ordered a hacienda built down by the sea. One of his guys got an air medal for flying all over the Pacific trying to find him a porcelain toilet. Called in a warrant officer out of headquarters and told him that the movies could not start until we had serenaded him. We had to sing before the movie because this was a way to keep us happy. It was demoralizing and degrading. The idea that we had to entertain him like he was the master of the plantation was upsetting. Well, the word got around and not a one of us ever sang on key.

Some black soldiers were so demoralized by the constant racism, overlaid with the wartime conditions in the South Pacific, that discipline completely broke down. Howard Hickerson recalled the period:

> Over in the jungle, the farther away you are, well, the people get demoralized. Everybody is edgy and jumpy. You don't want to take nothing from nobody. It's tough living, and some officer is giving you hell and you haven't gotten a letter from home. Pretty soon somebody gets the idea, "Hey! We're being picked on. We're being treated like crap here."

On this one island there was a roped-off officers' quarters down on the beach. One soldier had decided that he'd had enough, so he threw two hand grenades into the officers' quarters. Boom, Boom! About 10 o'clock at night they both went off and completely demolished the tent and injured one of the officers. The first thing we thought was that we were being attacked. Everybody was blowing whistles and running for cover.

Hickerson said "all hell broke loose" as the injured officer and the enlisted men scrambled to find out what was going on. After the officers figured out that the attack had come from within their own camp, an investigation began. Investigators uncovered a footprint in the mud beside the officers' tent and surmised the grenade-throwing culprit had left an imprint of his foot. They made a plaster cast to determine the culprit's shoe size, and as in the story of Cinderella, everyone was tested to see if the shoe fit. When the investigators found a match, the man was court-martialed and sentenced to prison for ten years. Hickerson said the investigators had an idea of who the culprit was before they began looking into the matter, so they mainly focused on the "discontents." Two of the white officers who were residing in the tent were transferred out. The rest of the black soldiers in the unit were put under heightened scrutiny, because the army assumed that every one of them knew the man had been planning the attack, and thus they were all guilty as accomplices.

Several of the men in the 93rd later served in the Vietnam War. They noted that the World War II "fragging" of officers was different from the type of outright attacks in Vietnam. The general insubordination was different, too. Officers in World War II might get a warning shot; in Vietnam they were more likely to be shot at directly. Several men remembered sniper attacks by enlisted men on officers in the South Pacific. At one point, the men of the 93rd were instructed not to fraternize with the Filipino women. The white soldiers in the area were not similarly warned. Walter Green commented:

The colonel [who had issued the order] was the only person who had a generator to furnish light in his tent at night. That night several men cut loose with their .30-caliber rifles on that light and the upper part of his tent. Man, he came crawling out of that tent screaming bloody murder. The whole thing was settled without another word.

Green said the colonel rescinded the order in the morning.

In another unrelated but similarly provocative incident, a commander ordered all of the live ammunition to be collected from a unit of soldiers in the

93rd. Howard Hickerson said that no one particular incident provoked the recall order, "just a general fear about some type of uprising was in the air." Though the men were in enemy territory, albeit not a heavily active area, none of them had ammunition for their weapons, which they were allowed to keep. After officers collected all of the rounds and clips and locked up the heavy artillery, they held surprise inspections, trying to catch the men secreting ammunition. Hickerson said:

> It was just demoralizing. To think we had gone through all this training, and they didn't trust us to have live ammunition. That we couldn't conduct ourselves as soldiers. This island was fairly good sized and we said, "Hey, what if somebody attacks?" And they said they would just issue it back out to us. Well, in a war zone things happen pretty fast. We were pretty damn nervous. Any time you are beyond the secured perimeter you are exposed. In jungle warfare, unless you search every hollow tree you can't be sure the enemy isn't around. We were unprepared, no ammunition, period. We did not get the ammunition back until we had moved onto another island—about four months later. Our morale was so low. If it hadn't been for military discipline, oh, well, I just don't know what would have happened.

"WE DID HAVE SOME FUN OVER THERE ..."

Not all wartime experiences were demoralizing. War definitely builds a bond, and the relationships in the 93rd were not all forged under fire. Some of the bonding occurred because the men enjoyed playing silly pranks. They called it "playing the dozens" or just simply "funnin'." Hickerson talked about the verbal games they would play on the Australians.

> Playing the dozens usually starts off with one guy saying something about your momma. Then the next guy picks up and so on. Real insulting, but fun kinda stuff. The Australians didn't really understand us, and they didn't know anything about the dozens, so we'd get a kick out of just asking one of them, "How's ya momma?" and then we'd all snicker.
> They would think we were being polite, so he would reply, "Oh, me mum's doing fine. Thank you for asking." Of course, we would just break out laughing at that and then continue on by talking dirt about the next one's momma.

The men found numerous other ways to keep themselves entertained. Donald McNeil wrote about the ingenuity of the men in his unit who made "Raisin Jack," or moonshine, out of dried fruit and sugar and "Jungle Juice," out of grain alcohol and water. They created a whole new language to describe their surroundings: chow, SOS, Maggie's Drawers, Brown Nose, Torpedo Juice. They tried to live life to the fullest. "We were living on the edge and that caused us to view things differently when we were there," Bill Payne recalled.

> Like if you were having a good time, you really had a good time. If you were going to drink, then you would really drink. If you played ball, you played to the maximum. Because all the time you thought this could be the last time.

The men could be rough in the way they played. Howard Hickerson recalled a fierce game of "teasing the tent mate."

> There were so many mosquitoes over there and so much malaria. Your bunk beds had to have a frame built up for a mosquito net over you. You'd go to bed at night and roll this net over your bed and tuck it in. In the morning you would roll it up real tight and stuff it in a brown GI-color thing. Everyday you would roll it and unroll it. We were on one of the islands, and we had to do something to keep from going crazy. So you'd do some jokes and stuff. They were actually pretty terrible.
>
> On this occasion, one of the guys had found a Japanese skull—which wasn't very hard to find. You just go out and pick it up. So he put the skull in the guy's mosquito net thing over the bed. We'd been up on a hill sitting outside with some candles, and then we came on in to go to bed. The guy pulled that string to unroll the net and the skull rolled right into his rack. Well, you know what happened. Well, Jesus Christ. He ran around the whole tent screaming and hollering. Everybody thought we was under attack or something. Wild things like that always happened.

Some soldiers took advantage of the terrain, and others just "got used to living like pigs and accepted our conditions out there in the jungle." Ted McCullough told a story about fishing in the South Pacific.

> Our biggest job was dynamiting fish out of the water. There was a stream that was running into the ocean. The stream was about 16 feet deep, and you could see all the way to the bottom. We'd float quarter sticks of dynamite on two- and three-foot strings and then throw some

bread crumbs out to get the fish to come to the top. By the time the fish started telling each other that bread was there, we'd set off the charge. Then we'd jump into the water and start throwing fish in the boat. Now out in the ocean we did the same thing, only we were much faster. Because once you blow the charge you're gonna tear up some of the fish, and then the sharks will be there. We had natives with us who would tell us which fish you keep and which fish you sleep. The Australians had been paying them about 75 cents a day and we started paying them about two-and-a-half dollars. They said I was ruining the economy in that place.

Howard Hickerson described another occasion where his tent mates quickly bonded over a prank that could have gotten them all court-martialed.

We would sit around the tent getting bored until somebody would say, "Hey, let's go steal something out of the mess tent," and off we'd go on an adventure. Soldiers are survivors, you know, and we just weren't getting enough to eat. We took turns going to the supply area in the back of the mess tent to get things. We would ease up there real quiet like and get ourselves a big can of peaches or something and bring it back to the tent.

One day a guy went up to the tent, and after a few minutes we heard this big commotion. He was screaming and hollering and tearing back toward our tent. He was also dragging half the mess tent with him. Apparently when he'd been feeling around among the cans trying to sneak the peaches, he'd felt this big python snake on top of the cans. Well, that's when he started screaming back to our tent. We went back up there and killed the thing with machetes, but then the officers wanted to know who broke the supply tent. Ha! We all said we didn't know nothing; didn't know anything about it at all.

Ted McCullough also recalled other "special provisions" or "midnight requisitions" that kept the men occupied.

We had a guy who lived in this town on one of the islands who had a barbecue set up at his home. My fellas would go out every Tuesday, about five of them, with automatic rifles and shoot the wild boar and bring them back in for this fella. He'd cut them up and soak them overnight in his goo. The next day he started barbecuing and slopping on this goo with a new clean mop we'd given him. We'd go down to this shack that the natives had built, open on all sides, situated on a hill. There was a movie screen with a little roof over it in case of rain. And we'd sit there having our barbecued pork and some beers and watch a movie.

To keep themselves entertained, some men built clubhouses, and other enterprising soldiers set up temporary gambling casinos. Bill Payne said that he was always good with his hands, so he and another similarly talented soldier built an officers club out of some extra materials they "rounded up" in the area. Payne built tables and chairs, and his partner painted the place. During quiet times, his partner wrote poetry, and Payne read. At night the clubhouse was a little more lively—the usual drinking and shooting the bull associated with military life. The army also set up makeshift theaters on some of the islands.

One night, Nelson Peery and Bill Payne, although they did not know one another at the time, attended an outdoor screening of the movie *Rhapsody in Blue*. It was nearly their last picture show. The men were seated on one of the logs laid out in rows over an abandoned airstrip that served as theater seating. Without warning, a Japanese "Betty" bomber interrupted the movie with a series of stair-stepping bombs headed directly toward the crowd. Machine gun fire from the plane ripped up a nearby control tower and tore through the crowd. Payne said the attack was in retaliation for the loss of an important Japanese pilot. Peery said utter pandemonium took over as everyone ran for cover, jumping over logs and crashing through the makeshift theater. The crowd picked up Payne, all 6 feet, 3 inches of him, and dropped him in the movie projection pit, probably saving his life. Peery ran with the crowd to the protection of nearby dugouts. Both Peery and Payne very clearly remember the incident, but neither of them remembers anything about the movie.

Ted McCullough talked about a very sophisticated gambling operation that kept many men busy.

Some of the fellas set up this super-duper gambling "casino," as we called it. I don't know where they got the wheels and the equipment, but it was set up for gambling on one side, and on the other side there were training manuals and that sort of thing. This was a bunch of black enlisted men who had set up the thing, but even the white officers came down there and gambled. I mean guys were coming in from all the different islands and drinking the Raisin Jack and playing cards all night long. The guys from the regimental headquarters would let us know when an inspection was coming from division. You know, when they can't think of anything else to do, they'll have an inspection. It cost a little money, but the division guy who alerted the regiment guy would get $200.00, and the regimental guy would get $100.00. And it looked like everybody was just sitting around reading training manuals.

McCullough did not gamble; he just "loaned out money and got a little interest on it" from his friends.

Actually, more men in the 93rd Division were busier taking classes than gambling. The army instituted a series of both academic and trade classes available to anyone in the division. Anywhere men could gather in a classroom setting, the army supported instructional training. Bill Payne said men would even "gather in the gun emplacements and have a little class." Nelson Peery claimed that the 93rd established the largest nonuniversity school in the Pacific islands during World War II. He taught Shakespearean literature and other English courses. Howard Hickerson was an expert typist who shared his knowledge with his fellow enlisted men. Bill Payne taught courses on "just about everything, from sex education to writing skills." The "instructors" wrote home to their high schools and received textbooks to assist in teaching. Many men talked about the educational opportunities as a benefit of serving in the 93rd. Most of the instructors like Hickerson, Payne, and Peery took it upon themselves to improve their minds and the minds of their comrades during the endless hours of overseas service.

Other entertainment for the men included the traveling USO shows. Reporting on the first "Flesh Show in the Pacific," Vincent Tubbs produced an entertaining and descriptive column for the Baltimore *Afro-American*.

When the first colored USO attraction in the Pacific reached New Caledonia, so many men sought glimpses of "the women" that a special detail of MPs had to be dispatched to the area to clear the roads. Next day work for Tan Yank troops was almost stopped because 8,000 soldiers either on pass or AWOL from work turned up in the camp to see the show. The hot midday sun beamed down mercilessly on the backs of the audience . . . [when] Julie Gardner crept unobtrusively across the stage with her accordion. They did not greet her appearance with applause. . . . the men were dubious for Julie is more than pleasingly plump; she's heavy. But when she grabbed her squeeze box and began to sing "Hit That Jive, Jack," that locked it up. She is the star of the show. To the boys she's a whole constellation. They had to join in, and whole hillside jumped.

Julie finished her set with "Kow Kow Boogie" and "Don't Cry, Baby" and then gave up the stage to Ann Lewis. Tubbs described Lewis "with flaming red hair swept up into a wavy pompadour atop her head . . . the throaty-voiced blues singer, sauntered Mae Westishly onto the stage." She danced the "boogie" and the "shorty George" and then rallied the crowd with her special version of "St. Louis Blues." She sang:

> Uncle Sam, Uncle Sam, when does my man get his furlough? He's been away a long time, and his baby can't stand this much more. Since you went away, baby, I sure do miss your loving face. But, don't worry daddy, No 4F Joe is gonna take your place.

A DOUBLE-EDGED SWORD

Reporters from all of the major newspapers and magazines followed the men of the 93rd around the South Pacific. *Time* and *Life* magazines both wrote pieces on the fighting black soldier. The language of the reporting relied on racial shortcuts and stereotypes. "There had been gibes when units of the 93rd landed on Bougainville, on the heels of the Americal [white] Division," wrote the *Time* reporter.

> The Americal knew by then what jungle fighting was like. They doubted that the Tan Yanks would stand up under the jungle's strange and silent horrors. It was animal-like warfare on Bougainville. The Negroes did not like it, any more than white men did. . . . The Negro doughboys helped extend outposts. Sometimes their officers had to tongue-lash them into action. But unseasoned white troops had gone through that first paralyzing terror of jungle combat.

In many ways this heightened interest in the combat readiness of the 93rd was a double-edged sword. The actions of black soldiers could be uplifting to the folks at home who were waiting to hear that black soldiers were participating in the war, but it also focused a spotlight of attention on the men in the combat zone. Bill Payne described the situation. He said: "Walter White [NAACP chairman] came down to the South Pacific to meet with MacArthur and find out why we weren't being sent up to the front. My feeling at the time was well, why don't you just get your little tail right on back to the United States and leave us alone." Nelson Peery commented on a common feeling about the press. He said: "The black newspapers, in a minimal way, kept us informed, [but] we infantrymen did not trust them. Before we were through basic training, they set up a howl to commit us to combat." Bill Payne said, "nobody wants to go into war and get killed. And if somebody wants to, well go on ahead." Peery and Payne were disgusted with the constant appeals of the black press and others to commit the men to front-line combat. They felt like they were seeing enough action.

Despite the exhortations of black spokesmen and inspirational articles in the black press, many men in the 93rd Division were not eager to get into any heavier action than they had already seen in the South Pacific. The men were not terribly concerned when they were not assigned to the front line. They wanted to contribute to the war effort, but like nearly every soldier, they wanted to avoid heavy combat. Howard Hickerson confirmed that sentiment.

> We were glad we were not being sent up into the main line of fighting. We wanted to survive. I mean there were places out of the secured perimeter where the enemy was shooting at us. And we got into some firefights out on patrol. That was hot enough for me. None of my friends volunteered or wanted to go up to the front part. We knew we were performing an important job repairing the communications equipment and setting up telephone, teletype, cryptograph, and de-coding units. We were also keeping the supplies moving to the troops ahead. We worked day and night assembling tanks and guns, building warehouses and supply areas. All of this was of utmost importance.

Some of the men of the 93rd resented their assignment as boat loaders or construction crew, but they were adamant that it was the nature of the task and not a desire to be in combat that gave rise to their complaints.

Despite the racialized policies that prevented black soldiers from being fully utilized, the men felt they were contributing a great deal to the war ef-fort in the Pacific. Most of the men felt they experienced enough combat doing the type of patrolling, mopping-up, and perimeter control that the units engaged in until the end of the war. In addition to fighting for their na-tion, and despite the military's policy of segregation, the men felt pride in their unit, and they fought to protect their war buddies. After several years of training and working together as a unit—and now with the added matu-rity gained under fire—the men developed a deep attachment to one an-other. Nelson Peery said the relationships forged in the infantry were in-tense emotional bonds that would remain with the soldiers throughout their lives, a testimony to their ability to love selflessly.

"PRAISE THE LORD AND SWING INTO POSITION"

Spencer Moore said he was "anxious to see action." He thought everybody who was trained for combat, but had never seen any action, was anxious to get into it. But, "once they get in, they wished to hell they'd never seen it."

Moore said when he got into combat he "just followed orders. I wasn't pro or con. I was just in the army doing what they told me." Jehu Hunter said he believed black soldiers were ready to go into combat. "I think when it came time to go overseas, we wanted to go. We had just come from maneuvers and we did well. The men wanted to go." Even though the 93rd was in action in the Pacific, the 92nd was still under evaluation. Military commanders were evaluating and calculating where they could be utilized. As they waited for an assignment, the war in Europe escalated.

In the summer of 1943, Allied forces had been pushing into Italy from the south, starting in Sicily and moving up to the Italian mainland. Destabilized, the Fascist government capitulated, uniting Italy with the Allied rather than the Axis powers. After Hitler's troops captured Rome, Italians declared war against Germany. Throughout the next year, Allied forces blasted through German strongholds, liberating cities on the Mediterranean peninsula. In June 1944 as Allied forces began the Operation Overlord D-Day invasion of France, the American Fifth Army entered Rome. In Normandy, Allied forces were throwing everything at the Germans—everything except black infantry soldiers. The 92nd Infantry Division was still stateside waiting for a combat assignment.

Although no black infantry soldiers were used in the D-Day invasion, some black service and support soldiers participated in the campaign. Their contributions are generally overlooked—they are not in the photos, movies, or history books. Lawrence Johnson described life in a transportation unit that got sent into action. "When they trained us, they said that the ordnance was a rear-echelon unit, and we wouldn't have to go into combat," Johnson recalled.

> But it wasn't like that in the war. They used us for contact and patrol. Our vehicles had to get to the recon units. Recon would go out look- ing for the enemy, maybe even draw fire. We had to get the vehicles to them. We would go through the towns pretty much by ourselves. We were very well armed, but we were on our own. A lot of those Ger- mans took shots at us.

Fred Hurns was in a medical unit, but like Johnson, he was also fired upon and taken into active combat zones.

> The Germans would just point those V-bombs, and they wouldn't know what they were going to hit. We weren't combat, we were all adminis- trative troops, but they would just point it out there and shoot. Those things could go 200 miles with a sound that was just unbelievable. One

dropped right out in the street by the hospital warehouse I worked in and just blew everything up out there.

Fred Watt was in a engineering unit that saw action in Europe. His unit was not in the first or second wave of troops to land on the beaches of Normandy, but he said it was "still pretty hot" when they waded out of the water and started laying down steel matting for use as temporary roads. Watt recalled being in England before D-Day and seeing an amphibious engineering outfit that would go out every day for about a month and work "across the channel." He said: "One morning they did not come back. But still we didn't realize what was going on." Then Watt's unit was instructed to get ready to move out, so they began loading all the trucks and other equipment and soon departed across the channel toward France. "I landed in the Omaha Beach area, and there we could see what was happening. All that we could see was ships and land barges. We had loaded rifles, and we started crossing. We had to go through barbed wired to get to the area where we had to lay down the roads for the tanks and trucks to use."

Cleother Hathcock also served in a support group in Great Britain and was alerted to prepare for the invasion. His fumigation and bath detachment unit got word just prior to D-Day to get ready to "cross the channel," but a strange confluence of events prevented their departure. "Our major made a mistake one day and said that he didn't like 'niggers,'" recalled Hathcock. "One of our lieutenants said to him, 'You've got no business going to France with us then.' The lieutenant called the adjutant general, and they sent out an investigating team." Two weeks later the major was moved to another unit, and Hathcock's group shipped out. It may be one of the few occasions when discrimination worked to the soldiers' advantage. The men missed most of the killing fire of the invasion.

Lawrence Johnson was not as fortunate. He was in the D-Day invasion in a trucking support unit.

> We crossed the Channel about four days after D-Day. When we were in Glasgow, Scotland, they drilled us on waterproofing our vehicles. We had no idea what it was about. We never even thought about going through the water or anything. But we found out when we crossed the Channel why they needed the vehicles treated. The water, this was in June, the water was real cold, and it was real rough. As rough as the Atlantic Ocean is, this was rougher still. It was 3 o'clock in the afternoon when we got on the other side. We were on this barge, and the bow of this thing opened up and the gang plank went down, and we had to drive our vehicles off that ship.

We had to go through the water, at least 500 yards, and then come up on the shore at Omaha Beach. The beach was littered with all kind of debris from the war. Ships, wreckage, weapons, bodies, everything. You could smell it, it smelled like stockyards when we got there. When we got on the beach we were told to drive up to this hill. We stayed up there about a month, maybe longer. The Nazis were throwing everything at us, and we had to be on alert in case we had to evacuate France and make it back to Great Britain. Then the Allies started bombing the Germans out of their positions. For three days, you could look up in the skies and just see waves and waves of planes in formation. You could see them bombing. That cleared out the Germans, and we moved on again.

In their retreat, Germans soldiers moved into mountainous regions in northern Italy and continued their campaign of terror from strategic high points. In August 1944, the first combat team of Buffalo Soldiers arrived in Italy after a brief stop in Casablanca. They were immediately dispatched to join the First Armored Division, where they began the fall campaign to pierce the Gothic Line. The last of the Buffalo Soldiers arrived in Italy in November 1944, and then all of the men were added to the forces of the American Fifth Army. They joined the Allied push from the coastal areas of the Ligurian Sea, through the valleys and plains, to the Apennines, fighting all the way to rout the Nazis and their Italian sympathizers.

There was speculation that the Buffalo Soldiers were sent into Italy, rather than to England to take part in the D-Day invasion of France, because Italy was a less important area in terms of military strategy. Bill Perry expressed the feeling of many men: "Italy wasn't a glorious moment for anybody really. Everything was in France." Despite its less-important status in terms of military strategy, there was nothing low profile about the fighting there. Black soldiers engaged in pitched battles to clear out firmly entrenched Nazi strongholds. Even if it was not the "glorious" campaign of other locales in Europe, at least most of the men felt confident with their own abilities. They even noted how their campaign utilized new military strategies. Perry commented: "The Fifth Army was coming up from the south [of Italy] to take the north, and that was the first time it had ever been done. Even when Hannibal came through with his elephants he came from the north." The men felt they excelled at the job they were assigned. The Italian campaign, following on the heels of Operation Overlord, caught the Germans in the middle of a strong Allied force pushing from the north and south. The enemy retreated toward Germany—routed from the shores of France and Italy.

When the first group of Buffalo Soldiers arrived at the dock in Naples, the men were cheered on by hundreds of black service-unit soldiers who were in the area waiting to greet them. Ulysses Lee of the army's Historical Division related the story of their arrival.

> Rumors of the arrival of the Buffalo Soldiers had preceded them. . . . As the thousands of black fighting men, in single file, debarked from the crowded troopships, they presented an impressive and awe-inspiring spectacle. Armed with basic weapons and full field battle dress, proudly wearing the circular shoulder patch with the black buffalo, they moved smartly and efficiently into their unit formations. As they marched away, every man in step, every weapon in place, chins up and eyes forward, a low rumbling babble of sound came from the troops on the dock, then swelled to a crescendo of thunderous cheering which continued until the last Buffalo unit had disappeared from sight.

Allen Green remembers the trip to Italy in the most poetic terms. His unit left the "pastel yellows of Casablanca" and came across the Mediterranean into Italy. "It was like crossing a sea of glass," Green remembers. "I mean there was not a ripple. The Bay of Naples was stunning. Just outside of Naples was all olive groves, and that was beautiful, too." Robert Madison remembers celebrating his twenty-first birthday onboard the ship. "And when we landed in Naples we bivouacked out in the King's hunting grounds!" Most men recalled the name of the troop ship they traveled on, and whether or not they were pursued by German U-boats.

Dennett Harrod vividly recalled how his troop ship made a 180-degree turn in the Atlantic and started heading back toward the United States. "We knew we were being tracked by submarines," he said. Allen Thompson remembered dodging submarines and that his ship included a detachment of Puerto Rican soldiers. Bill Perry remembered crossing the Atlantic Ocean in a converted cruise ship, *Mariposa*, a top-of-the-line Matson ship. "We didn't have an escort because they told us that ship could outrun anything," recalled Perry. "You could look out the window and zoom! It was moving." When Perry and Spencer Moore landed in the harbor they saw "nothing but ships, ships, ships—sunken ships." They got off the *Mariposa* by walking across a ramp that was built from one sunken ship to the next.

Many of the Buffalo Soldiers were not sure whether or not they would be assigned to combat missions. Robert Madison described the paradox. He was with the 370th Combat Team, the first group of Buffalo Soldiers to be sent into action. They were heading north of Pisa along the banks of the Arno River, pushing toward the German strongholds in the mountains. "When

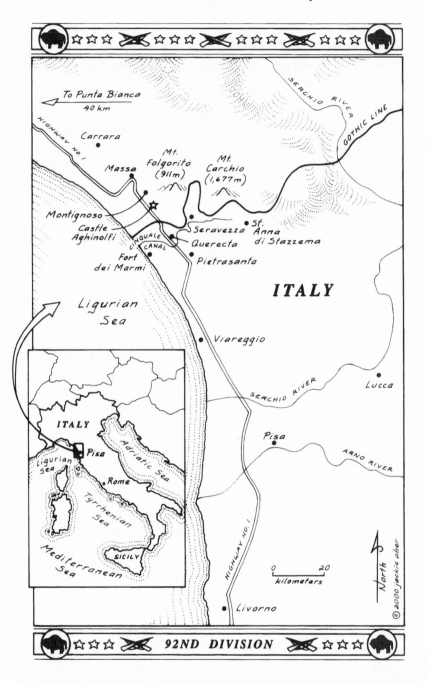

they started issuing us ammunition that's when it really hit us—we're going to work. We thought maybe they would parcel us out to do dock work or perimeter control. We were going to the front." Journalist Ollie Harrington captured the horror of a day in combat with the 92nd Division. He filed his report from "a grape arbor, somewhere in Italy."

> Three men and I went out to bring back a wounded comrade. Protected by a single mortar and tommie-gun fire, the patrol was able to inch its way between a clump of buildings. It was difficult to locate the exact hiding place of the Nazi gun. We finally found protection beneath a grape arbor, which also served as camouflage for the patrol. The Germans are holding all the surrounding hills in the Battle of the Gothic Line. We listened to the screaming steel from .88s; the men were subjected to the most terrible .88 gunfire. One can hear the shell for a split second. One must dive into the nearest depression. It is murderous fire, evil bits of screaming steel. Each man has his own front line, and he who shoots first moves on to shoot again.

Black soldiers in Italy recalled numerous attacks and casualties and many acts of bravery. Dennet Harrod remembered a particularly gruesome assignment with the 366th Infantry at the end of 1944. They received their mission assignment directly from General Almond, who told them: "You're to wade through the ocean about 400 yards, come inland, kick everything you see and take names as you come in. And bring me a prisoner." Harrod said they encountered German troops and they "got into a few firefights." Harrod's outfit sustained light casualties—fifteen men were captured. The black soldiers killed thirty Germans and brought back one prisoner. "Almond said, 'bring us one,' and that's what we did." The men were featured in the military paper, *Stars and Stripes*, but the best accolade came from men in surrounding units, who sent over all their whiskey rations to Harrod and the other soldiers who had been on the patrol.

Sometimes black soldiers engaged the enemy while out on patrols; other men were under fire in their daily operations. Robert Madison described one such daily encounter. Normally Madison rode in the passenger side of a jeep, but this one day he gave his driver a rest. "I said, 'you just stay there and rest,' and that saved my life," Madison recalled. As he was driving up a mountain road, the Germans shelled his position with ".88 shells." Madison was blown out of the jeep and onto the ground. The passenger side of the jeep was completely destroyed, and the entire vehicle was precariously perched on the edge of the mountain road. Had he been in the passenger seat, Madison's life would have been over.

In addition to seeking shelter in the grape arbors or shielding their movements in the waterways, soldiers were able to take advantage of other aspects of the Italian landscape. Much of the countryside had been terraced
for agricultural production, which provided the men with depressions they
used as protective defilades. Masonry structures predominated in the small
country villages the men passed through, and, as Bill Perry commented,
"some of those buildings were a thousand years old." He recalled running
from a field and diving head first into a masonry shack when he was under
fire from a German machine gun. He and another soldier waited there in the
building until after dark and then rejoined their company. Charles Hanson's
experience with the aging masonry structures landed him in the hospital.
Hanson said he was sent to observe the artillery of the enemy fire around an
Italian villa. When Hanson found the villa and entered it, he noticed that the
marble steps on the third floor had been blown away, and only the iron supports were visible. As he ascended the steps, one of the supports gave way,
and he fell two stories to the ground. He "cracked up everything" and was
sent to the hospital. But he was soon "fixed-up" and sent back to the front.

Spencer Moore recalled that soldiers used the haystacks in the fields to
keep cool from the sun. The Italians sometimes used the haystacks for other
purposes.

Soldiers of Company D, 365th Infantry, 92nd Division,
in Italy, May 1945. (Photo by Spencer Moore)

Some of them would hide stuff in the haystacks. Like one time there was a car hidden in there. I'm serious. When the Germans shelled us and hit that haystack it just exploded, and the men around it were injured.

Perry described the landscape as easily defensible because of the natural protective barriers of hills, valleys, and mountains. "You can run from one natural barrier to another one and defend it," he said. Cullen McKissock noted how efficiently the Germans utilized the terrain. "At this one area, the Germans had a huge cannon on a railroad car, and they would run it back and forth into this mountain. We couldn't knock it out. Consequently, anyone who came up from the flats would just get wiped out."

The push north in 1944 placed the Buffalo Soldiers in the mountains in the middle of winter. Many men commented that the terrain around the Apennines reminded them of Fort Huachuca, and they were pleased to have had training in a mountain environment. However, they encountered problems never experienced in their stateside training. German shelling, freezing conditions, and too few rations plagued the men. Bill Perry explained: "They sent us up in the mountains, and what happened is we outran the supply train. They could only reach us by mules. For many days we were too far ahead of everything, just outrunning the supplies." At one point, Perry got separated from his unit, but he caught up with them as they started climbing into the mountains.

The company was strung out for a ways. . . . We walked past this one area and we heard, "Comraden, Comraden." And all of a sudden everybody began to roll to the ground and chamber a round. We had walked past a German machine gun nest that these Czechoslovakians were manning. These were troops that the Germans would just chain to the equipment and tell them to fire. We unchained the guys and took them back to interrogate them.

Spencer Moore expressed the feelings of many of the men in a letter to his parents on November 20th, 1944.

Dear Mom and Pop:

The Jerry artillery and firing keeps you very jumpy and you are not so at ease of mind. Five officers (Colored) have been killed in action so far. Two were my classmates at OCS. Has the 92nd published any casualty lists in the colored papers? We are all getting a raw deal. We have been on the line 82 days and we don't know when we are going to get relieved. We thought the election would change it but it hasn't. The men are lousy, sick, frostbitten, shell-shocked and scared. It's good

Jerry doesn't know the condition of some of us or we would be in a lot hotter water. I wish some of the colored papers could get a hold of this and ask the War Department when we were going to get relieved. It looks as if they want to annihilate the all colored 92nd. The all means all colored on the line and a few on the staffs. I don't know what the papers are saying but it's really tough. A couple of the colored officers have been or are up for courts-martial because they refuse to lead troops into death traps. I just wish some of us here could get back and tell what we know. I guess they are all afraid if some of us get turned loose there will be too many "mulattos" in the world. I am really disgusted with the whole setup. It looks as if they don't even expect to give us a break. We can look right out of the hole and see Jerry parading around on the skyline and it takes half of the day to get artillery on it, because we have to conserve ammunition and yet Jerry shells hell out of us. It's no joke to see men you have known, lived with, eaten with, and slept with blown up or shot down before your eyes. The majority of the men are too tired to fight. Well, Mom, I've blown off enough steam for now. The NAACP should know this situation. Jerry is beginning to shell again so I'll sign off for now.

Your loving son, Spencer

Moore's wartime letters to his parents reveal his anxieties about the war against "Jerry," the election and subsequent death of Roosevelt, and conditions for black soldiers. They also include a description of the hardscrabble existence of many Italians. As he traversed the landscape, he wrote his impressions to his parents. He wished they could see the beauty of the sun reflected on the snow-capped Italian mountains. He witnessed four distinct seasons, all recorded in letters to his parents and wife. At the beginning of November, Moore wrote to his parents about the mild temperature in his new Italian surroundings. He thought the weather was colder in his home state of New Jersey than in the northern provinces of Italy. By the middle of November he had changed his tune. "The weather here is very cold and damp," he wrote. "At present we can't see very far because of the fog and drizzling rain. You have to keep alert for Jerry in this kind of weather." He asked for mittens—leather on the outside, wool on the inside.

Moore recalled what he saw and felt as the men pushed northward into the heavily fortified German-occupied territory.

We weren't really prepared for winter. We had winter equipment, but it wasn't like later in the Korean War where they had parkas and that kind of thing. In Italy we had high-top shoes and leather leggings.

Sometimes you could get boots, like with a rubber bottom and a leather top. But you had to fill in the soles of both of those shoes just to try to keep your feet warm. You always kept a second pair of socks inside your shirt keeping warm, and then, when you got to a foxhole, you would switch socks.

In December, when he was hospitalized for frostbite, he wrote that "the mud and water really hampers the progress of the war." By the spring Moore was able to appreciate the landscape again. "The flowers are beginning to bloom and if it weren't for the war this would be a beautiful country." At one point he was watching the unfolding of the season from a "dug-out way up in the mountains." He observed: "You can look out from the dug-outs and see for miles around." He noted the twinkle of lights from the houses in the "quaint little villages."

Just before Moore shipped out to Italy, his wife, Susie, told him she was pregnant. It was their first child. Naturally Moore was anxious to get all the news from home.

Dear Mom and Pop:

I haven't received any mail from you all in quite some time. How is everyone? Have you heard from Sue lately? I haven't heard from her for about three weeks now and my morale is slowly decreasing. What is the latest news at home? I haven't much to say because everything I know I am not allowed to write. Write soon.

Love, Spencer

He moved around so much that the mail was sometimes slow getting to him. For the twenty-eight days he was hospitalized with a gunshot wound and frostbite, he received his mail a little more regularly.

I am now in the hospital. Don't get excited I was wounded slightly in the heel and I am doing fine. Now don't you all get excited because you know if it was serious I would tell you. I have been awarded the Purple Heart. It is really a beautiful medal. I am going to send it home as soon as I can. I can walk fairly well but not very fast. My heel is quite sore but I am getting very good treatment.

Moore's letters reflect the general anxieties of the combat soldier. He was homesick, a common sentiment among American GIs. "Mom, it really makes you feel swell to know the folks back home are thinking of you," wrote Moore, after he received a package containing presents from home. In May

1945 at least one of Moore's worries ended when his baby boy, Roscoe, was
born in perfect health.

Because soldiers suffered from a host of injuries and illnesses brought on
by combat, unsanitary living conditions, and environmental factors, most of
the men had some experience with the aid stations. Several soldiers, like
Moore and Charles Hanson, were hospitalized—many of them repeatedly.
The second time Hanson was sent to the hospital, he had company.

> My brother had gone into the army and was also in Italy. He had fool-
> ishly asked to be put in my company. I didn't want to have our whole
> family blown up in one action, but there he was when we were in Italy.
> One night we spent the night in this stone house, and we were at-
> tacked. I got shot in the arm, my brother was shot, and the captain was
> injured. We all went to the hospital, and I recovered fine. My brother
> had some shrapnel that had gotten deep in his arm, so they kept him
> in the hospital.
>
> That night we were both in the hospital, and when we were laying
> in the beds we started going on about "Your momma this and your
> momma that." Playing the dozens. Actually, I started it. I said to him,
> "I got a letter from your momma," and of course everybody knew that
> was the way you started the dozens. The other men were ready to run
> out of the room, because they thought we'd start getting into a row, but
> then they realized his mother was my mother and we were just having
> fun. The next day I was sent to the rehabilitation center. They kept him
> to get the shrapnel out. But when they put him to sleep for the oper-
> ation, he never woke up again.

Many of the men related stories about looking for family members at the
different places they were posted. Brothers often served in the same units or
at least in the same theater of war. Sometimes their sisters served in nursing
or WAC units stationed nearby. Few brothers were in the same unit and in
the same battle, and even fewer of them died in the same combat scenario.
However, being in the minority was certainly no consolation for Charles
Hanson when he lost his brother. Back at home, many families were proud
to display a blue star—one for each member of the family serving overseas.
Bill Perry's family had three blue stars on display in their living room.
Spencer Moore had one brother and one sister who were serving overseas at
the same time he was there. They were all lieutenants at one time, an ac-
complishment that made their parents proud. Madine Davis Lane had a
brother in the service. When Clyde Whitted found his brother, he was
greeted by a sibling who outranked him. At first Clyde saluted his brother,

but then they just hugged. Captain William Banks encountered the reverse scenario when he met up with his brother, an enlisted man.

AMORE IN THE LAND OF MICHELANGELO

The Buffalo Soldiers passed through much of the Italian landscape, including some of the traditional tourist locations such as Rome and Florence. They engaged in battles, but in the lulls between the fighting, they took time to enjoy the scenery and the local culture. For instance, some of the men commented about the difficulty of passing through the mountainous, stony terrain around Pietrasanta while also noting that it was the area where Michelangelo first extracted the marble for his famous sculptures. Spencer Moore wrote home to his parents: "I am near a former marble foundry and there are plenty of men who do beautiful work. I even had a souvenir made." The Buffalo Soldiers took their scheduled leaves and rested and relaxed among the Italians. They attended operas, visited magnificent chapels, and generally immersed themselves in Italian culture. Many of the men went on R&R—rest and relaxation—jaunts to Rome and stayed in Mussolini's elaborate summer home. They toured the Vatican and the Sistine Chapel, viewed the art in the Uffizzi Museum, and took advantage of outdoor concerts.

During the year that the 92nd worked its way through Italy, many positive relationships were forged between the Italian people and the Buffalo Soldiers. Some Italians acted as interpreters and guides for the men. Many Italian children assisted the soldiers by doing odd jobs. And of course, many women engaged in numerous types of relationships with the "Yankee soldiers." Each relationship was first predicated on determining the sympathies of the Italians. Because the Italians had been on both the Axis and Allied sides of the war, it was difficult for the Buffalo Soldiers to ascertain which Italians were Nazi sympathizers. Although a partisan movement of freedom fighters emerged after the demise of Mussolini's fascist government, Italians on an individual basis still had to "prove" their loyalties to the Buffalo Soldiers. Spencer Moore described the Italians as "wishy washy."

> I remember going into a village and running the Germans out. The Italians would start ringing the bell, and the priest would come out. They didn't know whether to give you this salute or that salute. You know, the "Heil, Hitler!" or the GI-Joe salute.

The Italian government under Mussolini had invaded areas in Africa and buttressed its imperialist aims with notions of racial superiority. Although the alliance between Fascist Italy and Nazi Germany was not explicitly based on racial notions, the pre–World War II Italian campaign to overtake some African nations left many black Americans with an uneasy feeling about Italian sentiments. Added to that unease was the fact that Germans were known to dress as Italian partisans in order to infiltrate Allied lines of defense. The Buffalo Soldiers were naturally distrustful.

Amazingly, both groups came to live side-by-side, relying on one another and, in fact, enjoying each other's company during the Italian campaign. Once Italians and Buffalo Soldiers became acquainted, both groups rejected the notions of "otherness" and the hierarchy of racial categories that marked one as superior and the other as inferior. Spencer Moore described an interaction that illustrates the complexity of the relationships. Moore was assigned to a pack-mule detail, supervising fifty-five Italian workers. A black man supervising the work of white men, even way up in the Italian mountains where no one would notice, worked to break the entrenched barriers of segregation and hierarchical racial thinking.

> I was hanging out with this British guy, and a Scotch man, you know in a kilt and everything. We were hanging in this bar having a good time. Some Americans came in and said something nasty to me, and a couple of those Italian guys I supervised in the mountains stood up and told the Americans where to get off.

Two other personal recollections of positive interactions between Italian civilians and Buffalo Soldiers are instructive. The relationship between the two groups was especially critical as the soldiers pushed north toward the Italian mountains. Dennett Harrod said he distrusted most Italians, but he changed his mind after one man showed him where the Germans had placed land mines. Harrod avoided the "castrator-type" antipersonnel mines because of the assistance of his Italian comrade. "He taught me more in five minutes," Harrod said, "than I had learned in two years of training." Edward Price called his six-year-old Italian comrade, Marino, a "guardian angel." Price noted how Marino had a sixth sense about where German artillery was going to land.

> This kid would hear the German .88s come over and just by the sound he could tell you where they were going to hit. One day they began to pour over this mountainous area around Pietrasanta, and Marino came and got me. He said, "Here," and he moved me out to another area. Well, where I had been standing was where that thing landed. From that day on that kid never had to worry about a thing. I got him food, candy, clothes. Everything.

Italians who found their way into the American encampments and worked in some capacity were able to slightly improve their own living conditions. Spencer Moore wrote to his parents about the poverty and hunger of the Italians. "The Germans really stripped this country of everything. Few houses have running water and the women carry all the buckets of water. I really feel sorry for some of the people here who don't have sufficient food and no way of earning it, except maybe working for Uncle Sam." Italy was a war-torn country plagued by twenty years of Fascist rule and the recent Nazi occupation. Bill Perry recalled: "One time down in Naples, this guy got in the garbage can of one of the army places and was eating something. Another guy was trying to get him out of there, and there was a bunch of fighting. People were that hungry!" Many Italians learned how to rig up a wire and a tin can and use it to scoop food out of the army garbage cans. What they also learned is that the Buffalo Soldiers would give a hungry man "a little more than leftovers" scraped right from the plate into his tin. "The white troops weren't that humane," Perry said. "They just threw it in the garbage can." Spencer Moore told the men in his unit to "give them what you don't want, give it to the people."

Many soldiers extended their humanitarianism by "adopting" Italian children and their families. Moore described one situation.

> The woman who owned the building [where they rested] had a little daughter, Anna Maria, four or five years old. We Americans sat her down with us and fed her. We'd take a lot of others in, too. Like a kid, a teenager, who would know the area, we'd adopt him. Give him boots and a shirt and feed him.

Albert Burke concurred, relating another story.

> I had this young Italian kid, twelve or thirteen years old, working for me in my company. I had him dressed in a uniform with medals pinned on him. One of the officers asked me if I knew that was illegal, and I told him that this boy had worked just as hard as any American soldier had. I believe he was honored to wear that uniform. That kid ran to help me, even getting the medics when I got hit with shrapnel.

It seems the men felt especially responsible for young children. Burg Turner elaborated: "I would go into town and take candy and gifts for the children. They called me 'Tony' instead of Turner, and they always called out 'Tony's coming!' when they saw me. I loved them." The families of the children welcomed the relationships and even "adopted" a few of the Buffalo Soldiers. Edward Price recalled a special relationship.

I knew this one family well. I would leave the area and not come back for two or three weeks. When I knocked on the door and said who I was, they would just jump out of their beds and let me have the whole place. The brothers loaned me their civilian clothes, nice things, because I had been in my uniform for so long.

In addition to these wholesome, family-style activities, some of the men also engaged in amorous relationships with local women. There was of course the usual prostitution that goes along with any army encampment. Jim Williams described the culture of prostitution surrounding the Buffalo Soldiers.

The army did not condone prostitution, it was just they wanted the men to be protected. But don't get the idea that prostitution was rampant in Italy. It wasn't. They are devout Catholics. For a woman to talk to you in the streets was risky. But, like any other area where soldiers are stationed, there's some prostitution. One of my duties was to mind the pro[phylactic] station, make sure we had ample supplies.

Many of the men dated local women, and many of them fell in love. Edgar Whitley was so inspired by an Italian romance that he wrote a play called *Time Is the Enemy of Love*. In it, an Italian woman falls in love with a Yankee soldier, but when he returns after the war to marry her, alas, she is married to another. Some soldiers were skeptical about the love Italian women professed for them. Allen Green said that some of the women "would do almost anything to get to America, including marry a soldier—including marrying a black soldier." Marriages did happen between Italian women and men of the 92nd Infantry. Spencer Moore, reporting on the situation in a letter to his parents, wrote in somewhat coded language:

The "spooks" over here are raising plenty of sand and really trying to make a democracy of this world. They stay with Italians, have Italian girlfriends and take them to movies and so forth. Some are even marrying them. Of course, that's the rear echelon soldiers. The ones on the line don't have the time or the opportunity for that.

RACIST PROPAGANDA

Initially, Italians also felt uneasy with the Buffalo Soldiers. Wherever the black soldiers traveled, racist propaganda preceded them. In one case, propaganda from a surprising source appealed to Italians to refrain from any contact with black Americans. Written in Italian and posted on bill-boards throughout Naples, the racist poster threatened Italian women with violent reprisals if they engaged in any type of association with black soldiers. Translated into English, the placards read:

> Do you not know that the Negro is a man of the colored races; that he must live in America only among his own; that he is an inferior human being, if not in name, at least in fact? The machine gun will cut down the prostitute who sells the honor of her race, and the people will seek revenge upon her and her black son when this crime has been brought to light.

This appeal was so blatantly racist that even some white Americans were shocked by the tone of the placards. The chief of staff of the Mediterranean theater of operations, General David Barr, ordered an investigation. The findings appalled everyone. The investigation revealed that no Italian was responsible for the posters; indeed, three white American soldiers were re-sponsible for printing, financing, and distributing them. All three were con-victed by court-martial.

Germany waged a propaganda war with black soldiers as well. Edward Price remembers an incident when they got some news about a "race riot in the States." He said the Germans took advantage of that strife by "shower-ing us with pamphlets saying we had nothing to fight for." Spencer Moore still has one of the pamphlets the Germans dropped to the Buffalo Soldiers. It reads:

> To all members of the colored Division: After they got you into the army they shipped you off to a foreign country to fight in a rich man's war. As for you fellows, you have nothing to gain but you may lose your lives or get your limbs smashed up. Don't wait for that. Better say goodbye to war. Slip over to Jerry's some night, as many other colored boys have done before you. They are now safe in a POW camp waiting for the end of the war.

Another postcard from "your loving wife, Hazel," enjoins the men to "stay alive for your folks and don't die for empty promises." Moore said some guys "used those leaflets as toilet paper."

The U.S. government also engaged in a war of racial propaganda. They exported segregation to all the locations where the black American soldiers were located. This was especially true in Italy. The officers clubs were off limits to all officers of the 92nd—black and white. However, a white officer had only to remove the buffalo patch from his shoulder to enter the club. A black officer had to remove more than his patch. One particularly revealing photograph that Spencer Moore sent home to his parents illustrates the extent to which the commanders were willing to go to segregate the black troops. Two units of white nurses and WACs were stationed in an area close to where the Buffalo Soldiers were bivouacked. One commander got it in his head to prevent the men from visiting the boulevard where the women were living. He posted a large sign which read: THIS STREET OFF LIMITS TO 92ND DIV TROOPS. Moore says the sign was not up for that long, "just long enough to be photographed and start a little controversy."

TOO MANY TACTICAL ERRORS

In the many pitched battles at the Italian front, the most common sentiment among the men was dissatisfaction with the leadership. Joe Stephenson and Jehu Hunter both said they believed that General Almond and his upper tier of commanders made too many tactical errors in the Italian campaign. Stephenson described the command failures.

Off Limits to Black Soldiers in Italy. This sign was taken down shortly after it was posted. (Photo by Spencer Moore)

They just ran the 370th up and down the hills over there, and then they ran them through the plains over here. The Germans on the hill could shoot down on the plains. Almond didn't have sense enough to realize you've got to take the hills first and the plains second. Really, a lot of our men were really just shell-shocked, discouraged, angry, because they had been so mistreated tactically.

Hunter continued the commentary:

The men were just scared to death. They didn't want to fight anymore. That was a direct reflection of Almond's poor tactics. He would send people up night after night, no relief. Maybe you'd go into another sector, but every night you were getting shot at. After a couple of times it makes you wonder why they couldn't find another route.

Maybe they did try to find different routes, but as Joseph Hairston noted, "some of those guys couldn't even read a map." Hairston described one incident in which a commander heading in the opposite direction questioned him as to why Hairston was heading the wrong way. Hairston took out the map and showed the man where they were supposed to go—the direction in which Hairston was heading. The commander disagreed and continued to head down the road in the opposite direction. "He drove right along that other way and got shot at. When he came running back our direction his driver gave me a big high-five and a wink."

Some of the white commanders listened to and respected their black officers. William Banks described this occasional phenomenon.

In one combat action, or rather seize-and-hold position situation, the battalion commander and I were in constant communication. He asked me where I was and what I was doing. He wanted me to describe the situation and assess what we should do with both flanks. So I told him we had gone on quite a bit in front, and he asked should we turn around; and I said, "No, I don't think so." He said for me to stay where I was and hold. At least that man believed in my ability to make the right decision.

In fact, he believed in Banks so much that he recommended him for the Silver Star medal—a high commendation for bravery in action. At the time, few commanders recommended black officers or enlisted men for commendations. Banks's medal was one of only 102 Silver Stars awarded to Buffalo Soldiers for gallantry and valor during the war.

However, most of the white commanders kept their own council and sent their men into poorly planned operations. Tactical errors and general mismanagement affected the combat performance of the black troops. Many of the men who served in Italy described the Cinquale Canal debacle in February 1945 as a complete tactical failure caused by poor leadership. Dennett Harrod said:

> We got clobbered. You can imagine if twenty-three of the twenty-five tanks were disabled, you can imagine what they did to us. They were using those long-range coast defense guns and shooting .88s at us. Our guys were firing from the water with artillery fire, but it just lit up the area where we were. In other words, "Hello, Herman. Here we come." It was just stupid. We were under siege. I said to the executive officer, "Captain, you don't belong out here."
>
> And he told me, "I've got to," and that's when we both got hit. I got jerked around from the impact, and I saw the captain lifted up off the ground and slammed down, like he'd just been thrown to the ground. I knew he was dead. I didn't know what I'd got, but I found out some shrapnel passed through my helmet, and I got some in my hand and in my legs. I thought there was no point in calling a medic, I better just take myself to the aid station. I didn't know where it was, but I started dragging myself back through the canal.
>
> I ran into the major at the base of the canal, and he was all busted up with a femoral artery-type injury. I helped cut the rain suit off of him, but I told him my hand was all messed up and I couldn't do more. I would send the medics when I found them. There was this kid who was holding his stomach in his hands, and he started following me, saying he was going wherever I was going. We both got across the canal, and there was a jeep to take us to the station. We made it, but the major did not. And not the captain either.

Robert Madison experienced what he considered poor troop management, or outright command failure. He was assigned to lead some men across the Arno River at night. He wanted covering artillery fire to precede his advance, hopefully clearing out the enemy. Madison went to battalion headquarters and asked about the timing of the artillery fire. The major told him there would be none that night. When Madison asked who had given that order, the major said he received it directly from the general. Madison said, "Then get him on the phone right now." Madison admits he was a brash young man, and he recognizes that his demand set him up for future problems with the major. The men were sent out to cross the river without any protective artillery bombardment. Madison remembers:

> So I went down to the bank of the river. We were ready to go across and nobody, this is a true story, nobody was following across. Only the chaplain and I went out there wading across the river. We finally got over to the other side and looked around a bit, stayed there for a few minutes, maybe ten minutes. Then we came back. Nothing happened. And I reported back to the battalion commander that it's all clear. The next morning I was demoted because I had the audacity to ask for the general. The fellow who came in to take my place, a white officer, was absolutely incompetent. He was sent from a white regiment because he was incompetent over there. And they sent him in to take my place.

Dennett Harrod noted a change in the tolerance among the black troops. He said: "A whole lot of us were not as subservient as they thought blacks should be." Spencer Moore told a story confirming that sentiment.

> Our acting CO said, "Get some rest because you're going out again tonight." I told him I wasn't going out tonight. He said, "What did you say?"
>
> And I said, "I ain't going out tonight. I ain't going no GD place at night." I said, "You've got me doing all the patrolling. Why don't you send some of your buddies out? Some of your first lieutenant [white] buddies?" So he reported me to the battalion commander, and I got called in.
>
> I said, "Well, Major, look at the S2 Intelligence Reports. Who's been doing all the night patrolling? Me, me, me. That man's trying to get me killed out there."

Moore also remembered an incident where several of his men lost all sense of military discipline. They "drank the dregs out of some kegs and let loose." One soldier wore a derby hat and sported an umbrella. Another man wore a high-top hat that he had "lifted off" some Italian. Moore said: "They were all drunk up and everything. They were walking up and down the river-bank, shaking their fists at the Germans on the other side, shouting, 'Shoot you motherfuckers, shoot.' I had to go out there and get them."

Most crazy stunts like these fortunately did not result in death or dis-memberment, but a few "fragging" stories illustrate the tense situations and hostile tempers of the abused infantryman. Jim Williams described a situa-tion with one much-hated captain.

He was very cruel. Say on a hot sunny day, we would be laying under the vehicles trying to find the shade or something. You would see his company going through calisthenics with rifles. He was real mean, always putting them on extra duty. Well, when we all moved out from the staging area to the bivouac area we learned that he had been shot, killed in his tent and someone threw the rifle in on top of him.

This kind of direct hit was most uncommon the men reported. Most of the insubordination happened in another manner. Joe Stephenson described a sporting incident.

We were on this kind of reserve line, and we had an observation post on a hill that overlooked the front. I got an instruction to take the colonel up to the observation post, so I said, "Yes, sir," and I started out with the colonel. About halfway up the hill, I got down on the ground and started crawling. I looked around, and there was the colonel crawling on the ground just like me. We crawled all the way up and crawled right into a bunker. We looked out, and I pointed different things out to him. Then we came out of the bunker, and I just stood up and walked all the way down the hill. Ha! He looked at me real hard, like why were we crawling up there, but he didn't say anything.

Bill Perry summed up the command failures. He said, "Italy was a bad moment for everybody. But it was more of a bad moment for us than it was for [General] Almond because we were there. He was just sitting back looking at maps." Perry criticized the way that the units were constantly moved from one region to another. The theory of using a regiment in warfare relies on using two forward-thrusting battalions and one in the rear maneuvering left or right. Perry said they never fought under that kind of theory. The battalions were spread all over the Italian countryside, fighting at distances that allowed enemy troops to outflank and expose them. "We might be on the coast for two or three weeks, and then they would tell us to pack up and move to the mountains. They kept shifting us around constantly." Perry also complained about the lack of information available to the infantry soldier.

They never told you nothing. All you ever heard were rumors. The first thing when you wake up in the morning and the last thing at night, there's a rumor. Some kind of rumor about something. That's all you ever got, rumors.

Lack of solid information was distressing to the men, but worse was the lack of infantry replacement units. The commanders of the black divisions did not adequately plan for casualties. Because the troops were serving in segregated, black-only units, the replacements could only be black. This posed a problem when both the 93rd and the 92nd starting taking casualties, because a back-up pool of replacements was virtually nonexistent. Perry said the Japanese American outfit, the 442nd Regiment, which at one time was attached to the 92nd Division, had a larger replacement pool than *all* of the other regiments in the 92nd. Segregation policies prevented Japanese American men of the 442nd from replacing black American men of the 92nd.

Still, some replacements were trained, albeit in a hasty fashion, and sent to Italy to relieve the war-ravaged Buffalo Soldiers. Edgar Whitley was one of these. Pulled out of high school in Cleveland and taught to shoot a rifle, he had less than six months of training before being sent to the Italian front. He says he was naïve at the time—more than green, he was a "baby-in-arms." He remembers meeting his first black officer on the night he finally reached his unit.

We were up in these mountains in a castle, and I was introduced to this black sergeant. He said he was from Cleveland, too. Then he told me to get in one of the rooms and get some sleep. I came back out after a while, and I said, "Sir, where are the lights, and which room has the beds?"

He said, "Soldier, are you kidding? Get in there and sleep on the floor!" I just didn't know anything at the time.

Whitley also remembers his first enemy encounter.

I remember our Company had to attack Hill X. As we got to the crest of the hill, they told us to stop. "Don't go over." Because night would overtake us, and the enemy could be sending down some fire. But our officer said, "We've got the enemy on the run. We're going to keep pushing him." We kept going, and we got right over the top of the hill and then he had us to dig in.

As we started digging in, I heard something land on my right. My helmet kind of blew off me, it was held on loosely with that strap underneath. It was too big for me, I was kind of small at the time, and it just choked me. My buddy was on my left here. Something went off again, and after we laid there for awhile, he said, "Are you hurt?"

I said, "I don't think so." I asked, "How about you?" He said, "Yes. I'm hit in the leg. I'm hit in the thigh. I'm hit all over." He was a newcomer like me, and we had just met right there. It was amazing. Nothing touched me. It just flew over me, landed on my right side, went over me on the left, and got him.

THE VOLUNTEERS

In the winter of 1944–45, Allied forces in northern Italy began to break through the German strongholds, but the Germans mounted numerous counteroffensive attacks. The battles exacted a toll on both white and black troops. The black troops had only a small replacement pool to draw upon, but even the white troops experienced shortages of replacement personnel. The troops were exhausted, the weather was harsh, and the Germans were hard to dislodge. German commanders identified a weak spot in the Allied line of defense around the area of the Ardennes Forest. They mounted a ferocious counteroffensive, pushing the Allies back into Belgium. In that brutal campaign, the Battle of the Bulge, General Dwight D. Eisenhower noted: "The hardihood of the Allied soldier was never tested more thoroughly."

As replacement units from the United States began filtering up to the front lines, Eisenhower and his deputy commander, Lieutenant General John C. H. Lee, devised a plan to use black rear-echelon support troops as infantry replacements, in both white and black regiments. Lee directed a memo to all commanders of black support units, such as quartermaster, transportation, and signal corps, asking for men to volunteer as infantry replacements. More than 4,500 black men volunteered, and 2,221 were accepted. The men were asked to give up their rank in order for all of the volunteers to enter at the same level. They received a quick but rigorous refresher course on weaponry and the basics of infantry service. Woodrow Walton volunteered to move from a trucking company to the front line, because he wanted "to see some action." The black volunteers were sent to the front in small units and integrated with white troops. It was a bold step toward integration. Milton Hale said: "We were accepted very well by the white GIs. I guess what was uppermost in their minds was whether we would run the first time we were on the point." When the new replacements proved their mettle, Hale said, "we were accepted as part of the company."

Many men, like Hale and Walton, volunteered to go into combat. In contrast, Lawrence Johnson expressed another common GI sentiment. He said: "A good soldier doesn't volunteer for anything." He had already been reluctantly conscripted to go on the D-Day invasion, taking trucks and other heavy vehicles to the front. He recalled how his unit got "volunteered" to participate in the Battle of the Bulge.

> Our company was already in France, split out into platoons about 60 miles apart. One evening this first lieutenant from a white infantry company came to our platoon lieutenant and said he wanted some volunteers to go with his infantry men into the Ardennes Forest. And nobody would volunteer in my platoon. Nobody wanted to go on to the Ardennes Forest, because he said there were SS troops that were sited in there. They were terrorizing the civilians in all the surrounding areas, and they wanted us to go in there, with what they call a mop-up action. But it was more than that.
>
> They wanted us to go into the Ardennes Forest, shoot them or capture them, whatever it would take, you know. Well, just nobody volunteered. So, this infantry lieutenant asked my lieutenant, he said, "Can I take the whole platoon?" And our lieutenant said, "Yeah, go ahead. Take the whole platoon." We didn't have a choice.

After Fred Watt's experience in an engineering unit that supported the D-Day invasion, he decided to answer General Lee's call for volunteers to the front. "We received a memo that was asking for Negro volunteers from all rear-echelon outfits," stated Watt.

> It was posted on the bulletin board. At that time I was a T-5 and the sergeant told me, "If you volunteer you're going to get busted down to PFC [private]." At that particular time, rank didn't actually impress me that much. Also, I felt like if I was going to be getting shot at while building bridges and fixing roads, well, I might as well just go on in and get into the whole thing. I'll either get killed or I'll get out quicker—that was my thinking.

Watt was fighting against the Germans in a little village when he was caught in a crossfire. As he was trying to escape through a house, he was shot in the upper part of his leg. The bullet severed a nerve in his leg but fortunately missed his femur. Another soldier fighting nearby was shot in the thigh and also in the lower part of his leg.

> Up comes this sergeant, white. He told those of us with wounds to go to the basement of this house. So we crawled to the basement, but within a few minutes they started tossing phosphor shells into the

house to set it on fire. When the building caught on fire, that sergeant came down there and pushed both of us out that basement window. He carried me on his back down to the railroad and put me on a jeep. I had never seen that sergeant before, and I never saw him again, but he carried both of us to safety, one at a time.

In May 1945, the war in Europe ended. Like their white counterparts, black soldiers were pulled off the front lines and reassigned to other duties. Needless to say, most of the men wanted to go home, but the army had other plans for them. The war in the Pacific was still going on, and some black soldiers were shipped there from Europe to finish the fighting. Spencer Moore expressed the anxiety of many men waiting to hear about the next assignment. He wrote to his parents on May 5th: "Dear Mom and Pop: I just hope we don't have to go to the SW Pacific." Moore said he would not mind an assignment in Europe as part of the occupation forces, but he was not interested in putting in more combat time. Felix Goodwin was in Europe when the war there ended. He wanted to stay in the service as a career, but he was not so sure he wanted to go to the Pacific and get into more fighting.

We got word that we were going to be sent to the Pacific. They had already taken some troops from Europe over to the Pacific. We were on that list to go. While we were waiting on those orders luckily, we got on a list to be disbanded.

Still, Goodwin did not go home. His group got reassigned as a quartermaster unit heading into Germany to "clean up."

Clyde Whitted had been serving in England and France, driving personnel and weapons carriers. He wanted to go home to be with his wife and their four children. He did not volunteer to go to the Pacific; he prayed to the Lord to be good to him and get him on a ship back home. "But then they carried me direct to the Pacific," he said. "The water was rough, and I was seasick the whole way. I just felt like I wanted to go and jump overboard." Cleother Hathcock knew he was getting shipped someplace, but only when he was issued khaki clothes did he figure out that he was moving to the Pacific. He said: "We heard we had dropped the bombs, and then we heard the war was over, the Japanese had surrendered. We were in Panama, so I thought we would just turn around and go home. Two of our three ships did head back, but as luck would have it, mine was the ship that did not turn around."

In the summer of 1945, the 93rd was in the South Pacific preparing for what everyone assumed would be inevitable—an invasion of Japan. By

August, white divisions in the Pacific campaign were worn out, and the men of the 93rd were certain they were going into combat as the first wave of the invasion of Japan. Rumors ran wild. When Japan sued for peace in August, the men rejoiced. The end of the war in the Pacific had come in a blaze of death: the strafing and firebombing of Tokyo and the atomic bombing of Hiroshima and Nagasaki. Donald McNeil expressed the prevailing sentiment of the men fighting in the Pacific. "We were very happy about the use of the atomic bomb, because we were told that we would be in on the invasion of Japan, and they expected two million casualties for us. Since we did not start the war, I would rather they be killed than us." Bill Payne said everyone was shouting and carrying on. The men were "just elated that the war was over." He said they had heard about the bombs, but they "didn't know the magnitude of the thing until later."

Black soldiers of the 93rd were among the first Americans to accept a Japanese surrender. They became peacemakers, dropping leaflets on South Pacific islands telling the Japanese the war was over. As they traveled from island to island they dumped their unused equipment into the Pacific Ocean. Howard Hickerson said: "We didn't want any old bombs to harm the natives or anything, so we just dumped the equipment into the ocean." Cases of guns, radios, and medical supplies and even tanks were discarded.

Madine Davis Lane described what it was like in Okinawa at the end of the war.

> You could still see the kamikaze planes in the bay. Planes, floating bodies, and everything there. Once we got ashore, we saw where they had staged one of their biggest battles around this university area. They still had dead soldiers right where they had been machine-gunned or blasted; they were still there. No one had been able to move them. We were placed in a camp that had been for refugees from the islands around there. A lot of the military people were arriving at Okinawa because it was going to be the staging place for invading Japan. But then after V-J Day everything stopped. So we just stayed there until we were assigned new ships to come home.

Lane went out with a bang. "A few days before we were to leave, they had a big typhoon that tore down all of our tents and tore the top off the Red Cross place. We were in this building with the rain coming in and all. Finally, we boarded ship heading home." Davis was one of the lucky ones who returned straight to the United States. For many of the men in the Pacific, and for those still waiting in Europe, the end of World War II brought not only relief, but also a whole new set of anxieties centered around returning home.

COMING HOME

"I'LL BE HOME FOR CHRISTMAS . . ."

Everybody wanted to go home. Few men were eager to stay on and serve as part of the occupying troops. In Europe, the men were hoping to avoid additional service in the Pacific. Spencer Moore wrote to his parents in June 1945.

> Dear Mom and Pop:
>
> Glad to know Europe is OK. Don't have to go to the Pacific. I can hardly remember what it's like in the States. You would be surprised at what a numb feeling I have. I guess it will take a couple of months to really realize that I am home. Well it won't be as long as it has been before all of us are back home. That will be "Victory at Home" day for all of us. You know I have 98 points and am on the waiting list to come home.
>
> Love, Spencer

Moore was one of the lucky ones. He returned to Magnolia, New Jersey, and joined his family before the end of the year. Over in the South Pacific, all of the soldiers were hoping to get home by Christmas too. Most of them did not make it. Some of the men, like Howard Hickerson, made the best of the delay. He wrote to his friends back in the San Francisco Bay Area: "Hey, I'm out here taking a nice, warm dip in the Pacific Ocean here on Christmas and New Year's Day." Hickerson's upbeat reaction was not typical.

The deactivation delays set most of the men on edge. Donald McNeil said he knew of three men in his company who had to be treated for nervous breakdowns; "one even shot his foot off trying to get home." The men began the difficult readjustment of trying to live each day without the turmoil of warfare, yet their psychological recovery was hindered by a slowdown in the army's deactivation procedures. The army adage "hurry up and wait" was in full effect at the end of the war. As the men waited, boredom and anxiety set in. A soldier had to acquire a certain number of points before he was eligible to return home. Soldiers acquired points by their length of time in service, length of time in combat, medals awarded, and rank.

Because the 93rd was predominantly used in mopping-up operations, its men acquired fewer combat points than many white soldiers. Though they had defended their nation by holding strategic locations, they were not awarded the higher points of "active combat." And because so few black men held any rank above first lieutenant, they acquired fewer rank points than whites. Some individual men got out early, but most of the men in the 93rd waited in the Philippines until 1946 to come home. In Europe, the 92nd was leaving to go home in piecemeal fashion. When Charles Wesly finally got back to American shores, his friends asked, "Where the hell have you been? There's been people got out here months ago that had lesser points than you." Fred Watt expressed the anxiety of waiting to come home: "All the rear-echelon outfits were regrouped after the war and sent into Germany to clean up the mess that we had made. I had enough points to get out of the service—I had volunteered to go to the front, I had the Purple Heart, the Bronze Star and four Oak Leaf Clusters, and I had spent enough time in to get high points—so I said, 'No way am I staying.'"

Madine Davis Lane recalled her experiences of waiting to come home. She remembered the readjustment process most soldiers experienced as they decompressed after the daily regimen of life in the wartime army. "Up there in the jungle and every place we'd been to you didn't have to worry about polished brass, or army protocol," she said. "You didn't have to polish your shoes because they were mildewed, things were just more lax." One Friday afternoon at the end of the war, as Lane was waiting to be mustered out of the service, she and a girlfriend got into a little trouble on an army base. It was about 5 o'clock in the afternoon, and the ladies were walking and enjoying the sunset when they heard a loud "Boom!" Lane said she noticed some soldiers trying to get their attention, but the ladies figured they were just flirting.

When you're twenty-three, you think everybody's flirting. Anyway, we're waving back at them, blowing kisses. But pretty soon we heard this screech of tires. A jeep stopped along side of us, and this officer says, "Lieutenants, didn't you hear the cannon sound for retreat?" Well, we had heard it, but we'd forgotten what it was for. Those soldiers weren't flirting, they were trying to warn us to stop and salute as the flag came down.

Lane had gotten used to life in the jungle, where army protocol was not as necessary as saving lives. During her wait to get out of the service, she began the difficult readjustment to civilian life that most soldiers experienced.

Rumors circulated that the army was holding up the discharges of black troops so that they could be used to rebuild bombed cities in war-torn areas of the world. Many black soldiers and their families contacted their government representatives asking for a clarification of the deactivation policies. Some also contacted the press. When could the boys come home? Why were white soldiers coming home quicker than their black counterparts? Was there any truth to the rumor that black troops would be retained overseas to rebuild war ravaged areas? The Office of War Information (OWI) drafted a form letter to respond to the inquiries. "Negro soldiers who are eligible for discharge under the plan will be returned to the U.S. with the same promptness as all other soldiers of their particular credit status."

The OWI denied discrimination existed in the discharge policy. The office refused to admit that black soldiers with enough points to go home were being moved around rather than being sent home. The military leadership rejected criticism of its policies of assigning most black soldiers to service-and-support tasks, rather than to combat assignments, and they refused to acknowledge that this policy discriminated against the men. They also refused to acknowledge how the restricted opportunities for black officers to advance limited the number of points each black officer could acquire. The men were caught in the ultimate "Catch-22." They could not get enough points because of the policies, and even if they somehow managed to acquire the appropriate points, they would be moved to another area and only rarely sent home in a timely fashion. The military leadership attempted to squelch rumors that black troops were to be used for clean-up in the war-torn areas, but it did nothing to readjust the point system to compensate for prior discrimination. The troops remained anxious. Keeping the men overseas for so many months after the end of the war only aggravated the situation.

The restlessness of some soldiers turned into militancy as they waited—and waited—for the point system to make the deactivation process more equitable. Some of the men mutinied. Fred Watt explained:

They sent us to these camps in France called Lucky Strike, Philip Morris, and so on. I was in this group of 101 other guys in Philip

Morris, and we decided among us that we were not going back into Germany. There was a lawyer in the group, and he got a hold of the laws of the armed forces, and he told the colonel that we weren't going back. We had enough points to get out, and that's what we wanted. They were sending the white guys home, but they weren't sending us, and we had enough points. The colonel said, "You know this is a form of mutiny."

And we said, "We know that." We knew they couldn't court-martial all 101 of us without notifying Congress. We didn't answer reveille, didn't pull KP, no rations, we didn't do nothing. We stayed in that mutiny state for three months. The colonel just let us sit there until he got tired, then he sent us out when the next ship was leaving.

Fred Hurns described a similar situation: "I was high up enough on the point system to have gone home a week after they put the point system out. But it took me three months." He recalled how he was moved around and reassigned to several different units that were all supposedly staging to come home. He said he was "zigzagged" around until he finally got to a unit that was shipped out. On the ship, Hurns noted that many of the soldiers had lesser points. He summed up the policy: "The point system really didn't mean nothing. It didn't mean nothing at all."

Black soldiers in the Pacific were suffering from the same mistreatment. Ted McCullough worked in division headquarters, and he was well aware of the unrest in the ranks of men waiting to come home.

We were keeping records on the island of the black and white soldiers who had so many different points. All the white soldiers down to 65 were going, and we still had some black soldiers in the 90s, and they weren't going. So that was the reason our commanding general was pressured to go see MacArthur and find out what was wrong with the point system. And while he was gone, I think the second night, we got word to prepare all troops with 70 and above to be ready to leave in 48 hours. Well, that was almost the whole division.

But it was not the magnanimity of MacArthur that put the men on the "going home" list. Some members of the press, as well as notables like the Reverend Dr. W. H. Jernagin, director of the Fraternal Council of Negro Churches, were told of the deactivation problems, and they pressured the White House to deactivate the men. Charles Wesly remembered that the reverend—who was in the South Pacific visiting the soldiers—pressured the commanding general, who in turn pressured MacArthur to get the men back home. The reverend threatened to wire the president, and of course, at that point the orders were cut. "But the real crowning ignominy," Wesly recalled, "was, after being over there, suffering all these indignities, when we got to the port with our orders to board the ship we got turned back around." Wesly said that a captain looked at "all the black faces coming on to his ship and waved them back off." When the men were returned to shore, Jernagin turned the threat into action and wired the White House. Within a few hours the men were boarding the ship for the trip home.

Although the trip home was not as dangerous as the wartime voyage to the South Pacific, the men still encountered some hazards. Howard Hickerson recalled a heart-stopping moment in the Pacific on the way home. He was happy to be heading home to the States, and he felt fortunate to be traveling back with his good friend Sandy.

Howard Hickerson with war memorabilia. (Photo by David Weintraub © 1995)

You gotta picture this now. We're coming back on this converted troop ship; it was better conditions than going over. As we were coming out of the South Pacific, Sandy and I were out on the deck. We always liked to be up high and dry. We were telling stories and this-and-that. Sandy's looking out, and I see him pointing at something. Sandy stuttered, you know. The more he got excited, the more he stuttered. Da, d-d-d-d, like that. So he started looking out, pointing and saying: "How, How, Howa, How-w-w-aard."

I said, "What's the matter, Sandy?" And he goes, "Ma-ma-ma-m-m-m. Mi-mi-mi-MINE. MINE." And there was this mine floating out ahead of the ship. He just barely got it out of his mouth that a mine was bobbing toward our damn ship.

So I saw it, and I looked up to the brig, and I hollered, "Hey, hey, there. Turn now, there's a mine." So right then you could hear the horn, "Hoot, hoot" like the sound they make there. They turned the course around, going slowly past this mine. Then once they got past it they exploded it. But Sandy, we still laughed about it till the end. He would say: "You-you-you di-di-didn't even knowed-da what I was tal-tal-talking about. We could-could-coulda gotten ki-ki-ki-killed, and you wouldn't a even known what I was saying."

Hickerson could almost always make light of any situation. He was happy to be alive and happy to be returning to his prewar job. Other men returned home embittered from the indignities that they could not gloss over. Bill Payne remembered how the point system worked in his favor, but the color of his skin worked against him. He was in one of the first batches of soldiers returning from the Pacific. Approximately 120 black officers from the 93rd were the only passengers aboard a large Kaiser ship heading home. In the thirty days it took to travel across the ocean, Payne said they watched movies and played cards. He remembered watching the movie *Gung Ho!* and, without a touch of irony, noted how he always enjoyed combat chronicles—movies, books, anything to do with war stories. Out at sea they hit a couple of storms, which interrupted the entertainment schedule, but eventually they arrived safely off the coast of California near the port of Long Beach.

The whole ship was held out at sea for three days, because no surrounding military base or civilian community wanted to accept black soldiers. The military leadership scrambled to find them accommodations. They called all the neighboring towns to try and locate lodging for the men. Finally the leadership at Camp Hahn, near Riverside, California, agreed to give the black soldiers temporary refuge. These American men who had bravely fought for their country for two years in the jungles of the Pacific returned home to face second-class citizenship in a society that was still segregated.

Bill Payne at the San Francisco Presidio. (Photo by David Weintraub © 1995)

This example is not an isolated case. Other black soldiers experienced similar indignities. Perhaps the most demoralizing aspect of the deactivation program was the boundary zones set up to restrict the soldiers once they reached American shores. The official government policy called "Redistribution" defined areas in America where soldiers could return and deactivate or take some needed rest and relaxation if they were going back overseas. Even after the successes of limited integration of some troops in Europe, official policy designated separate areas in America for white and black soldiers to rest and regroup. Secretary of War Henry L. Stimson spelled out the policy in a memorandum: "The recently published decision to provide separate redistribution stations for colored returnees was based on the War Department's long-standing policy not to force the intermingling of races. The placement of Negro Redistribution Stations in the vicinity of large Negro populations will afford the individual soldier an opportunity to be received and entertained by his own people." The War Department believed that black people wanted to return to their own neighborhoods in Harlem and Chicago rather than the beaches and resorts where white soldiers were sent to relax. Although many black soldiers did want to return to their "own" neighborhoods, being denied access to beaches or other more glamorous areas within an America they recently fought to defend was a shameful example of discrimination.

By the end of World War II, so many black citizens had loudly complained about the unequal treatment of returning soldiers that the War Department was forced to look into the matter. To prevent confusion, a map titled "Zones of Influence: Negro Troops" was attached to an explanatory memorandum and circulated around the military leadership.

> The attached map shows a boundary zone of varying width. In this zone conditions for Negro troops returning from overseas will probably be found tolerable. In the other areas conditions on military posts are frequently found to be undesirable, and conditions in the civilian environment intolerable, for Negro troops returning from overseas. In the light of the existing pattern as broadly outlined, it is held that precautionary measures must be taken against tension situations based on race.

When twenty-six members of black high society in Harlem sent a telegram to the president complaining about the redistribution policy, the War Department quickly convened a meeting to review their complaint. The Reverend Dr. Adam Clayton Powell Jr., Walter White, and City Commissioner Austin—among others—signed the telegram.

> The undersigned citizens of Harlem take this means of registering with you as Commander-in-Chief of the Army and Navy our most vigorous protest against the Jim Crow arrangements for Negro soldiers under the rotation furlough system. We learn that White soldiers brought back from overseas for recreation and relief from battle strain are to be given approximately two weeks each at government expense at luxurious hotels and resorts at Lake Placid, New York, Santa Barbara, Cal, Miami Beach, and perhaps other pleasure places. But Negro soldiers are to be required to go to New York's Harlem or the Pershing Hotel on Chicago's south side. The population density of these two hotels will add greatly to already overstrained housing. The action of the United States Government in segregating Negro soldiers . . . in northern communities where it is both illegal and contrary to public opinion is reprehensible.

After the usual hand-wringing and denials of inappropriateness, the "confidential and secret notes" reveal a slight modification of the redistribution policy. In addition to the Hotel Theresa, another hotel in Harlem was added to help out with overcrowding. In Chicago, a new redistribution center at the Congress Hotel allowed returning white soldiers to use the hotel on a voluntary basis, but they would be instructed that it was primarily for the use of returning black soldiers. However, the War Department decided that it would be inadvisable to allow black soldiers to enjoy the beaches of Del Mar, California, a favorite recreation area for white citizens.

MAKING A CAREER IN THE ARMY

No matter the restrictions or other humiliations of segregated service, many black soldiers still considered a career in the military as a worthy goal at the end of World War II. Allen Green recalled his own decision to stay in the service:

> When I got home they had this debriefing. As part of the spiel they said there was still trouble in the world, and there may come another war. We were still needed, and if we decided not to reenlist, then at least look at the reserves they asked us. That's what I did, stayed in the reserves. It made sense. I kept my five stripes, and I stayed in long enough to retire as a master sergeant.

Staying in the army was the sensible choice for Joe Stephenson, too:

> On the boat home I was thinking, "Well, what do I want to do when I get home?" I thought the job market would be real tight because so many people were going home. I said, "Well, I like the army." And the only thing I wanted to do was train and have a good platoon.
>   When I got to Fort Meade, the man told me that I had a good record. He said: "If you want to stay in, the only thing you will have to do is go to the orderly room and sign out, and we will send you your orders. If you want to get out now, then you'll have to stay here until Monday, and we will process you out then." So I went down to the orderly room and signed out, and caught a cab to my sister's. That was the beginning of my leave, and the continuation of my army career. I made it for twenty years.

Joseph Hairston made the decision to stay in as well. After "re-upping," both Hairston and Stephenson were assigned to duty at Fort McClellan,

Alabama, a place neither one of them enjoyed. Hairston said he experienced "another series of racist type of actions," because he outranked some
of the white artillery men in his unit. Within a few months, a junior officer
gave Hairston a low rating on an evaluation. Hairston said: "The guy didn't
dislike me, it was just a matter of black officers weren't worth anything
more than a 'satisfactory.' We couldn't even get 'very satisfactory,' and never
'superior,' on our reports." Hairston was reassigned to Fort Knox, and from
there, within a month, he was transferred to Fort Benning, Georgia. Finally, he applied to go to flight school, and by late 1946 he was off to his
next army career, although racialized restrictions continued to plague him.

Soldiers were offered perks to stay in the service. Some of the men were
offered advanced commissions, and others were offered the continued adventure of overseas employment. Alex Pitcher was offered a chance "to make
officer overnight" if he reenlisted and went to Japan with the occupation
forces. Pitcher declined, because he said he was "conditioned to go back to
college." But other men took the opportunity. Lawrence Johnson wanted the
steady employment guaranteed by the work of rebuilding Germany. He
noted how all the Germans called him "Yankee," even his Jewish girlfriend,
and commented about the number of people who distanced themselves from
the Nazi regime. "None of them wanted to be Nazis then," Johnson said.

Ezell Jackson, like Johnson, signed up to go back to Europe. He expected
to be put to work repairing the war-damaged areas, but he was detached
from his unit and reassigned to a transportation unit in Germany. "I was just
a loose soldier then," he recalled. "They assigned me to driving some officers
back and forth to this mountain place they called 'Hitler's Home,' and I did
that for a while." All of Jackson's assignments were temporary. He was detached and reattached to several units. Jackson drove an ambulance for a
while and then a school bus for officers' children. He had been a chauffeur
for a prominent Spartanburg, South Carolina, family before he was inducted
into the army, and he knew he had that job waiting for him back at home.
He figured there was no reason to be working in the army doing something
he could do on the outside.

> I lived a crazy life in the army. I guess I was the most unassigned sol-
> dier that ever served. When they asked me to reenlist again I did not
> do it. I came out simply because they didn't do what they said they
> were going to do at the beginning. I didn't trust them; I lost faith so I
> came on home.

A range of sentiments regarding continued service prevailed among veterans after the war. Clyde Blue went into the army "strictly as an interested

observer," expecting nothing from the army and getting nothing. He was not interested in continuing life in the military after the war. Bill Payne's wife asked him to come home after the war and forget about a career in the service. He tried it. He worked two and three jobs a day for about five years and then decided to reenter the army. Ultimately, the military life conflicted with Payne's family life, and his wife left him.

Each soldier's decision about staying in the service was as individual as the person, but perhaps Madine Davis Lane's mixed feelings about continued service express the difficulty of the decision. She said she was sorry she did not stay in, because she loved every minute of her duty stateside as well as overseas. The man she met at Fort Huachuca and agreed to marry after the war sent her a letter asking her not to stay in the service. She took the discharge, and then, "wouldn't you know it, he decided to stay in and make a career out of the army; he went back to Italy, and we never got married." Shortly after that mistake, Lane thought about reentering the service, but she said that all of her friends who stayed in were on the verge of court-martials. She decided to try and make a go of it as a civilian instead.

Most black soldiers decided to come home and rebuild their life as civilians. They were not enchanted with army life anymore. There are so many stories of disenchantment—from poorly handled deactivation policies through redistribution foul-ups—it is a wonder that any black soldiers stayed in. Alex Pitcher's discharge illustrates the individual soldier's disillusionment. He recalled coming home from the Pacific, how the train whisked them out of the Bay Area and dumped them at a Texas train depot on a Sunday evening. Hundreds of soldiers were departing the train to the sounds of a white sergeant shrieking commands over a bullhorn. "'I want all the white soldiers over here,'" Pitcher recalled, "'and all the niggers over there.'" Even if he did not have plans to attend college, it would be hard to imagine why he would have wanted to stay in the service.

Spencer Moore was on the verge of staying in the service when he encountered the same racist remarks. He was at the deactivation center in Fort McClellan, about to get on a bus, when the driver told him to go to the back. "Who are you telling to get in the back? This is America," Moore recalled yelling at the driver. "You see the medals on my chest? I don't have to get in the back for nobody. In fact, I'm gonna sit right down here and breath down your neck." Shortly after that indignity, Moore attended an officers meeting during which he was given a pep talk about staying in the army.

> This old Southern colonel got up and told us, "Well, you know, you're down here in the South, and you've got to abide by the social structure of this community." He was talking with this southern drawl that just

got on my nerves. "And you've got to do this and you've got to that," he says. I jumped right straight up, and I said, "No, sir. I don't have to do it." I said, "I'm gonna sign to go home now."

"A RAMPART, FOREVER SEPARATING US . . ."

The black Americans who fought in the jungles of the southwest Pacific and in the mountains and valleys of Europe during World War II were changed by their experiences in the war. The changes individual soldiers experienced were not uniform, but each man or woman's life was altered as a consequence of serving overseas in a combat zone. They were prepared for hardship by their prior experiences in the Great Depression of the 1930s. In that period many black Americans lived under harsh conditions—few job opportunities left little money available for basic living expenses. Added to the overall poor economic conditions were the hardships of living in a segregated Jim Crow society. But the economic deprivation that was the hallmark of the Depression, as brutal and demoralizing as it was, did not compare to the daily indignities of segregated service, or the fear and brutality of warfare. Black Americans who served in World War II fought under segregated conditions, sometimes without appropriate housing, equipment, or supplies, against an enemy with a simple battle strategy: fight to the death. The type of fear experienced in war was unlike anything the men had experienced in Depression-era America. Thus, black soldiers who lived through the war, who fought in segregated units for a nation that treated them as second-class citizens, were permanently altered by their World War II experiences.

Fred Hurns said he was a different type of person after the war. "I carried myself in a different way after I came back, and people could tell I had been in the service." Nelson Peery summarized the difficulties the returning veteran faced:

> For four years we had been molded by the army and the war. Socially disoriented, and as unsure of civilian life as we had been of army life four years before, we began the process of discharge from the army. We were going back to try and weave 1946 to 1942. We would try to bridge those four years. But we knew they would remain as a rampart, forever separating us from those who never served in the infantry.

Howard Hickerson was one of those black Americans whose life was altered by his army experiences. He had trained for combat, but when he arrived at

Guadalcanal he realized there was no preparation for what he encountered. Some twenty-three thousand dead Japanese and fifteen hundred dead Americans required burial. "We buried the Americans as best we could, and the Japanese, we would just put them in trenches, the best we could bury them. It was a very gruesome, stinking place to be. And that was my first introduction to war." Two years later Hickerson returned home to the San Francisco Bay Area and tried to put the war behind him. At first an eager soldier, he came to realize that "wars just don't make sense." He had matured, and he had learned that life can be cruel. Hickerson wondered why nations had to settle their differences by killing each other: "Nobody wins, and pretty soon it's over and then there's all these negotiations."

World War II veterans—black and white, male and female—returned matured by the years of military discipline and sobered by the horrors of war. As they returned to segregated communities and rampant racism at home, some wondered what the war had been about. Henry Peoples commented:

> When I entered the armed forces of my country, I sincerely believed in my government as it is supposed to be—a democracy that protects all of its citizens. My beliefs haven't changed, but I do wonder . . . just what World War II was all about. Our government is supposed to represent all of the people. I killed—I repeat I killed—other men in the name of democracy. Could the joke have been on me for being naïve enough to believe in my government?

Walter Green expressed similar feelings:

> If I had to do it all over again, I would take off for Canada like many of the fellows have recently done [Vietnam]. We were brave; we did whatever job was assigned. We had no instance of cowardice or mutiny. But the officers could have made life more bearable and left us with a little dignity.

Green characterized segregated service in World War II as a terrible "racial thing" that should not have happened to American citizens. The pattern of discrimination against black soldiers during the war set the course for continued racial friction in many communities across America.

Some of the veterans have never forgotten the bitterness of segregated service, nor the indignities perpetrated by white racists. Others learned they could tolerate rough conditions, including widespread discrimination, in a disciplined, stoic manner. Bill Payne said he could have come out of the service antagonistic toward white people because of the conditions of the segregated service. "I could have been hard-nosed about things, but that's not my personality," he said.

> I was there to learn to be a soldier and to be a man, and basically, I developed my personality while in the army. I learned how to take care of myself, mentally and physically. I learned how to be a leader. I learned how to deal with people, and I learned how to get around problems. Rather than butt heads and get into a big confrontation, I would just sit back, take note, and figure out the best way to resolve something.

Payne said he learned that hate destroys the hater; time has tempered his bitterness.

Alex Pitcher acknowledged that growing up in Louisiana had taught him his "place"; he said he did not have full consciousness of the country's racial situation until after he had served in the army. He was a minister's son—a good law-abiding Christian. He was shocked when white soldiers would routinely call him "boy" or "nigger." Wearing the uniform of the U.S. Army, he thought, would give him and his fellow black soldiers more respect, but he soon learned how little it meant. He said he became a man in the army. He also developed a strong "racial consciousness." The lessons Payne and Pitcher learned during their years in the army serve as the foundation of their personal character. Most black soldiers experienced World War II as the defining moment in their lives.

BLACK AMERICANS ABROAD

One of the experiences that inevitably defined the character of the veteran, and ultimately altered the social fabric of America, was the experience of foreign travel. For many Americans, World War II provided an opportunity to travel abroad. While all of the black soldiers who traveled were sent to conduct a war, as a by-product, many of the men engaged in a range of cultural activities and exchanges with the local people. They met foreigners who treated them respectfully. They listened to new music and visited tourist sites. These cultural exchanges altered both groups' perceptions of each other.

Most of the cultural exchanges in the Pacific happened at the end of the war. The men stationed there had spent two years mostly cut off from any civilian life, so the cultural exchanges with other peoples was minimal. That changed at the war's end when the men were stationed in the Philippines waiting to come home. Howard Hickerson said the local people were so glad the war was over that they treated the soldiers like kings: "We had parties with the girls. It was good living. It was heaven." Of course, other black soldiers remember the clash between the white Americans who were angry over the black soldiers' attention to local women. But in Europe, where black troops could mingle with the local populations and even go on rest and relaxation jaunts (R&R) to other European capitals, cultural exchanges were frequent and life altering.

Fred Watt said traveling to Great Britain was new and exciting: "The people, the way they spoke and acted, it was amazing to me because I had never seen any other nationality except Americans." The locals were often just as amazed when they met black American soldiers. Watt elaborated:

> I'd go to a billiard hall over there, and usually we were about three men in a group playing on one table. We were playing the game called "Black Ball," a rotation game. One day this guy walked up to me and asked me, he says, "I don't want to be insulting, but here's three of you fellas here, and now all three of you are a different color. And you all three say you're American Negroes?" I had to laugh and explain it to him.

Many of the veterans were impressed with English mannerisms. When Dennett Harrod went on R&R in Italy he noted that it was run by English soldiers. "The British really know how to occupy a place," he remarked. "You could just sit on the porch in those chairs, and all you had to do was crook your finger, and you could get a drink." Fred Watt liked doing things the British way. He was in England with a group building a hospital.

> We had tea time about twice a day. I don't care what they're doing. They're stopping for tea. About 10:30 in the morning and 3 in the afternoon. The ladies would come out and say, "Aren't you gentlemen going to take a break? It's tea time." They would bring us little flavored cakes and a pot of tea with a cover on it. We'd pour it in our canteens and drink it. We loved the whole bit.

Cleother Hathcock remembered how the English people loved the black American soldiers during the war. "At that time the Jitterbug was in, and the blacks would get a buggin' and the English just loved that. We would go into a dance hall and just take over the place because everybody wanted to learn how to do that American dance, the Jitterbug. They went wild over that."

Bill Perry recognized how the travel experience advanced his own personal growth during the war years:

I think that World War II changed my whole life. Things happened to me that would have never happened if it had not been for the war. I would never have gone to places. I'd have never gotten to Arizona; I'd have never gone to Italy.

Cleother Hathcock said the army allowed him to explore the world. He had enough time off in Europe "to tour around some museums and cathedrals."

Some soldiers hated all the traveling. Woodrow Walton said he traveled too much:

I had enough of moving around. They would just say "pack your bags," and I'd be off. It just broke me down. Sometimes now my wife says "let's go someplace," and I just tell her I don't feel about traveling too much, I traveled so much then.

But most of the men recognized their time abroad as one of their most formative experiences. Fred Watt expressed what travel abroad meant to him:

I think that it was one of the greatest experiences that I have ever had. And I think every human being should go abroad if they get a chance. See how other people in the world live. Because we have a certain way of doing things in the United States that other countries do not put up with. By me not being able to go to college, I still consider myself as knowledgeable as anyone else because of all my knowledge from traveling.

Although American-style segregation was in effect at some locations in Europe, many black soldiers experienced unfettered relationships with local people. Generally, the only time black soldiers ran into blatant discrimination was when they encountered white American soldiers. William Banks remembered traveling to Switzerland for a little R&R. He was worn-out from active combat. In Switzerland, a local family struck up a conversation with him as he walked through the streets of Geneva. Later that evening, at a dance party held at a USO club, Banks danced with the daughter of the family. Although the father had approved, several white soldiers took offense. One soldier began bumping into Banks on the dance floor.

I thought it was accidental, but it kept happening over and over. So finally one of the security people at this pavilion came up and tapped him on the shoulder and said, "We'll have none of that. Clean that up." Evidently some American racist was resenting the idea that a black man was dancing with a white woman. She was Swiss, not even American!

While that story describes an unpleasant aspect of the black experience, many black soldiers stationed in Europe talked about the feelings of freedom they experienced there. They commented how the local people recognized them as Americans or "Yankees" first, rather than seeing them primarily by color. This attitude would prove to be a strong influence on how the men expected to be treated once they returned to America. Many black soldiers who traveled abroad felt that their American identity was reaffirmed. Joe Stephenson was most emphatic about the experiences of the war and the cultural exchanges. He said: "There was an impact, of course there was. It was the biggest thing that ever happened, and it touched everybody's life who was around at that time." The men experienced different cultures and different lifestyles, and they returned to the United States feeling more American and less willing to accept discriminatory treatment. In World War II, black soldiers had been trained to fight for what they believed in, and the experience of combat had formed strong bonds between the men. Once they returned to American shores, the veterans began changing the social structure of America.

A RISING TIDE OF EXPECTATIONS

Many of the black veterans returned to America determined to change their status. As Nelson Peery noted, the soldiers had not fought to preserve their way of life; they had fought to change it. Robert Madison concurred:

> We went into combat because that's what we were supposed to do. And black troops have always done what needs to be done. We hoped that the residual effect would be better treatment at home after the war. We hoped that would be true.

Peery summed up the difficulties the returning black veteran faced in postwar America.

> In a thousand subtle ways, in a thousand brutal ways, we were taught we were not part of American culture and history. Here we were making history. We were part of the vanguard of a new revolution—part of

the struggle. This was the ramrod that straightened the shoulders and lifted higher the heads of the young Negroes who made up the ranks of the infantrymen.

Peery expected to be treated as a full-fledged citizen after he returned from the war, and he found that many other black veterans returned to America on a rising tide of the same expectations. The men had answered the call to protect their country—they expected to be treated with respect. When they were denied their rights and actively discriminated against, many veterans became involved in the black movement for racial equality. Peery said: "The Negro troops got a taste of racial equality in foreign lands. As they came home, that had to be beaten and lynched and terrorized out of them before they would go back to building levees and picking cotton."

Journalist John Gunther traveled across America in the 1940s and reported that nearly every lynching victim after World War II was a veteran, some even still in uniform. Alex Pitcher believes the lynching of veterans came about because the men would actively resist any sort of racist act. "They went in to the army unaware of the racial problem, but they came out belligerent." Burg Turner said he was well aware of the resentment many white Americans felt toward black soldiers "who had been overseas with white women." He explained the problem. "You see that was a terrible capital crime. The best thing to do with them is get rid of them, but the veteran who had traveled overseas and fought in the war was just not going to take that crap anymore." Nelson Peery said he learned the fundamentals of evaluating life while he was in the service. He explained, "war is an experience that leaves one with a sense of responsibility: the veteran never forgets the meaning of force or loses his sense of organization."

One of the reasons the men would no longer tolerate racism in America was because they had met white people from other countries who did not treat them in a discriminatory manner. Another reason was that the army provided a training ground for collective thought and action. And finally, and perhaps the most important reason, the U.S. government provided a GI Bill of Rights to every World War II veteran, black and white. Black veterans expected to be treated as soldiers and citizens of America. With the new veterans' benefits, every World War II soldier was eligible for financial assistance to complete an education or buy a home.

The GI Bill of Rights became the great equalizer in postwar America. The army promoted the GI Bill at its deactivation centers as well as in its newspapers. *The Buffalo*, a newspaper for the 92nd Division, printed a special edition in October 1945 outlining the provisions of the program. Black veterans were encouraged to take advantage of the new education benefits.

Here are the education provisions of the GI Bill of Rights. Those of you who were 25 years of age or under at the time of induction or enlistment for service in the present war are presumed under the law to have had your education or training impeded, delayed. The course of study must start within two years after your release from the army.

The men were told that they could receive as much as $500 per person per year for every year they were in the armed forces, $750 if they had dependents. The men received allotments of either $50 or $75 for a ten-month academic year. While no veteran got rich off the largesse of the U.S. government, the gains in personal growth and enrichment cannot be measured in dollars.

Alex Pitcher said the GI Bill helped him finish college and allowed many black men who would never have had the opportunity to learn a profession and pursue higher education to do so.

Before World War II, there wasn't too much interest in any of us. Maybe if we got to college we could do a little teaching or something like that. Maybe if your parents had money you could go to Howard University or something. But most of us didn't have the chance to become doctors or lawyers.

All of that changed with the equal opportunity provisions in the GI Bill of Rights. Pitcher said: "So our eyes were opened all across this country. And we became aware of the racial problem, and we became aware of what to do about it."

College was not the choice for every veteran. Yes, Uncle Sam assisted veterans who wanted to attend college, but the new scholars found themselves on tight budgets. Fred Watt found that he could not go to college and support a family, even "with Uncle Sam's help," so he gave up on furthering his education. Jim Williams studied music for two years, and then, he said, he "became an addict—I was addicted to eating at least one hot meal a day. So I had to go to work." Still, Watt and Williams enjoyed the benefits of the GI Bill for a period of time. Other men tried to use the GI Bill, only to discover discrimination in school acceptance policies.

Robert Madison made up his mind to enroll in the Western Missouri School of Architecture with his GI Bill money. "Let me tell you a story," Madison said.

In July of 1946, I made an appointment with the dean and went up to the school to talk about getting in. And the dean said, "Well, you know,

I'm sorry. But we don't have colored boys study architecture here because there are just no jobs for them. Anyway you'd just be taking up the seat of a white boy." So I was quite disappointed. I went back home, and two days later I put on my uniform with all my battle ribbons and my Purple Heart. I went back up there, and I said, "Let me tell you one thing. I spilled my blood on the soil of Italy to make this country free. And you're telling me I can't enter this school of architecture just to study?"

Madison was shunted off to a few other departments and finally given a series of tests every Saturday for a month. When he passed every test, the school finally relented and let him in the program.

Bill Perry experienced similar discrimination with his GI Bill education. He had entered a life-drawing class at Western Reserve College in Cleveland. He said when he got to the first class, everyone "seemed kind of apprehensive." The instructor approached Perry and said he could not register for the class.

I said, "Why not? What's the problem?" The teacher said, "Well, we use, uh, we use live models." I still couldn't figure out what was the big deal. Finally, the guy said, "We use white women." Well, then we had a little discussion. And I went home and talked to my father about it. I don't think they wanted to mess with us. So then I went back into that class, and you know, of course I didn't disrupt everything like they thought I was going to.

Allen Thompson noted that black soldiers in World War I did not have the educational benefits of the returning World War II veteran. He commented on the impact of that policy change. "You see, you have to have an educated society before you can make any moves at all toward progress," he said.

You can't make progress with an uneducated man. You can control him, but he doesn't think anything about progress because that's the way it's always been, that's the way it's going to be. He's satisfied, and he's happy. But a person who has an education won't take that kind of malarkey. He's thinking, he's wondering, "Well, where is my piece of this whole pie?" This guy that came out of World War I, he went back to his normal way of life of getting kicked in the behind and run over by the Ku Klux Klan. He didn't have the ability and didn't have the communication skills to mobilize an effort. I'm not talking about energy, we've always had that. I'm talking about the political will to change.

The NAACP recognized the benefits of an educated black population. They were also keen to press any case in which a black veteran was denied access to education. Alex Pitcher joined the NAACP right after he got back from the war, and he commented on their organizational strategies: "The NAACP wasn't just talking to veterans, but they realized that the black veterans had the GI Bill of Rights, and they could use that to go to graduate schools." Most graduate schools, including law, medical, and other professional schools, generally discriminated against blacks. The NAACP began filing antidiscrimination lawsuits. "That's the way to get followers," Pitcher explained. "Get people to try things and then become plaintiffs if there was any discrimination. The eyes of the world were on discrimination then in America."

Pitcher claimed that veterans were more sensitive to discrimination and were willing to work with the NAACP:

> We had the impetus for the movement coming out of these people who were able to press for their rights. We were making an impact. The whole world was opening up. The political process opened up like never before. You see expectations were high then, not only me, everybody else, especially blacks from the South. I was just a typical southerner, one out of thousands who were just like me, whose eyes had become opened and who had become conscious.
>
> Well, now the rationale for the NAACP, especially at the end of World War II, was the focus on education. We realized that black people never could really accomplish their dreams unless they had education. Even now that's the most important force we have, education. Once you have an education, then you're able to help yourself, and you can help so many thousands of other people.

Pitcher had decided to become a lawyer, but his home state of Louisiana would not allow blacks to attend its only law school, Louisiana State University. Pitcher said: "That was at the time Thurgood Marshall and the NAACP were filing lawsuits across the country. They were filing lawsuits against the various state universities to get blacks admitted to medical schools and to law schools." The Louisiana government settled the matter temporarily by setting up a what Pitcher called a "makeshift law school." They set up the new program at the predominantly black Southern Baptist University, where Pitcher was getting his undergraduate degree.

> Now Louisiana had a different situation than what you have in other states in the country, because our state and parishes are governed on the Napoleanic Code. And that system of law is different, particularly

the civil law from criminal law. There were no black lawyers in the country that had ever graduated from a Louisiana law school, so no black lawyers knew Louisiana law in order to teach this new makeshift class. So what they had to do at Southern, for my three years at law school, was hire the white professors from down at the LSU law school. So you get my point? We had the same professors and the same education as the white students over at LSU!

Pitcher said the white professors quietly encouraged the black students to press the legal system for equal rights. He said his professors knew they were training soldiers for a battle. Fifteen of his fellow students were black veterans of World War II. Five of them successfully graduated, passed the state bar exam, and went on to practice law in Louisiana.

Alex Pitcher started fighting antidiscrimination battles in Louisiana with the backing of the NAACP and the tactics of his former military training. He was using his newly developed skills as a lawyer, pressing cases for black plaintiffs. However, in a strange twist of southern-style irony, the local Ku Klux Klan helped Pitcher get his law practice started.

When I first started practicing law, my biggest help came from the Ku Klux Klan. Mostly judges and people in the district attorney's office. Also, some of the white side of my family, the white Pitchers, were in the Klan and they'd help me out. They were all Klan members. At that time, the Ku Klux Klan had a hold on the whole political structure, and you better not get out of line. They had ways of getting retribution against you. They'd kill you. They'd put the threat of death in you, even the white guys were afraid. They used the same tactics to keep the white guys in line as they used on the black guys. So a lot of white guys just sort of stayed with the Klan, but maybe they weren't so supportive.

Some of those guys used to call me secretly and give me a briefing on what to do and everything. Told me some points of law to use in my cases. In my area, all the courthouses were controlled by the Pitcher family—the white Pitchers. They wouldn't let anything bad happen to me—they would call me and warn me about things. One of the leading judges was just like a grandpop of mine at the time I finished law school. He wouldn't let nobody do nothing to me. He used to be one of those grand wizards or something at that time—he simply looked after me for a long time. Of course I didn't publicize that too much back then. I was one of the first black lawyers in the area, and naturally I was not too familiar with everything like any new lawyer would be. So that judge used to send over his assistants to help me prepare my cases.

Ultimately, the grand wizard died, and Pitcher got a late night phone call telling him to "stop pressing all those damn civil rights cases and get out of town." He packed up his family and moved to the West Coast.

FOOT SOLDIERS IN THE FREEDOM MOVEMENT

The coming together of one million black men during the war was a significant community-building event, one that would be the precursor to the modern black freedom movement. Bitter veterans, indifferent veterans, and military "lifers" all commented on the heightened sense of responsibility and power resulting from their wartime experiences. Newly acquired skills and life-lessons prepared black veterans for a new life in America. The returning soldiers came home with their American identity fully developed; they felt they had earned their citizenship. They articulated their newfound "Americanism" by demanding all the rights and privileges of full citizenship.

In the army, Allen Thompson had learned how to take orders and comport himself with discipline.

> We learned to understand peoples' folk ways and mores, and we learned how to get along with each other. We are not a democracy; we are a republic, and most people don't understand this. Certainly, the army is not a democracy. It's far from that. It can't be a democracy to operate efficiently. You learn these things in the army, and you learn more about your responsibility to the nation. You have a responsibility as citizens. You must participate in the political process.

When the men returned to America they were not content to live within the constraints of segregated society. In the nationwide movement for civil rights and black power, the black veterans of World War II became foot soldiers in the fight for equality.

Ironically, the experience of serving in segregated divisions enhanced the men's "racial consciousness," an effect the army never expected. William Banks said that he returned from the war more sensitized to the shortcomings of American society toward its black citizens. Envisioning black empowerment through direct involvement in the political process, Banks agitated for change within his own community in Georgia. In 1941 when Harold Montgomery enlisted in the newly expanded armed forces, he realized "fully well that the army was segregated and that the leaders were all from the South." Believing that one man could not change the army's racial policies, he chose to adapt to the situation rather than to fight. He came to believe that the fighting spirit that was the hallmark of the civil rights movement of the 1960s came directly out of the contradictions the war raised for many black soldiers.

In 1943, when Nelson Peery wrote to his mother about a race war that was sure to follow the current world emergency, he felt his fellow comrades-in-arms from the black divisions would join him in the future fight.

> After all the hell that these men have been through, you can bet that few of them are going to feel content to return to that little farm in Georgia, and none of them will remain satisfied for a very long time. This army is a most wonderful thing for education of the mind as well as the body. It makes one think in an objective manner. America will be forced to make a drastic change in policy toward the Negro in the very near future.

With prescience, Peery predicted the future for black World War II veterans.

By the end of the war, there were many chinks in the armor of the army's segregation without discrimination policy. Government officials, military planners, and individual soldiers all questioned whether segregation was the most effective way to use human resources in the military. It cost money and energy to maintain duplicate facilities. The policy was temporarily disregarded when black soldiers were allowed to volunteer for frontline action at the end of the war in Europe. Milton Hale was one of the 2,221 black soldiers who volunteered to go to the front in the Battle of the Bulge. It was the army's first attempt at integration, and Hale said he felt it was a success. But other black soldiers in that group of volunteers commented that the troops were not completely integrated.

Fred Watt explained:

> Two of us volunteered from my platoon. They grouped a bunch of us up and made a platoon out of us and sent us right up to the front line. They said they were integrating the army, but that wasn't really true. My platoon was black, and we had a French platoon on one side and some English troops on the other side. I didn't sleep or eat with the white soldiers. One platoon at a time would spearhead; sometimes it would be us, sometimes one of them.

Still, the attempt to utilize white and black soldiers together demonstrated a major shift in military thinking at the command level.

After the end of World War II, on some army bases new behavior began to emerge. Some returning veterans—black and white—began to challenge the army's policy of segregation. Oglesby Barrett described a situation on a troop train that foretold the end of segregation in the military. As the train headed south from New Jersey to North Carolina, white soldiers started segregating themselves. One white soldier was sleeping. When his white comrades woke him up to get him to move to a whites-only car, he responded angrily, "What for?" His friends reminded him that the train had passed Washington, D.C., and he was "down South now." Barrett said the soldier, who was from Mississippi, yelled out: "You mean to tell me you've been over there fighting with these fellows, and now that you're back here you're not going to sit with them? Forget it. I'm not moving." These cracks and chinks in the armor of segregation turned into fissures of resistance.

Joseph Hairston described an incident that happened in Georgia in 1946. Several black officers who reenlisted after the war were assigned to Fort Benning. The men served under the command of a general who had been reduced in rank to colonel because of the army's postwar troop reduction policy.

> This former general was mad at the army for getting busted down. He was an avid golfer, and he liked his black troops. And two black officers in his combat team played golf, but they weren't allowed to play at the main golf course on post. In order to play on the course you had to be a member of the club, and you couldn't be a member of the club if you were black. Now, a member of the club could have guests. So the commander invited the black officers to be his guests. Well, this angered the others so much they built an entire nine-hole golf course just for the black officers! The army got these earth movers and flattened out those rolling hills around the base and just built an entirely new, professional golf course so those men would not play at the main course. And then those two black officers got transferred out shortly after that. Ha!

THE SLOW WALK TOWARD DESEGREGATION

The political and economic cost of maintaining segregation escalated. In October 1945, newly appointed Secretary of War Robert P. Patterson commissioned another study on the army's use of black soldiers. Even after all the studies, reports, investigations, inquiries, memoranda, and edicts regarding "the Negro soldier," the new secretary apparently felt another study was needed. His new commission was known as the "Gillem Board" because it was headed by Lieutenant General A. C. Gillem, wartime commander of XIII Corps. The commission conducted a five-month study and concluded "that for the sake of national security every available and qualified man should be used in an assignment for which there is need, for which he is best suited, and for which he has been trained. Negroes should have full opportunity to fulfill their responsibilities as citizens in national defense."

The final report of the Gillem Board also recommended that black Americans constitute at least 10 percent of all enlisted men. It called for the abolition of the two all-black divisions, but it did not call for integration. It recommended the maintenance of all-black units, such as regiments, groups, or combat teams, which could be used in both combat and noncombat assignments. These "composite organizations" represented the army's new way of using black soldiers in the postwar military. The report did not call for changes in the segregated living and dining situations on military bases where "composite organizations" would be stationed.

In 1946, the Adjutant General's Office weighed in with its policy on the use of black soldiers. Because of escalating tensions with the Soviet Union, there was a critical need for manpower in the army. A War Department directive circulated to every military establishment acknowledged that induction of black Americans would remain at the stated goal of 10 percent, but "enlistment of Negroes in the Regular Army [would] be accepted without restriction as to their numbers." The War Department outlined its new policy in a "discussion format" column in one of its regular circulars. The column, entitled "Utilization of Negro Manpower in the Postwar Army," indicated a shift in military policy.

> First of all, the Army holds that it is its duty to teach American ideals, but that it is not an agency of social reform in matters either of race, racial relationship, or anything else. In time of war its business is fighting. During peace its job is preserving the peace, keeping itself ready to fight, and doing all the other things that an army does beside fight; but in no case does it set out to bring about social reform in the life of the nation. So far as questions of race are concerned, the basic interest of the Army is in its own effectiveness. In its off-post relationships with civilian communities the Army recognizes local laws and customs with respect to race and does not attempt to influence them. Within its own jurisdiction, the Army holds that every member of the military establishment should respect all other wearers of the uniform, irrespective of race.
>
> The Army realizes that equality of opportunity and treatment irrespective of race, is essential to military effectiveness. To keep racial

friction among troops to a minimum, the Army approves the organization of racially separate units; but upon the basis of experience, modifications of this practice have been announced as current policy. These modifications authorize the establishment of "composite" organizations of small Negro units and small white units, and also the establishment of racially mixed overhead and special units. The policy means that there will be in the peacetime Army a larger percentage of Negroes, doing more things, in closer association with white personnel. Personal adjustments of attitude and effort may be necessary. The revised policy and the Army's attitude in matters of race are based neither upon sentiment nor upon any special social philosophy, but upon the need for employing most effectively all manpower allotted to the Army.

In December 1946, President Harry Truman issued an executive order that established a committee on civil rights. The committee pressured the White House to institute a civil rights bill as well as to review the discriminatory practices in the armed forces. The idea for expanded civil rights, especially in the form of integration, resonated among black veterans who had fought to "make the world safe for democracy." After the war, black activists such as A. Philip Randolph established the "Committee against Jim Crow in Military Service and Training." The committee's stated goal was to end segregation and discrimination in the military, and its members vowed to use civil disobedience when necessary.

When it became politically expedient, Truman pushed for a civil rights agenda. Republicans swept into Congress in the 1946 election. The Democratic Party faced a challenge from its communist-leaning members who subsequently formed the independent Progressive Party. Also, the party encountered a threat from its southern members who followed Senator Strom Thurmond of South Carolina into his newly formed States' Rights (or Dixiecrat) Party. The Dixiecrats organized around an ideology of segregation. Meanwhile, the Republicans nominated Thomas Dewey, who made a campaign pledge to integrate the armed forces. Truman knew he needed to act boldly, because black voters, needed for his election, were concentrated in twelve of the most influential electoral states. Three weeks after the Democratic Party convention, Truman used his presidential prerogative and issued Executive Order 9981, desegregating the U.S. military. Political expediency and a hotly contested upcoming election prompted Truman to issue the executive order. What has been interpreted as "forward thinking" was really a way for Truman to get control of his party and stay ahead of rapidly changing political attitudes.

Some army generals interpreted EO 9981 as an end to segregation. Others interpreted it as an end to discrimination, but not segregation. The wording of the declaration was ambiguous.

It is hereby declared to be the policy of the President that there shall be equality of treatment and opportunity for all persons in the armed services without regard to race, color, religion, or national origin. This policy shall be put into effect as rapidly as possible, having due regard to the time required to effectuate any necessary changes without impairing efficiency or morale.

Truman held a press conference three days after issuing the executive order to clear up the misunderstanding. He said he envisioned the end of segregation—this executive order was the first step toward that goal. Black leaders rallied to support Truman in the November election, and in a famous upset, he beat Dewey and the renegades in his own party. Between the announcement of the executive order and the election, however, the military command took no steps to implement the policy outlined in EO 9981 in any branch of the armed forces. In fact, the president's own Committee on Equality and Treatment of Opportunity in the Armed Forces did not even convene until after his term began in January.

In general, when presidents issue executive orders, they do so for political reasons. Certainly, Truman's reasons for issuing EO 9981 were political. The order was issued before an election—an election "surprise." Also, at the time Truman issued the order, the military was *already* beginning to integrate some of its troops. Perhaps most importantly, the government perceived a crisis in terms of segregation and military efficiency, and thus changed military policy to reflect a new integrationist thinking. Overall, the order was a presidential grand gesture aimed toward political and social equality. However, the gesture, political and expedient as it was, resulted in a change of culture within American society and started a movement toward equality in all social and political settings and institutions. EO 9981 was in many ways the political precursor to the civil rights movement. The executive order to integrate the armed forces had long-term and long-reaching effects.

Truman appointed Charles Fahy of Georgia to head the Committee on Equality and Treatment of Opportunity in the Armed Forces. Fahy knew that many military leaders opposed integration, so he asked Truman to let him work out agreements with each branch of the service in order to smoothly implement EO 9981. The committee worked for two years, trying to nudge the armed forces toward integration. The newly formed air force was the first organization to end race-based assignments and promotions. In

May 1949, the air force implemented an enlistment plan based on merit and ability, rather than on race. The army was more resistant. Its leader, Secretary of the Army Kenneth Royall, believed the old adage that military efficiency would suffer if black men were integrated into white units. After he resigned, the new secretary ordered the integration of all army training facilities. By March 1950, the army had officially ended its race-based quotas and limitations. Also in 1950, Truman sent American troops, black and white, into Korea to support a United Nations resolution aimed at stopping a communist takeover.

In the first stages of the Korean conflict, all of the U.S. soldiers—white and black—performed poorly. The postwar military had downsized and was unprepared for serious warfare. Many of the early engagements were lost to the North Korean communists. One all-black regiment, the 24th Infantry, reportedly "melted away" in action. (The 24th Infantry's performance is currently being reevaluated, and it may turn out that the regiment's "failure" was caused by poor leadership rather than poor troop performance.) The 24th, like their white counterparts, was unprepared for war.

Truman ordered the troops in Korea to immediately integrate, so that black soldiers could not be criticized as a group. Truman did this only after he relieved General Douglas MacArthur of his command. MacArthur's chief of staff, General Edward M. Almond, former commander of the all-black 92nd Division, had been actively slowing down the "composite organization" integration that had been going on. Almond was a bigot by almost everyone's standards, as evidenced by one of his more infamous comments: he said that blacks and whites were different and should never serve together. He had commanded black troops in World War II and had nothing good to say about their performance. (He declared his ideas were not racist.) His questionable decisions as commander of the 92nd in the Italian campaign should have gotten him demoted, but for some unexplainable reason he had been promoted into the inner circle of MacArthur's most trusted advisers. From that position, he did everything possible to delay integration, even though that was a direct violation of his commander in chief's executive order.

Almond's slowdown represented the norm. To be fair, very few generals were integrating their troops. They were still wringing their hands and undertaking new studies. In fact, the army commissioned an entirely new and heavily funded social survey to determine the impact of integrating combat troops as well as soldiers-in-training. They hired civilians from Johns Hopkins University to conduct the study, which was called "Project Clear." Not surprisingly, the study showed "substantially the same frequencies of desirable and undesirable combat behavior [in black soldiers] as white soldiers. 85 percent of the officers said that blacks in integrated units performed as well as white soldiers." On bases in the United States, military leaders were following orders to desegregate, but at a deliberately slow pace. In some locations very little integration occurred, but in others, such as Fort Jackson, South Carolina, black and white troops had already been training together for some time. By 1951, all of the army training centers across the United States had integrated training. By the end of 1954, all of the remaining all-black units had been integrated or disbanded. It is ironic that the army, albeit reluctantly, integrated its forces even as much of American society remained staunchly segregated.

At the fiftieth anniversary of EO 9981, hosted by the Department of Defense, all of the usual historical facts about integration in the military were repeated by officials. What has never been discussed, except by insiders who were there, is the manner in which the executive order was carried out. Despite the presidential edict, the army did not fully integrate its troops until well into the mid-1950s. This noncompliance or slow implementation has never really been highlighted, other than to say that U.S. troops in Korea were integrated shortly after the executive order was issued, primarily to improve efficiency. Some World War II veterans were still in the service when the executive order was put into effect. They have a different story about how integration happened. The evidence suggests that integration of the troops, when finally carried out at bases at home and overseas, was conducted rapidly within a 24-hour period, albeit years after the executive order. The army was not completely integrated until six years after Truman's order.

EO 9981 was slowly instituted in the combat zones of Korea, but on noncombat military bases, the order was even slower to be enforced. Joe Stephenson noted that the troops were not integrated in the Aleutian Islands in Alaska when he had the misfortune of drawing an assignment there. "They were dragging their feet. They didn't want to integrate the army. The Congress didn't want to do it and the military, they didn't want to do it, either." But within the army, black World War II soldiers started pushing for changes. Joseph Hairston described his part in changing the culture of the army.

> One of the reasons I became a lawyer was because I always read all the rules and regulations. For instance, I knew the regulations governing the duty roster assignments. It is strictly a rotational thing. Everybody comes up in turn, but in one place we noticed that all the black officers were getting the weekend duty. So I wrote up a protest about that and got myself into a little hot water. It embarrassed the commanding officer because it was his job to make sure that all the procedures were working properly.

For Reuben Horner, integration came about on a single day in 1951 when he was stationed at Fort Dix, New Jersey. One day, the men were ordered to remain on post until they got their orders for reassignment. The new assignment schedules were posted at twelve midnight. When the men woke up the next morning, they had to look on a board to find their new assignments. Horner went to bed as the commander of a black artillery battalion, but he woke up as an executive officer in an infantry unit, with some white junior officers under his command. He said integration had happened overnight.

Harold Montgomery said the same thing happened in his all-black company in Germany.

In 1952, I was assistant chief of staff for training and operations for the 43rd Infantry Division. I was the only black member on the staff. My commanding officer was from Georgia. He called a meeting of the entire staff. He stated that he had just received word on an executive order. They call it DP orders, Directive of the President. He said, "The division will be completely integrated by retreat that day." That means when the flag comes down at 5 o'clock.

Later, from my staff office where I could look out on the parade ground and onto the helicopter pad, I could see these helicopters coming in and landing just about every three minutes. Every one of them was filled with black troops. They were bringing the black troops from all over Germany, bringing them in, integrating that division. And just like the general said, that division was completely integrated by retreat that day! That means they were dragging their feet from '48 when the president put out that executive order, but when he put out the presidential directive saying he wanted it by this date, boom, it was done.

Felix Goodwin agreed that the EO 9981, by itself, did not bring about integration in the military: "That Executive Order didn't mean a thing in '48." In Goodwin's experience, the executive order was carried out slowly at the two segregated bases where he was assigned.

At the time they started investigating whether to integrate or not, I was in Germany commanding an all-black truck company. We got word about a report [the Gillem Report of 1946] about this so-called integration, but we didn't have any part of that at all. We had practically all black troops there, all service companies—quartermaster truck, quartermaster service, the honor guard for the general, all black. At the same time as this report, they gave us some information about VD to pass on to the men, and we did that, but they gave us nothing about integration to pass on. Then they shipped me off to another truck battalion, and those men were all black except the white officers at the headquarters company.

Anyway, by this time it was in the spring of 1952, and I was told we were going to integrate the battalion. We had four or five companies from the battalion. And only one company, mine, had all the black officers and enlisted men. So I was called in, and we were told that the companies would be broken up. The new integrated companies were going to be 10 percent black, and they were bringing in white fellows from all around to form this mixed company. They would move out 10 percent of the white boys out of a company and move in 10 percent of the black company. Well, there was no problem as long as they had 10 percent of privates or corporals. But where the problem started was with your black first sergeants and master sergeants and lieutenants, of course.

Even after the troops integrated there were still problems. Goodwin continued his story:

I got moved to headquarters—that was all white guys from Lubbock, Texas. The sergeant major owned a store in Lubbock and everybody in HQ had worked with him back home. But it ended up I was pretty well running things. Our first inspection was a mess, though. Some white replacements had come in from Mississippi and Georgia and then we had about six or seven black soldiers integrated into the unit. Our guys were mostly cooks and others working in the motor pool, no black noncommissioned officers.

For the first inspection, the white soldiers had taken big sheets of white paper and drawn flags on them. There was a Confederate flag and on the other wall there was that old flag with the curled snake that said, "Don't tread on me." And they were all standing there when I walked in to inspect the area. I didn't say a word, just started inspecting the stuff in the lockers. I cited them for scuffed shoes and stuff not hung properly, but I did not say anything about those flags. I went into the next room, and it was the same thing—the same flags. The third room was like that too. The fourth room was not, and I said, "Where's all your flags?" and they said, "Sir, we are Yankees." So I didn't question them, I just moved on. But the next room had flags.

When I got to the last room I found my colored cooks, colored mechanics, and so forth. I asked one man, "Why aren't you in the room with the mechanics?" The first sergeant started stammering and told me there was not enough room for the men in the mechanics area. And I said, "Well, dammit, you better find some room. You've got six stripes on your arm, and I can take them away." He tried to tell me I could not understand him, because colored people were Protestants, and he was Catholic, but I told him, "Hey, I'm a Catholic, too." I had a reputation of being one hard man, and mostly I lived up to my reputation. So I told the sergeant to get his men assembled around the steps of the building. They all came running, and they had this grin on their faces, like oh, yeah, he's gonna be raising hell about our flags.

"Soldiers," I said, "we have a problem in our company. I see we have a very patriotic company that loves flags. But I'm mad as hell because I didn't see a United States flag up there. We've got a Confederate flag and a 'don't-tread-on-me-Revolutionary-War flag,' but I don't see the flag of our country. So starting at the front door and into every room, we are gonna have all three flags—the American flag, and then those other two that you want. Which means we are going to have to get the stands and enough flags for every room. Now in your footlockers, you're gonna have to take down your mama's pictures and your girlfriend's, and put those flags in there, too. I can't force you to buy the flags, but we'll just apportion the cost across everyone here. I think it will cost about 500 dollars. So all the men who do not want to pay for the flags, just step over here to my left."

Well, that left about fifteen guys to my right, and they were looking at me like I was crazy. So I told them that they had about three hours to raise the money. When we met again in three hours, of course those men did not have the money. But they could tell I wasn't going to take any of that mess. I told them they would all be privates if this thing didn't clear up. I said, "This is the United States Army. I don't give a damn if your daddy is Robert E. Lee or J.E.B. Stuart or whoever. It makes no difference to me. The Civil War is over."

But I was tough on the black guys, too. When they complained I told them, "I don't care how high up you are in the NAACP. We have an American company here in Germany, and you are going to obey the army regulations. I don't intend to have any racial problems in my company." When we had our reinspection we made a 97 out of 100. We continuously got the highest grades in the corps. Those fifteen guys just fell in line and became military after that. They may have muttered among themselves but not to me.

FAMILIES ON THE FRONT LINE OF EQUALITY

No executive order or presidential directive could spell out the proper procedures for integrating the social settings on military bases. At least the soldiers had their instructions, but their dependents—spouses and children—
were left to manage the process on their own. Harold Montgomery
remembered what it was like when he and his wife, Helen, attended the first
formal party held after integration. At such parties, the soldiers and their
wives customarily lined up inside the ballroom by rank or grade to form a
greeting line. The base's commanding general would be at the top of the
configuration, and his deputy commanders would be flanking him. That
would have placed the Montgomerys far down the receiving line. But all that
changed at the spring ball of 1952.

> I was standing by my wife when the general and his wife came in. He
> had the deputy commander behind him, and he had the artillery com-
> mander behind him. He was supposed to go right in and get in line,
> but he didn't. The general took the other officers with their ladies and
> walked all the way across that ballroom where I was located. He said,
> "Major, I'd like for you to introduce Mrs. Montgomery to the general
> officers of my division." In other words, that was a signal to all of the
> officers in there: "Look, I brought this black officer in here, and he's
> the only one on my staff. Don't give him a hard way to go." That was
> the signal. He walked all the way across that floor. And I hadn't any
> trouble after that.

As slowly as the work and social settings were integrated overseas, it was
nothing compared to the slowdowns at military bases across the South. After
helping to integrate a military base in Germany, Felix Goodwin and his family returned to the United States for a few years of stateside postings. In
1953, six years after Truman's executive order to integrate, the Goodwins
found the military bases in Louisiana completely segregated. Naturally,
Goodwin challenged all aspects of the segregated system. But now, unlike
his first postwar assignments, Goodwin had support; the general who had requested that Goodwin be assigned to his staff wanted Goodwin to spearhead
the changes. A new day had dawned in Louisiana, and the old guard was vir-
ulently resistant to the changes.

When the Goodwin family first arrived in Louisiana, they stayed at a hotel
in New Orleans that catered to blacks until they could get officers' quarters.
When Goodwin asked for housing at the base, he was driven to an empty,
dusty, and unused barracks. He said the barracks were boarded up and about
90 degrees inside.

I told the sergeant to drive me back to HQ. When we pulled up, I saw the captain standing in the window looking out at us. Then he slipped away. I told the sergeant to take me to the back door of the building, and when we got there we met that captain coming out his door. We had a little talk, and finally he said he was going to take me to the VIP quarters. And that was funny, because when we got there, a black maid was there and she told me right off, "You're in the wrong place."

I told her to please get out of my way and let my children come in, and she was just adamant, telling me that I could not come in there. Finally, she said, "Well, we never had no colored officer in here." And I said, "Well, now you do."

Goodwin, almost single-handedly, had to integrate every place else on the base, including the bars and the toilets.

They wouldn't serve me in the officers' bar. I don't drink, but I was just checking it out to see what they would do about me. They wanted me to go to the colored NCO [noncommissioned officers] club, but I said, "I'm an officer, and I will not go to any back rooms. I expect to be served." This old white-haired man in civilian clothes jumped up and called me a black s.o.b. I asked the bartender who the old white-haired bastard was, and he jumped out of his chair. He said, "You want to know who this old white-haired bastard is?"

And I said, "Yes, I want to know. You are the one that called me a black son of a bitch, so I presume that we should know each other." He said he was the commander of the base, but you see he was retiring. That's how come I was there. I was brought in with the new general. I had just gotten there a little early.

The commander told me, "By God, if I wasn't retiring I'd court-martial you," but I told him, "Sir, if you weren't retiring I wouldn't be down here. I didn't ask to be here. The general wanted me here."

When the general got there we had all kinds of things to fix up and integrate. Like, they had segregated toilets. There were toilets for officers, enlisted men, white ladies, white men, colored ladies, and colored men. The only colored man working there was the janitor! I told the general about the situation, and he called a sort-of spot inspection. Naturally I called attention when he walked in and I saluted him and all.

He said, "How many toilets do you have here, Goodwin?" And I told him. He said, "How many sexes work out here, Goodwin?" And I said, "Sir, as far as I know, only two." He said we would only keep two toilets, then, and which ones did I want to keep. I looked him dead in the eye and didn't crack a smile and said, "Sir, I have never been in the white ladies' toilet." He knew it was a lie, because I had been in there to check it out and see if we wanted to keep it. But we made a show of going over to look at it.

Let me tell you, in the white ladies' room they had a couch; they had a chest of drawers and a big mirror. They had dispensers and hand-towels. In the colored toilets they just had the latrines with a partition pulled between them. The partition did not even come to the floor; there was no privacy. So I told the general, "Sir, I would like to keep the other one for the ladies, and I would like to keep the white offi-cers' toilet for the men. We do not need an enlisted men's toilet." We set the other rooms up as supply rooms, and one was turned into a mimeograph room. Some of those white women had a real problem with sharing their space, but after a little adjustment and a few con-frontations, we just made it all work out.

All across the country, at a number of military bases, black soldiers and their families tested the system. As with the enemy in World War II, there were still pockets of resistance, and thus the fight continued. Joseph Hair-ston and his family encountered one of those pockets. They were traveling from California to Virginia for a new assignment. Hairston made reserva-tions across the country at guesthouses on military bases, because at that time, black people were not allowed to stay at some hotels. Hairston figured it was easier if he just planned the trip with stops at military bases. He ar-rived at Fort Benning, Georgia, after a full day of driving with a carload of kids. He was greeted by a white woman who said to him, "You'll have to go to the other side of the base for your guesthouse."

Hairston was tired and short-tempered. He shot back: "Look, I fought in a war, I'm in the army, and I have a right to stay anywhere on this military base." A white man came running out of the guesthouse and admonished Hairston for speaking so harshly to a white woman. Hairston recalled: "So I pulled out my notebook and said, 'Just who the hell are you two? I'm going to take down your names and get you thrown off this base for being un-American." Hairston got a room for the night, but he said he hardly slept at all, worrying about how they were going to get away from there in the morn-ing. He woke up the family at 5 a.m. and "very quietly snuck out of that place." His oldest daughter was posted to look out the back of the car to make sure no one followed them off the base.

By 1955, the military high command reported on the progress of integration in the armed services. The pockets of resistance had cleared, and integration was a success. The report signaled a clear shift away from the segregated culture of World War II. After the usual disclaimer that the Department of Defense (no longer the War Department) maintained no racial statistics, James C. Evans, the civilian assistant to the secretary of defense, wrote:

> The program of equity of opportunity for all personnel, military and civilian, is based on the concept of obtaining maximum effectiveness in the defense effort through full utilization of the maximum potential of every individual. Anything less is wasteful, especially in view of threats to our national security, besides being contrary to the basic tenets of our government.

The army would always defer to efficiency, and now the predominant ideology equated segregation with inefficiency. Allen Thompson attributed these sea changes in military thinking to contributions of black World War II veterans:

> You think about the number of men we had under arms; we changed everything when we came back home. We changed the political structure of this country. That's something we felt, that I have just as much stake in this society, in this republic, as anyone else. My ancestors were here before some of these people who are claiming to be citizens ever thought about getting here. It was a groundswell. It was a matter of a mass of people beginning to learn to read and to understand the political structure and what it means to get involved in the political structure that changes things. You don't go out throwing bricks and rocks. You get in the system, and you work within the system to change. That's what happened for the veterans of World War II.

World War II veterans changed the culture of the military and went on to change the social fabric of America.

From the official record it seems clear that military planners during the Cold War wanted to advance racial harmony on military bases in order to improve efficiency. They realized that racial disharmony within the military would lead to an ineffective fighting force. They also recognized that racial friction on military bases could spill over into nearby civilian communities, embroiling the public in unnecessary and unhealthy disputes. Within military compounds, integrated troops lived in integrated housing, went to integrated schools, and worshipped in integrated churches. In the 1955 progress report, Evans wrote, "the impact [of military integration] on civilian life is yet to be measured." Now we *can* measure the impact of military integration based on Truman's executive order: it paved the way for the advancement of African American civil, political, and social rights.

Despite its prior segregationist policies, the military was, remarkably, the first element of U.S. society to officially abolish segregation. Although committees were convened, investigations conducted, and recommendations written suggesting integration, no official change in military policy was instituted until long after World War II. As society struggled to deal with returning black soldiers and ensuing racial difficulties, the military became the first organization to engage in social engineering and address institutionalized racism in a proactive manner. After Truman's executive order, military bases around the world were incrementally integrated. Although neither the military hierarchy nor society at large was ready for full integration, the armed forces experimented with integration and ultimately proved that soldiers were soldiers, no matter their skin color. Many of the men who spearheaded military integration were veterans of the segregated combat units in World War II. This social experiment affected the consciousness of its individual participants, who were on the front line of integration. As issues of segregation and discrimination began to tear apart the country, ironically, the military became a weapon in the integration wars. A few years after the armed forces were integrated, President Dwight D. Eisenhower deployed troops to protect nine young students who were integrating a high school in Arkansas.

SOLDIERS FOR FREEDOM ONCE AGAIN

Black veterans joined and sometimes led the nationwide fight for equality. Oliver Brown (of the landmark *Brown v. Board of Education* decision), Medgar Evers, Nelson Peery, Alex Pitcher, Louis Stokes, and Coleman Young are just a few of the better-known World War II veterans who were involved in the civil rights and black power movements. These men, and many more like them, believed they had proved their loyalty to America and should be granted equality—the cornerstone of the American ideal. They would not passively accept discrimination. While some men joined organizations to battle discrimination, others responded in a scattered, noncohesive, and sometimes violent manner. Whatever the dominant ideology or tactic in their battle against discrimination, the veterans of World War II participated on the front lines. There was a range of opinions regarding the proper response to racism.

Bill Payne commented:

A lot of the sixties movement came from some of the veterans who came back after World War II with radical ideas. You know, they just

weren't going to take it anymore. They felt they were owed, and they
were going to get their just due. I wasn't one of those people; I was
never considered radical. But I say more power to those that were
radical.

Another World War II veteran, Jim Williams, agreed that black veterans took
action against racism:

I knew that the black veterans had a certain anger. We felt as though
we served our country, and we weren't going to stand for that nonsense
anymore. Many of them just rebelled. You had little pockets of rebellion all over the nation. But in essence they went about it in the wrong
way, because to fight it with force will get you nowhere.

Other foot soldiers in the battle for civil rights used tactics learned from
their days in the military to advance the movement. Joseph Hairston explained how his military training helped him. In 1963 Hairston was working
at the conservative Internal Revenue Service in Washington, D.C. A civil
rights march was planned by A. Philip Randolph, labor and civil rights
leader; James Farmer, head of the Congress on Racial Equality; and Martin
Luther King Jr., Southern Christian Leadership Council spokesman. When
Hairston's boss at the IRS heard that he was involved in planning the event,
he tried to prevent him from participating. But Hairston was a step ahead—
he used a preemptive strike to outwit his boss. "When he called me in,"
Hairston explained, "I suspected that he was about to forbid me to participate in the march. I beat him to the punch when I delivered a sermon on
Americanism and nonviolence. I said it was up to us to keep the peace, and
then I ended by asking him if he wanted to join us."

The organizers of the 1963 March on Washington worked with local
CORE people to stage the march. The local CORE president was a World
War II veteran who had served in Italy with Hairston. The organizers did not
want to be discredited by any sort of violence, and they were aware that a
heavy police presence might upset the marchers. Hairston and the CORE
president worked together to organize a military-like system of crowd control for the march. The elaborate security system was based on a military
regiment—three battalions with five companies in each battalion. Each
company commander was stationed at strategic intervals along the march
route. All of the commanders had radios that they used to keep in contact
with regimental headquarters, and HQ regularly reported to the local police.
And indeed, there was no violence at the 1963 March on Washington: black
veterans had organized security and kept the peace.

Some black veterans were less visible in the movement. Woodrow Walton had left the service by the time the integration battles started at high schools in the South. He decided to take a stand in the fight. "When integration started," he recalled, "I pulled the two older boys out of black schools and put them in white schools. I knew at the time it had to be broken down some way or another." Felix Goodwin was also more of a silent partner in the civil rights movement. He explained:

> As an army officer, I couldn't be out in the street, but I could put three or four hundred dollars into a cause that I felt worthy. I was a member of the local board of directors of the NAACP, and I was involved with my fraternity, Alpha Phi Alpha, the oldest black fraternity in the country. We were involved in civil rights and all those things. Still, many of the students at the University of Arizona, where I was the assistant to the president, had this idea that those of us who had been able to advance within the power structure had sold out. It was very hard for them to understand that if you weren't in the streets, you could still be doing something worthwhile. To the local kids I was an "Uncle Tom." They felt like they were making a big contribution to things.
>
> What most of them didn't know was that the changes only came when you got around the table, not when you were out in the middle of something. I had a problem trying to get through to the young black kids. They just didn't understand that you can be in the street with a broken bottle, but the white man doesn't give a damn about you. He is not afraid of you. I fought with him in North Africa, Italy, the Far East, and believe me, white Americans as a group have no reason to fear blacks. They have the weapons and the whole power structure, including the law, behind them. Why do you think being in the street with a brick or a bottle is going to scare him?

Goodwin's pragmatic approach did not always win him friends, but as he notes, he did get ahead. And, as we now know, the movement for civil rights was politically successful.

"Being in the armed forces, you're trained to have courage," Alex Pitcher said.

> It makes you a man. You get tough, and so you're not afraid. It takes the fear out of you. The thing that keeps people from fighting for their rights is the fear. The fear of what's going to happen to them. Fear of hurting their family. Fear of losing their job. Fear of losing the car and fear of losing the home. Fear will stop people from doing a lot of things.

Pitcher says the veterans learned how to work together as a group and how to push ahead without letting fear immobilize them.

In 1962, Levi Hill was stationed at Montgomery, Alabama, in a military procurement office. Most of the workers on the base, and nearly all of the civilian defense contractors, were white. Hill did most of his work over the phone.

> On the eve before the Martin Luther King march [in Montgomery], this one outside contractor that I had been working with for two years strictly by telephone said to me: "What do you think about that nigger Martin Luther King?" And you know he kept on and all. He'd never met me; we were always working on the telephone, and I guess since I was from the North or something, he didn't think I could be black.
>
> Anyway, I told him, "Well, I work for the U.S. government, and I am not free to comment on that matter," so pretty soon he was spent. A few weeks later over the phone he suggested that he could drop off something that I needed at my office. I said, "Okay" and told him how to get to my area. I saw him when he came in, and he walked right through my area. Finally I said, "Can I help you?" and he said, "I'm looking for Sergeant Hill."
>
> And I said, "I'm Sergeant Hill." Hell, I had my name-tag on, my desk had a big name-plate that said "Sergeant Hill." I wish I had a camera, because he just came unglued. Finally, he had to sit down, and he just couldn't even say anything except blubbering some kind of apology. Later, after he was back at his office and all recovered from the shock, he called and said, "Well, I guess that's the end of my contracts with your office?" And I told him, "No. You have good products and you do good work, and I won't let the color of your skin get in the way." And you know, he learned something. One person learned something about race and prejudice.

In 1963, after evaluating the Report of the President's Committee on Equal Opportunity, President John F. Kennedy wrote to Secretary of Defense Robert McNamara:

> We have come a long way in the 15 years since President Truman ordered the desegregation of the Armed Forces. The military services lead almost every other segment of our society in establishing equality of opportunity for all Americans. Yet, a great deal remains to be done. A serious morale problem is created for Negro military personnel when various forms of segregation and discrimination exist. Discriminatory

practices are morally wrong wherever they occur—they are especially inequitable and iniquitous when they inconvenience and embarrass those serving in the Armed Services and their families.

Kennedy then went on to request that all military officials adopt solutions to the morale problems noted in the report and implement them within thirty days. "I realize," Kennedy commanded, "I am asking the military community to take a leadership role, but I believe that this is proper. The Armed Services will, I am confident, be equal to the task. In this area, as in so many others, the U.S. Infantry motto 'Follow Me' is an appropriate guide for action."

From the U.S. House of Representatives, Congressman and World War II veteran Louis Stokes wrote in 1996 to his fellow servicemen: "Segregation is evil and divisive. We rose above it to be strong, courageous and cohesive both on the battlefront and the home front. May the lessons of those days serve all society well." The lessons Hank Williams learned in World War II have served him well in his life: "I think my time in the service did as much for me as it did for the country," he said. Even with segregation, black soldiers discovered many advantages to life in the army.

Felix Goodwin concurred:

> Life in the military was tough. Still I loved it. I made a life out of it for me and my family. We went through some rough times with the integration. I had some good white NCOs and some good black ones, too. Some of the men are still my friends today. There were also some very prejudiced officers. I had poor white officers and poor black ones, too. I mean people who did not have the ability to do their job well.

Goodwin stayed in the service, moving up and moving around. One of his last assignments as post information officer took him back to Fort Huachuca, Arizona, the base where he had begun his military career. Prejudice still prevailed in the 1960s as it had during the 1940s. Goodwin said the post commander told him: "You can't be information officer here. The folks around here won't accept a colored officer as the information officer." Goodwin said the commander "started in with all the standard myths and yip-yap about the ranchers in the area and black folk." They put him in charge of transportation, hoping to get him out of the limelight, but later he was promoted to chief of services, with transportation and communications both under his purview. His last position there was higher in command than information officer—the job they tried to discourage him taking!

Before they were sent into combat in World War II, many black soldiers struggled against segregated and unequal conditions on military bases and in

neighboring towns in the United States. The story of black soldiers who
fought in World War II against the Axis powers, and also against racism
within the military, is a story of individuals and their reactions to social and
political conditions. But the men were always more than the sum of their
segregation. The individual battles of black soldiers reveal a compelling story
of discrimination, resistance, camaraderie, and triumph. Whether they were
fighting for the Double V—democracy at home and abroad—or to be sent
into combat, or to be in integrated units, black soldiers were always actively
involved in battles. Some were fought with bullets, others with words and
deeds.

These last stories illustrate the number of ways that black veterans of
World War II continued to battle against prejudice after the war. Joe
Stephenson drew a profound lesson from one of those battles:

> I have a little grandson, and he is eight years old. He's a real bright lit-
> tle fella. He says, "Granddaddy, what would have happened to me if
> you had gotten killed in the war?" I said, "Son, I never thought about
> that."
>
> And it made me think of this time in Italy when we were sneaking
> up on this enemy house. I started to stand up, but I paused. And at the
> moment that I paused, a machine gun shot right over my head. If I
> hadn't paused it would have caught me right in the middle. When my
> grandson asked me that question, I thought about that—we wouldn't
> be here. Well, now I look at my little grandchildren, I've got four of
> them now, and I say, "I hope you never see anything like war."

6

AFTERWORD

The conflagration called World War II touched everyone in the world and forever changed international and domestic relations. The individuals who experienced the war, either stateside or in the international arena, were profoundly affected by their experiences. America and her citizens came of age in those life-altering years of the war. Young black men who were hardened by the Depression years were tested further in the battlefields of the segregated army. Black military wives and nurses forged a life in a world that was inhospitable and prejudiced at every turn. After their struggles and triumphs in the war years, these new Omni-Americans returned to change the social fabric of the regions they inhabited.

Several examples illustrate the way the war changed the individual foot soldier. Nelson Peery began developing his political ideology while he was in the army. From his last posting in the Philippines he wrote to his mother: "I doubt if I'm a communist but I do feel I have some leaning to the left and a little speck of red." When he got out of the service, he refined his ideology and began to apply his military skills to organizing workers to fight for human rights. Peery immediately joined the Communist Party because he was "very taken with their theory of 'Self Determination for the Negro Nation.'" He used the GI Bill to go to the University of Minnesota, but after eighteen months he came to the conclusion that he could not be a revolutionary while attending school. He left the university and began organizing his fellow workers in the bricklaying industry.

With its sense of mission and discipline, the Communist Party offered Peery a safe haven to recover from the bitterness of his war experiences. But by 1954 he was disillusioned with the party as an organization because of its class and racial composition. He was expelled from the party, along with many working-class blacks, for not abandoning their support for the Negro Labor Council, which the Communist Party disapproved of. He went underground for a few years, including a stint in Watts, California, during the uprising, all the time organizing workers to fight for more humane working conditions. By 1966 he had formed the Communist Labor Party, within which he continued to agitate for workers' rights. In the 1990s he joined other concerned organizers and workers in the League of Revolutionaries for a New America, finally focusing his battles against the labor disruptions of the new technologies of robotics and computerization in the global workplace. He says now, over seventy, he thinks someone else should be leading the movement, but you can still find him any day of the week actively engaged in finding ways to improve the welfare of the American worker.

Peery's motives for organizing for a better world illustrate one of the many ways the returning veteran tried to change his environment, but embracing communism was atypical for most. Other black veterans abhorred communism, actively engaging in military maneuvers against governments that espoused the ideology. Felix Goodwin, Bill Payne, and Joe Stephenson stayed in the service and fought against the communist governments of the Soviet Union and China in the battlefields of Korea and Vietnam. As a company commander and battalion executive officer in Korea, Joe Stephenson was on the front line of the battle. He returned to the United States to serve for a time as a paratrooper in the 82nd Airborne Division, finally ending his military career teaching ROTC to other army hopefuls at Howard University and A&T University. He retired from the army with twenty years of experience, and for the next twenty years he taught social studies to high school students in Prince George's County, Maryland.

Shortly after returning from the Pacific, Bill Payne began working for the U.S. Postal Service in Cleveland. He also held down a few night jobs just to make ends meet. When he got a letter from the army in 1951 asking him to come back to active duty for sixty days to umpire a war game at Fort Bragg, North Carolina, he decided to reenlist and make a career out of the army. He was stationed in Germany, did a stint in Korea, and a later tour of duty in Vietnam, interspersed with several stateside postings. After he was shot in the leg in Vietnam, he was awarded the Purple Heart and shipped home, where he retired from the army. After recuperating from his war wounds, he went to work for an insurance company and finally ended his career working for the State of California Employment Division. Now you can find Bill enjoying his life with his fun-loving wife, Vergie, in Indianapolis.

Felix Goodwin and his wife, Barbara, are enjoying "la vida buena" in Tucson, Arizona. It's hard to find them there, as they are always on the road traveling on holiday or to one of the many conventions they attend for their fraternity and sorority organizations. Although Barbara and Felix met long after the war, Barbara's mother used to work at Fort Huachuca during the 1940s. Felix stayed in the service and had tours in Germany, Korea, Okinawa, and Greenland. His last posting was Fort Huachuca, where he retired as a lieutenant colonel after thirty years of service. But that was not the end of his career. He received his doctorate in education from the University of Arizona and went on to serve the university as assistant to the president. During the black power struggles of the 1970s, he instituted affirmative actions to increase the number of black students at that campus.

After World War II, Spencer and Susie Moore resettled in Magnolia, New Jersey, where they live today close to their two children and grandchildren. Spencer tried college for a while, but he was plagued by combat nightmares from his time in the service. His father, "an old country doctor," advised him to get a job doing hard work to make his mind rest. He worked at a cinderblock plant for a while and then apprenticed with a carpenter. None of the labor unions at the time allowed black members, so he moved from job to job, from collecting trash to cleaning buses. The bus companies also discriminated against black workers, but he managed to advance and became the fourth black driver in south Jersey. He was simultaneously active with the National Guard, where he continued his military training and service, retiring after almost twenty years of duty. He finished out his working life with twenty years of service with the U.S. Postal Service. In October of each year, you'll find Spencer and Susie at the annual meeting of the 92nd Division World War II Association of veterans. They have quite a collection of Buffalo Soldier memorabilia, which they display at the meeting.

Every December 7th you'll find Hank Williams and Bill Perry at a fancy dinner ball in Cleveland, Ohio, sponsored by the Huachucan Veteran's Club. Bill attends both the Huachucan dinner ball and the 92nd Division annual meeting. Bill's personal collection of World War II memorabilia frustrates his wife's best efforts to keep the place organized, but it's a researcher's dream to drift through it. After the war, he was discouraged from taking art classes with live models, yet he persevered, completing his art degree at Ohio State in 1950. Still, he ran into discrimination at his first job after college. The surveying company that employed him asked that he work at home drawing his plots and plans, because his presence might disturb the white women who worked at the office. Fed up with that nonsense, Bill was able to land a position in the Cleveland Public School Business Department, where he worked for the next thirty years. He was a draftsman, an assistant to the business manager, and finally, the Equal Opportunity director.

Hank Williams started the Huachucan organization during the war just to get the Cleveland recruits together for "booze and broads." For a few years after the war, the club languished as the men pursued careers, but ultimately they reconvened the group. Hank worked in marketing, promoting everything from clothing to beer. When he realized he kept training new workers to become his boss, he decided to quit and open his own store. For twelve years, Hank and his wife ran a well-respected wine and beer outlet. Hank also worked days as a divorce investigator for the Cleveland courts. Later he moved to the Regional Transit Authority as the Affirmative Action officer. He is very active with church work, fraternity fellowships, and of course the Huachucans, whose members now include ex-servicewomen and female historians.

As you can see from this brief snapshot, the men and women who tell their stories throughout this book continue to play an active role in postwar America. Now in their seventies and eighties, all of the participants remember the war years as life-altering. This generation of black men and women

Telling war stories fifty years later. The author with Bill Payne
and Nelson Peery of the 93rd Infantry Division at Fort
Mason in San Francisco. (Photo by David Weintraub © 1995)

is usually overlooked in the history of the civil rights struggle, but in fact, its members were active participants. The war galvanized a whole new consciousness for them, and they returned home to demand their place within the fabric of American life. We have learned about ourselves as Americans from this generation of men and women. This enriched understanding of ourselves is their legacy and their gift to us.

METHODS AND SOURCES

In order to construct this previously unrecorded history, I first reviewed the literature of World War II. After reading a few grand narratives of the era, I was able to extract very little about the contributions of black soldiers in the war. My graduate advisers suggested a few secondary sources, and I diligently reviewed the monographs. Secondary sources record the findings of people who did not directly observe the events being described, but who probably investigated primary sources for the analysis. For the most part, the secondary sources I used, mostly academic or military manuscripts, relied on government records. Also, nearly every secondary source relied on an extensive tome by Ulysses Lee, a military historian employed by the government's Office of Military History. Lee's 1966 book, *The United States Army in World War II: The Employment of Negro Troops*, was re-released in 1994 in preparation for the fiftieth-year reunions of World War II. Lee's book was particularly helpful to me for guidance in locating primary sources in the government archives. Bernard Nalty and Morris MacGregor compiled an extensive collection of primary source documents titled *Blacks in the Military: Essential Documents*, which was invaluable in my work.

I traveled to the National Archives in College Park, Maryland, outside of Washington, D.C., and looked through official records of government and military departments. The military employs an "army" of workers to keep track of every matter—major or minor. They can really aggregate the minutia as illustrated in the numerous scientific studies they conducted during World War II. Official correspondence, memos, and documents of government departments and the military hierarchy are quoted in this book. For this work, I found particularly useful the records of the Office of War Information, the personnel files of the general staff located in the War Department records, the Office of Censorship records, and the Federal Security Agency records. I utilized the unit records of the 92nd and 93rd Infantry Divisions that I located at both the National Archives and the Military History Institute at Carlisle Barracks, Pennsylvania. The African American Museum and Library of Oakland, California, and the Fort Huachuca Museum in Arizona were instrumental in the formulation of this book. Several World War II collections were also helpful, including the personal collection of Anthony Powell, an independent curator in San Jose, California; the Huachucan Veteran's Association files in Cleveland, Ohio; and the 92nd Infantry Division World War II Association's documents and memorabilia in Washington, D.C.

I wanted to find evidence that recorded the actual words of the men who served in the segregated army of World War II. I looked for autobiographies, oral histories, newspaper articles, diaries, and letters but uncovered very few personal recollections in the National Archives. Only a small number of first-hand accounts from the men involved in the segregated service are located in those files. I located two out-of-print texts that partially filled in that gap: Phillip McGuire's 1983 collection of correspondence, *Taps for a Jim Crow Army: Letters from Black Soldiers in World War II*, and Mary Penick Motley's magnificent collection of interviews, *The Invisible Soldier: The Experience of the Black Soldier in World War II*. From Motley's book I have extracted parts of her interviews with George Looney, Willie Lawton, Lester Duane Simons, Wade McCree, Richard Carter, Clyde Blue, William Purnell Shelton, Albert Evans, Bill Stevens, and Henry Peoples—black veterans primarily from the Detroit, Michigan, area. One day on National Public Radio my husband heard an interview with Nelson Peery about his service in the 93rd Infantry Division. Nelson's autobiography, *Black Fire: The Making of an American Revolutionary*, had just been released; my husband knew I was searching for leads, so he duly noted the citation. I purchased the book, read it, wrote to Nelson's publisher, and began a life-long relationship with one of the men who had been there and, coincidentally, knew my father.

Locating the texts was a valuable first step in the writing of this book; however, it was my own personal interviews with participants that gave "life" to this story. For this project, I interviewed fifty black Americans about their experiences during the war years. Many of the veterans are still alive and eager to tell their stories. I collected oral histories, "stories," from previously unheard voices. Most of the stories are not familiar to the general public, but they have been bandied about, told and retold, for the past fifty-five years. The stories I collected are descriptive of the black experience during World

War II and represent a good cross section of the types of stories and recollections of the participants. They have been told for years between the men
who served and their families; among the veterans; or, in my case, to the his-
torian willing to listen. The people who participated in the interviews are
listed in alphabetical order: William S. M. Banks, Oglesby Barrett, John
Beavers, Sam Broadnax, Albert Burke, Roland Dix, Ruth Jones Earl, Arthur
Goodwin, Felix Goodwin, Allen Green, Joseph Hairston, Charles Hanson,
Dennett Harrod, Arnett Hartsfield, Cleother Hathcock, Howard Hickerson,
Levi Hill, Reuben Horner, Jehu Hunter, Fred Hurns, Ezell Jackson,
Lawrence Johnson, Madine Davis Lane, Robert Madison, Mrs. Robert
(Leatrice) Madison, Mick Marshall, William "Ted" McCullough, I.P.
McIver, Mrs. I. P. (Dorothy) McIver, Thomas McKinney, Cullen McKissock,
Harold Montgomery, Mrs. Harold (Helen) Montgomery, Spencer Moore,
Mrs. Spencer (Susie) Moore, William "Bill" Payne, Nelson Peery, A. William
"Bill" Perry, Alex Pitcher, Edward Price, Joe Stephenson, Allen Thompson,
W. E. "Burg" Turner, Woodrow Walton, Fred Watt, Charles Wesly, Edgar
Whitley, Clyde Whitted, Hank Williams, Jim Williams, and Mrs. Jim
Williams. From these interviews, I was able to combine individual recollec-
tions with official histories in order to reconstruct the story of life in the seg-
regated army during World War II.

In all of the interviews I used a tape recorder and some thirty questions,
more or less depending on the interviewee. I did deviate from the formality
and structure of my questions when I would hear a story that I knew would
make an interesting addition to the book. For instance, I would never have
known that razorback hogs ran wild over the camps where the men stayed
in Louisiana. Nothing in the archives or the military histories indicated these
sorts of difficulties.

I found the interviewees in a variety of ways. The first two men were from
Oakland, California, and I collected their stories as part of an internship that
I served at the African American Museum and Library at Oakland. That in-
stitution placed an advertisement in the newspaper, and two men answered
the ad and participated in interviews for an upcoming exhibit on World War
II. Those men gave me names of soldiers in other parts of the country, and
I began locating more men to interview. There is a large organization of veterans, the Huachucans, in Cleveland, Ohio, which started up in 1941 and
continues to this day. I had been communicating with the then-president,
Hank Williams, when I decided to go out to Cleveland and meet the men
personally. By the end of my stay there, the *Cleveland Plain Dealer* newspaper had come out to interview and photograph me interviewing the members. I was inducted into the Huachucans as an honorary member, and now
my membership placard sits alongside my framed graduate degree.

In Washington, D.C., Harold Montgomery, past president of the 92nd Infantry Division World War II Association, invited me to their yearly dinner celebration, where I met and interviewed a large group of veterans. I attended another annual reunion of black veterans in Greensboro, North Carolina, and conducted a few interviews between the numerous rounds of cards. On several occasions, I visited the area around Fort Huachuca, Arizona, to look through the military archives there, and I located a few veterans still living in the area where they had trained in World War II. The director of the museum and military archives, Jim Finley, was very helpful and, in fact, has added some of my transcribed interviews to the museum's collections for future researchers. I also interviewed some of the wives and nurses who were stationed with the men. At times, the women were more descriptive in their accounts of military life than the men.

Initially, I spent at least an hour and a half with each interviewee. More often, I spent several additional hours with each subject when the stories could not be contained on one tape. I would have spent more time with each person if I had it to do over again. I feel they deserved more time. Although Hollywood is able to condense extended periods of time into two-hour narratives, I found it nearly impossible. At times, I felt as if the stories were a burden, and I found myself oppressed by the poignancy of some of the tales. I felt rushed to get the men's words into print to provide a living legacy for their families and the general public. Sometimes I knew it was the last time that a man would ever tell his story and I felt a duty to the men and their memories. I asked the interviewees to tell me their beliefs, feelings, motives, and understanding of the facts. I asked them to explain to me their conscious reasons for their own actions. This is one of the ways this book is different from a simple retelling of war stories. In most gatherings of old men, feelings are generally not talked about.

Memory is a problem in the data collection process. None of the subjects prepared for the interview other than making a pot of coffee. We relied on their memory of events as the questions unfolded. I usually returned another day and continued with more questions. This gave the men another opportunity to "set the record straight," to clear up forgotten facts, or in more cases to relay another story they thought of while I was gone. Relying on a person's memory can be problematic, and I was aware of this as I conducted the interviews. Because many of the men have told their stories so often, I questioned the veracity of some, yet I continued to collect them. The stories have been corroborated with archival evidence where possible, and at other times multiple interviewees told the same story. Some of the stories could not be verified, and when I knew the facts to be in error, I did not include the narrative. I rarely included the name of an individual spoken about, although I may have retained their rank. I am aware that favorite stories take on a life of their own, but I believe this storytelling aspect enriched the archival evidence. Another potential problem I encountered centered on the events happening so long ago, and I questioned the memories of the men. I wondered if they had augmented their memories with secondary materials, but overall, the secondary materials are so lean as to be virtually nonexistent. I asked the interviewees to focus on their own personal experiences, rather than on a sequence of historical events. I never corrected the men; that was not my job or my aim. I collected the story, checked it against the records as best I could, fixed up the language, and went on to the next interview.

The interview setting was always predetermined and formal and held at locations such as the men's homes or clubhouses. Thus, my research methods were separated from the informal ethnographic techniques used by many researchers. I acted as the data collection instrument in this qualitative research project. I got signed permissions from all of the participants to use their words and photographs in my doctoral dissertation, in presentations, and also in this book. I paid typists to transcribe and digitize the interviews. I read the transcripts, highlighted components, and pulled together similar stories in order to construct intelligible narratives. Many men had photographs from the time period, and I used my computer scanner to capture those images, some of which you see here in this book. To set the mood for my research, I listened to the music that the men told me they listened to during World War II. You have read some of the lyrics throughout this text. I also read newspaper accounts of daily events, in an effort to understand and incorporate common slang and jargon. I watched several films about World War II to get a visual appreciation of the events of the day. I studied a 1943 military propaganda film by Frank Capra called *The Negro Soldier* and compared it with a 1995 Department of Defense (DoD) documentary titled *The African American Soldier in World War II*. Capra's film was part of the military series "Why We Fight," and it was specifically crafted to get black Americans to join the war effort. The 1995 DoD film was a self-congratulatory, but still instructive, example of historical revisionism. Some of the men I interviewed for this book can be seen in that film. I also evaluated popular movies about black participation in World War II, including the recent HBO film *The Tuskegee Airmen*, and a 1980s film version of the play *A Soldier's Story*. After all the hoopla died down, I finally studied *Saving Private Ryan*, and like others, I wondered why director Steven Spielberg did not position a few black soldiers as support to the archetypical white GIs. In this book, you have read that the experiences of war were as life-forming for blacks as they were for whites.

Conducting my research, I crossed race, age, and gender barriers, and I did so without a great deal of distrust or hostility. I knew the official history of black soldiers in World War II before I met any of the men, and this knowledge engendered their respect and trust. I am the daughter of one of their commanding officers, which could have worked against me—very few men have anything nice to say about their white officers. But in fact, my military status gave me added credibility with the men. Some researchers have detailed specific problems they have encountered when conducting research in "minority communities." They believe that minority scholars studying minority communities, "stand-point theorists," are less likely to encounter distrust and hostility from their subjects. Some scholars even take an apologist stance, "I can't know what it is like to be black," thus discrediting their own work. I did not live in the 1940s, I am not a black man, and I was never really in the army. However, I have studied, listened, and learned over the years, and although I will never know what it was really like to be a black soldier in World War II, I feel confident that I have portrayed the history from an informed point of view.

I engage in this self-reflexivity here to avoid what some scholars have characterized as deeply distorted research from those researchers engaged in "racial studies." Because much of the earlier scholarship concerning black people has been distorted, I take this opportunity to illuminate the reasons behind my engagement with the topic. I want to address the problems of my own biases and also to list the potential problems in the research. I have assessed two groups of black combat soldiers in a specific historical context, and I have drawn comparisons and conclusions that reveal similarities in their experiences. I have also pointed out the dissimilarities by using personal recollections from the men themselves. I have extracted information from government archives and other official collections. Initially, as a researcher with a new project, I was not completely knowledgeable about the topic. I have never been a "war buff," able to cite battles and strategies of past military maneuvers. Also, I did not know anything more than that my father had served with segregated troops. I did not know the history of the 92nd or the 93rd Infantry Divisions. Yet, I never felt as if these facts and histories could not be known. The story was not unknowable, or unapproachable, even for a white female scholar researching across race, age, and gender. I used standard historical methods, complimented with my own personal standpoint, and I believe this work adds another layer of understanding to black life during the war years. Any distortions observed are not because of my inverse positionality in the research process, but rather from my understanding of the history. My opinions and interpretations are fully my own responsibility.

Gunnar Myrdal, a Swedish social scientist researching the "Negro problem" in the 1940s, wrote in his treatise *The American Dilemma* that full objectivity was an ideal toward which we are constantly striving but which we can never reach. In the quest for objectivity, Myrdal understood that a social scientist is able only to create an analysis through the lens of his or her own background and biases. He recognized that historians are part of their own culture and environment and that this produces certain biases about the topics they study. Myrdal called these preconceptions and ideas a "web of conflicting valuations." *What* people study and *how* they develop their theoretical framework will always reveal the bias of the researcher. Myrdal understood that although objectivity is the goal, subjectivity is the reality. This does not mean that Myrdal's work was invalid, or that biased work is invalid. It simply means that bias is a component of everyone's research and should be duly noted. For Myrdal the cure to bias was direct confrontation, a sort of confessional approach where the researcher says, "this is my background and this is my bias or cultural valuation." Thus I confess my bias and reveal my own web of conflicting valuations that undergird this work.

INDEX

Watt, Fred, 14, 159, 181–82, 186–88, 199, 200, 203, 208, 237
Wesly, Charles, 33–34, 43, 44, 47, 61–62, 87, 123, 130, 144, 146, 149, 186, 188–89, 237
White, Walter, 100, 111, 112–13, 134, 156, 192
white officers, xiv, 28, 37, 58–60, 82–85, 90, 91, 93, 95–98, 100, 101, 104, 117, 132, 146–51, 159, 175, 177, 178
Whitley, Edgar, 10, 172, 179–80, 237
Whitted, Clyde, 9, 19, 100–101, 168, 182, 237

Wilkinson, Horace C., 110–11
Williams, Hank, 19, 32, 41–42, 60, 65–66, 72–73, 81, 135, 226, 231, 232, 237
Williams, Jim, 8, 48, 79, 119, 122–23, 172, 177–78, 203, 223, 237
Williams, Mrs. Jim, 237
Willkie, Wendell, 23
Women's Army Corps (WACs), 98, 168
Wood, Sterling A., 129
Woodring, Harry H., 4
work stoppages, 4, 101–2, 103

Young, Coleman, 222

ABOUT THE AUTHOR

Maggi M. Morehouse is a doctoral candidate in African Diaspora Studies at the University of California, Berkeley. She received her M.A. in history from San Francisco State University and has taught classes in U.S. history, African American history, and research methods. She was awarded a Fulbright fellowship to spend the 1999–2000 year in the Caribbean researching racial and colonial policies of Britain during World War II.

Voices and Visions

People and Events That Have Made a Difference
Series Editor: Robert L. Allen

Fighting in the Jim Crow Army
Black Men and Women Remember World War II

by Maggi M. Morehouse

Strong in the Struggle
My Life as a Black Labor Activist

by Lee Brown with Robert L. Allen